Music as Message

Constantin Floros

Music as Message

An Introduction to Musical Semantics

Translated by Ernest Bernhardt-Kabisch

Bibliographic Information published by the Deutsche Nationalbibliothek
The Deutsche Nationalbibliothek lists this publication in the Deutsche Nationalbibliografie;
detailed bibliographic data is available in the internet at http://dnb.d-nb.de.

Cover image:
Gustav Klimt: Die Musik I © b p k; Bildagentur für Kunst, Kultur und Geschichte

Library of Congress Cataloging-in-Publication Data
Floros, Constantin.
  [Musik als Botschaft. English]
  Music as message : an introduction to semantics of music / Constantin Floros ; translated
by Ernest Bernhardt-Kabisch.
    pages cm
  Includes bibliographical references and index.
  ISBN 978-3-631-66033-1
  1. Music--Philosophy and aesthetics. 2. Music--19th century--History and criticism. 3.
Music--20th century--History and criticism. I. Bernhardt-Kabisch, Ernest, 1934- translator.
II. Title.
  ML3845.F5613 2015
  781.1'7--dc23
                        2015020872

ISBN 978-3-631-66033-1 (Print)
E-ISBN 978-3-653-05301-2 (E-Book)
DOI 10.3726/ 978-3-653-05301-2

www.peterlang.com

Table of Contents

6

Foreword

As long as people have been theorizing about art, there have been diverse conceptions of music. Some take it as an art that follows its own laws, a play of "moving tonal forms," as the high priest of music Eduard Hanslick put it. To others, it is expression, an art of "inwardness," the "language of the soul." For some, music serves the purpose of amusement and entertainment, being an art designed solely for aesthetic pleasure. Others tirelessly point to its educational and therapeutic function – a function ascribed to it already in Greek antiquity. If in the 18th century it was widely held that music has a specific end in view, in the 19th the notion of music as pure, purposeless, so-called *absolute music*, began widely to prevail.

The words *message* and *code* denote basic concepts in the modern science of communication, in mythography and semiotics. Music, too, is a communicative phenomenon par excellence but has to date hardly been analyzed in terms of the communicative process. What do composers from Ludwig van Beethoven to Luciao Berio and Luigi Nono intend with their music? What do they want to say, and to whom do they address themselves? What is the nature of the messages they transmit, and how are they received and deciphered by the listeners?

The subject of music as message is one that has fascinated me for half a century. The book is intended as an introduction to the basic questions of musical semantics. Nearly all of my books profit from it (cf. section 3 of the bibliography).

The publication of the original German version in 1989 made a lasting impression in several European countries. The concept of the "message" established itself in musicological criticism and inspired several symposia on the subject: in Bratislava (*Hudba ako posolstvo*) in 1993, in Cracow (*Music as Message of Truth and Beauty*) in 2008, and in Vienna ("Music as Ideological Message") in 2011. The second chapter of this book appeared in a Spanish translation in *Quodlibet* Issue 39 (September-December 2007) and in a Polish translation in *Teoria Muzyki*, 6 (Cracow, 2015): 211–226. The present English edition has been brought up to date and expanded by the chapters "Public and Private Messages in Music," "Autobiographic

Elements in Schumann's Music" and "Franz Liszt's *Faust* Symphony. A Semantic Analysis," as well as some additions to chapter V and XVII.

For the past ten years, I have been collaborating intensively with my dear friend, Emeritus Professor Dr. Ernest Bernhardt-Kabisch of Indiana University. He has carefully translated a number of my books, functioning at the same time as a very conscientious copy editor, who does not miss a thing. He has once again provided an expert translation, as well as making numerous fruitful suggestions. My most cordial thanks go to him.

Hamburg, Fall 2015   Constantin Floros

I. The Concept of the Message in Music

"Croyez-vous qu j'entends la musique pour mon plaisir?" Hector Berlioz

The notion was, and is, widely held that the music of Arnold Schönberg and his pupils Anton Webern and Alban Berg is to be approached primarily, or at least predominantly, in terms of its constructivity. Schönberg himself protested against that notion. In a letter to Rudolf Kolisch of July 27, 1932, he stated emphatically that he did not want to be stamped as a constructor and complained that some of his adepts in analyzing twelve-tone music labored to realize how it was "made," whereas he had always sought to make clear what it "was." "For me," Schönberg writes, "the only valid analysis is one that identifies the idea and shows its presentation and development. In doing so, naturally, artistic subtleties will have to be considered as well."[1]

The more closely one studies Schönberg, Webern and Berg, the clearer it becomes that their nature, thought and work is characterized by a peculiar mixture of rationality and esotericism, calculation and intuition, conscious and unconscious elements. Thus Schönberg's hitherto published writings contain, besides numerous rationalistic considerations of the technical aspects of music, philosophical reflections that, while often immediately plausible, are subjective" in that they cannot be proved. Of special significance among these insights are Schönberg's ideas about art as message. "Message" (*Botschaft*) is a word that recurs in diverse of his essays.

Let us begin with the essay "Kriterien für die Bewertung von Musik" (Criteria for the Evaluation of Music), written in 1946, five years before Schönberg's death. Here we find the lapidary sentence: "We can conclude from the lives of truly great men that the creative urge answers to an instinctive vital feeling, solely in order to convey a message to humanity." And a little later we read: "My personal feeling is that music conveys a prophetic message that reveals a higher form of life toward which humanity is evolving. And it is precisely because of this message that music affects

---

1 Arnold Schönberg, *Ausgewählte Briefe*, ed. Erwin Stein (Mainz, 1958), 178 f.

people of all races and cultures."[2] This observation might help to explain the enormous effect of the music of Wagner, Bruckner, Mahler and Richard Strauss on people, for example, in Japan.

In another essay, entitled "Selbstanalyse (Reife)" (Self-analysis [Maturity]), Schönberg doubts that atonality or dissonance constitute criteria for the evaluation of music. What matters, in his view, is something altogether different. "True love of music," he writes, "and a true appreciation of it will ask: What has been said? How was it expressed? Was a new message proclaimed in the music? Was a new personality discovered? Was the technical representation commensurate?"[3]

In the context of the essay "Brahms, der Fortschrittliche" (Brahms, the Progressive), finally, Schönberg speaks of works created by great artists toward the end of their life, saying that such works represent far more than ordinary opera. One can assume, he maintains, that the message of a man who already dwells half-ways in the beyond will "advance to the outermost limits of the still expressible." Of such a work one could "expect an extraordinary degree of perfection," because mastery would manifest itself for once in its entire completeness when it is a matter of formulating "a message of such importance." On this occasion, Schönberg intimates that by message he means "a part of the wisdom" that a great artist has acquired in the course of his life. Such a person may feel the wish "to incorporate a word into the knowledge of mankind."[4]

Other composers of the 20th century, too, make use of the term "message" when endeavoring to make their intentions transparent. Hans Werner Henze, for example, tells of his composing during the ten-year span between the *Bassariden* and *We come to the River* – that is, the years between 1965 and 1975 – that it was a "continuous movement, away from the drunken, hedonistic world of the bacchantes and maenads and towards the contemporary, the murderers and victims of the new piece." It was, he says, a passage "full of difficulties, artistic and moral ones." "During this time,"

---

2 Arnold Schönberg, „Kriterien für die Bewertung von Musik," in *Stil und Gedanke. Aufsätze zur Musik*, ed. Ivan Vojtěch (Gesammelte Schriften I (Frankfurt a.M.: S. Fischer Verlag, 1976), 123–133; pp. 131, 132.
3 Ibid., 386.
4 Ibid., 69.

he professes, "my music became ever clearer and more definite and progressively a vehicle of messages and precisely nameable contents."[5]

Essential ideas on the subject of music as message are to be found in the writings of the French anthropologist Claude Lévi-Strauss. Lévi-Strauss spoke of a profound affinity between music and mythology, and compared the two areas on several levels. One of these levels is the relation to time. Both myth and a musical work are, he thought, languages "that, each in its own way, transcend the level of articulate speech" while yet requiring a temporal dimension in order to reveal themselves.

The terms with which Lévi-Strauss operates in his famous structural analysis of myths *Mythologiques I. Le cru et le cuit* are "scaffolding," "code" and "message." "Scaffolding" he calls the totality of the features that remain invariant in two or more myths. By "code" he means the "system of functions that each myth ascribes to these features." "Message" he calls the "content" of a particular myth. Elsewhere he specifies that the codes whereby messages are transmitted consist of a grammar and a lexicon.

Another common property of music and myth consists in the fact that both emit messages. Myths, according to Lévi-Strauss' basic thesis, "have no author: whatever their origin may have been, as soon as they are perceived as myths, they exist only as embodied in a tradition. When a myth is recited, the listeners receive a message that really comes from nowhere; that is the reason why a supernatural origin is ascribed to it." Music, too, is a language, "by means of which messages are formed, of which at least some are understood by the great majority, whereas only a very small minority is capable of emitting them." For this reason, the creator of music becomes "a godlike being" and music itself "the loftiest secret of the human sciences."

The kinds of messages composers proclaim through their music – or, put differently, into whose vehicles they make themselves – serve Lévi-Strauss as a criterion for the division of composers into three groups, between which there are all kinds of intermediaries and connections. The representatives of the first group (cited are Bach and Stravinsky) explicate and comment in their messages on the rules of a musical speech; Lévi-Strauss calls them musicians of the *code*. The composers of the second group (Beethoven, but

---

5   Hans Werner Henze, *Musik und Politik. Schriften und Gespräche, 1955–1975* (DeutscherTaschenbuch Verlag, 1162) (Munich, 1976), 251 f.

15

also Ravel) "narrate": they prove to be musicians of the *message*. The representatives of the third group (Wagner and Debussy), finally, codify their messages by means of elements that already belong to the area of story: Lévi-Strauss therefore calls them musicians of *mythos*. This distinction, he says, remains instructive even in dodecaphonic music, enabling us to relate Webern to the *code*, Schönberg *to the message and* Berg to the *mythos*.[6]

The term "message" is also used in genetics, in communication theory,[7] in semiotics and in sociology.[8] In Umberto Eco's *Theory of Semiotics*,[9] it is among the basic terms, along with "code," by means of which the author seeks to explain the process of communication between human beings and how messages are decoded.

Some startling observations were made around 1971 in rock and pop music. It was ascertained that some songs delivered two contrary messages. If the records were played at the normal speed, the texts proclaimed a "positive" message, for example, a commitment to Christianity or to Jesus. But if they were played backward, in "backward messaging," or at a different speed, the message became sinister and was taken in unconsciously by the brain. The development went along with a tendency toward occultism, a commitment to Satanism and the Black Mass. A famous example was the Pink Floyd song "One of these days" (on the LP "Meddle" of 1971). If one plays the record at a speed lower than the official one, one seems to hear the sentence "I'm gonna dance with the Devil's sister."[10]

What uses can be derived from semiotic literature for a discussion of "music as message"? A study of Eco's book makes clear that he uses the term message in a far more comprehensive way than Arnold Schönberg. To

---

6 Claude Lévi-Strauss, *Mythologiques I. Le cru et le cuit* (Paris, 1964), 23 f., 205, 218, 26, 38.

7 Hannelore Link, *Rezeptionsforschung. Eine Einführung in Methoden und Probleme* (Urban-Taschenbücher, 215) (Stuttgart/Berlin/Cologne/Mainz, 1976), 27 ff.

8 Kurt Blaukopf, *Musik im Wandel der Gesellschaft. Grundzüge der Musiksoziologie* (Munich/Zurich, 1984), 154 f.

9 Umberto Eco, *Einführung in die Semiotik*, (Munich, 1972).

10 See Helmut Rösing, "Heavy Metal, Hardrock, Punk: Geheime Botschaften an das Unbewußte?" in Rösing, ed., *Rock, Pop. Jazz im musikwissenschaftlichen Diskurs* (Hamburg: CODA-Verlag, 1992), 163–185 A list of pertinent examples can be found on Wikipedia under "Backwards Messaging."

him message means any signal, any advertisement, and indeed any sense, whereas for Schönberg and Henze the term refers to the highest human knowledge and thus has a humanitarian dimension. I myself would plead for a narrower definition, lest it lose in sharpness, and in what follows I take message to mean an extra-musical idea, a spiritual-emotional experience, a meaning that is conveyed through the medium of music. Three things above all are to be kept in mind:

1. The question what music is and what purpose it serves can, of course, not be answered once and for all. Opinions about it are too divided, art-theoretical and aesthetic positions differ too radically. The various conceptions are clearly dependent on the particular cultural sphere, on nationality, on the time and the zeitgeist, on the prevailing tastes and on the respective intellectual and artistic currents and tendencies. Thus music has been, and still is, defined as art for the ear, as the language of the heart, of feeling, as science of composition, as "moving tonal form." The mission of tonal art, it has been and still is said, is to provide pleasure, to educate, to teach, to move, to excite, to uplift, to transport, to interpret and deepen a text emotionally, to enhance drama, to convey an intimation of the other world, and so on. Perhaps we can agree that not every kind of music proclaims a message. The playfully concertante music of the Baroque and of Classicism differs considerably in this respect from Beethoven's Ninth Symphony.

2. Not every musical work that does proclaim a message is necessarily of aesthetic value. It would be a fatal error to confound aesthetics and ideology. Ideology does not determine the rank of a work of art. Robert Schumann, in taking position on the hotly debated question as to the value or lack of value of programs in music, expressed his conviction by saying: "First of all, let me hear that you have made *beautiful* music, then your program, too, will be pleasing to me."[11] *Mutatis mutandis*, Schumann's statement is valid also for the conception of music as message.

3. In the recent past, there has been much discussion about the contrast between so-called absolute and program music. The conception of a certain kind of music as message might help to partly reconcile the contrast. For a

---

11 Robert Schumann, „Sinfonien für Orchester" (1843), in *Gesammelte Schriften über Musik und Musiker*, ed. Martin Kreisig, 5th ed. (Leipzig, 1914), 2:129; hereafter GS.

musical message is something other than a musical program and pertains to a higher level of abstraction than the latter. Many works that do not seem to fit into the category of either absolute or program music can be placed under the rubric of music as message. Here, too, Beethoven's Ninth Symphony can be cited as exemplary.

II. Public and Private Messages in Music

I

"Alle Menschen werden Brüder." Friedrich Schiller

What is music? What is its function? According to an ancient tradition, music has an affinity with magic, with sorcery, with conjuration, with the realm of the arcane. Already the ancient Greeks extolled its educational, moral and therapeutic effect. They imputed to it the ability to turn the psychic powers, the motions of the listener's soul, to the good. We may remember the touching story of the singer Arion of Lesbos, whom evil mariners rob and are about to throw into the sea but grant him a last request, to sing and play a parting song. Lured by the magic power of his music, dolphins carry him on their back to a promontory. This legend should serve as a motto in every textbook about music therapy.

It is rather remarkable that certain ideas about the nature of music persist through the centuries. According to classical rhetoric, speech has a threefold function: to entertain, the move and to teach. That perception infiltrated the realm of aesthetics and for many centuries determined the thought of countless artists about the purpose of art. Every attempt however, to reduce everything in the history of art to a common denominator is bound to fail because art and music, as well as the thinking about music, are subject to constant change. For example, the Dutch cultural philosopher Johan Huizinga sought the origin of culture in man's play drive and in his much-read book *Homo ludens*[1] adduced proofs for his thesis from all eras of human history. Especially the culture of the 18th century, according to Huizinga, was a culture of play – a fascinating thesis, when on thinks of the art of the Rococo, but also of the flowering the concerto underwent as a genre particularly in the 18th century. For the 19th century, on the other hand, the formula "art as play" has only a limited validity. The French Revolution had confronted humanity with altogether new problems – a completely new sense of life developed. The music of the 19th century subsists, if I may say so, in close relation to

---

1   Johan Huizinga, *Homo Ludens. A Study of the Play Element in Culture* (London, 1949; orig. 1938).

nearly all intellectual currents of the time. Many composers put their music in the service of literary, religious social and political ideas and, in concert with writers, philosophers and politicians, searched for a new orientation. Oddly enough, however, it was precisely in this profoundly agitated century that the idea of the so-called absolute music emerged and found an eloquent champion. The Viennese high priest of music, Eduard Hanslick, defined musical art as a "play of moving tonal forms" (*Spiel tönend bewegter Formen*), formulated the aesthetics of the specifically musical, and combatted not only Richard Wagner and Anton Bruckner but also the adherents of program music, which experienced its very heyday in the 19th century.

After the First World War, program music went out of fashion and even got into discredit. Since the 1920's, the idea of absolute music won recognition almost everywhere, in line with a pointedly anti-Romantic outlook. Although several noted composers continued to write program music, the files were essentially closed on the genre. Many regarded the genre as obsolete, as a typical product of the 19th century, and as synonymous with second-rate music to boot. No less an authority than Ferruccio Busoni argued in favor of the view "that music is music in and for itself and nothing else."[2]

That was our tradition, the tradition in which we grew up. I recall that when I was a student, it was a sacrilege to pose question about the hermeneutic dimension of music. In musicological circles, it was for a long time part of the *bon ton* to cleanly separate a composer's life and work, his inner biography from his outward creation, to view the artistic creation detached from the personality of his creator.

Yet music – particularly "significant" music – is not merely form, structure and tonal play: it is more. It conveys spiritual and intellectual experiences, personal feelings and recollections, autobiographic elements. Thus Gustav Mahler held the conviction that in music the complete human being expresses itself: the feeling, thinking, breathing suffering human.[3] Music, in his view, also involves the intellectual. It addresses the entire human

---

2 Ferruccio Busoni, "Junge Klassizität," in *Von der Einheit der Musik. Verstreute Aufzeichnungen* (Berlin, 1922), 275–279.

3 Gustav Mahler to Bruno Walter, summer 1904. Gustav Mahler, *Briefe*, ed. Herta Blaukopf, new ed., revised and enlarged (Vienna/Hamburg, 1982), 293 f.; hereafter GMB².

being and expresses the entire human being: a position to put the merely formalistic firmly in its place.

As we have noted at the outset, the term "message" is one that 20th-century composers like Arnold Schönberg and Hans Werner Henze have employed to denote their artistic intentions. And many musical works of art that to us are surrounded by a special nimbus owe their renown in considerable part to the humanitarian messages they proclaim.

In this respect, a line of development extends from Mozart's *Magic Flute*, Beethoven's *Fidelio* and *Ninth Symphony* via the music dramas of Richard Wagner and the symphonies of Gustav Mahler to works like Alban Berg's *Wozzeck* and the *Soldiers* of Bernd Alois Zimmermann. All of these works can be regarded as appeals to intellectually and artistically interested human beings in their entirety all over the world.

Ludwig van Beethoven is the most prominent representative of committed music at the beginning of the 19th century. His intellectual world was anchored in German Idealism but was also affected by the spirit of the French Revolution. It centered in the ideals of humaneness, of political liberty, of inner freedom, the idea of hope and also in religious ideas. Beethoven revered Goethe but also felt drawn to Friedrich Schiller, whose fighting spirit and thirst for liberty fascinated him. A firm believer in the moral mission of music, he had also adopted the ethical maxims of Immanuel Kant.

The texts that Beethoven chiefly set to music circle about these idea(l)s. The libretto of *Fidelio* and Schiller's *Ode to Joy* are like focal points that concentrate primary contents of his weltanschauung. Generations have seen *Fidelio* as a fiery protest against despotic power, inhumanity and oppression, and entire generations have perceived the *Ninth Symphony* as a prophetic anticipation of a reign of joy and human brotherhood. Arnold Schönberg may well have had this work in mind when he spoke of prophetic messages through the medium of music.

Beethoven's *Ninth Symphony*, the decisive major work of the more recent musical history, is neither absolute music nor program music, but a prototypical example of music as message. The message it conveys is the key declaration of the *Ode to Joy*: "Alle Menschen werden Brüder," all men shall become as brothers.

Schiller's ode appeared in 1786 and deeply impressed the young Beethoven. Already as a twenty-three-year-old he conceived a plan to set it to music. Roughly twenty years later he drafted an overture that was to incorporate the ode. But it was only with the composition of the *Ninth Symphony* that he was finally able to realize his intention. The stanzas he selected from Schiller's long poem, and especially the way in which he composed them, help us to recognize that two proclamations of Schiller's above all were important to him: the address to heavenly joy, which intoxicates the soul, and the wish dream of fraternal union.

Freude, schöner Götterfunken,	Joy, thou spark of deity
Tochter aus Elysium,	Daughter of Elysium,
Wir betreten feuertrunken,	Drunken with thy fire we enter
Himmlische, dein Heiligtum!	Heavenly one, thy sanctuary!
Deine Zauber binden wieder	Thy enchantments bind together
Was die Mode streng geteilt;	What stern custom's law divides;
Alle Menschen werden Brüder,	All mankind become as brothers,
Wo dein sanfter Flügel weilt.	Where thy gentle wing alights.
Seid umschlungen, Millionen!	Be embraced, ye countless millions!
Diesen Kuß der ganzen Welt!	To all the world this kiss of love!

This text Beethoven set beneath the two main themes of the Finale, which are treated in the manner of a double fugue. The first theme is initially intoned by the baritone soloist. Later, in an *andante maestoso*, the very differently structured second theme is recited by the chorus, its solemnity being underlined by the addition of three trombones. In the penultimate section of the Finale, finally, an *allegro energico*, the two themes are contrapuntally intertwined, as the music assumes the character of a dithyramb.

Though it may sound paradoxical, the musical history of the 19th century can be understood in part as the result of composers creatively wrestling and coming to terms with the oeuvre of Beethoven, including his *Ninth Symphony*.[4] In 1916, Ferrucio Busoni, a composer of a truly European frame of a mind, wrote in his widely read *Entwurf einer neuen Ästhetik der Tonkunst* (Sketch of a new Aesthetic of Music): "The apostles of the

---

4 Cf. Constantin Floros, *Gustav Mahler*, vol. 2: *Mahler und die Symphonik des 19. Jahrhunderts in neuer Deutung* (Wiesbaden, 1977); english: Gustav Mahler and the Symphony of the 19th Century, Peter Lang: Frankfurt am Main 2014.

Ninth Symphony invented the concept of depth in music. It still has its full value, especially in Germanic lands."[5]

The message Beethoven directed at humanity in the *Ninth*, however, soon moved beyond the narrow boundaries of the German-speaking world. Piotr Ilich Tchaikovsky and Claude Debussy divined Beethoven's intentions but doubted whether his utopian vision human brotherhood through joy would become reality anytime soon. Edouard Herriot, the French prime minister, saw in Beethoven the apostle of *fraternité*, an incomparable creator, "who teaches us at once dedication to art, striving for moral perfection and an ardent passion for peace."[6]

The music of our time is marked by a remarkable plurality of directions. Music is conceived as technology, as science, as ideology and as mystical philosophy of redemption. While some composers are increasingly interested only in the technical aspects of music, for others music has meaning and a right to exist only as committed art. The shocks produced by the Second World War in many creative individuals had undreamed-of consequences also for the development of music. Numerous composers put their art in the service of humanitarian ideas, many protested against violence, brutality and despotism. Some of Arnold Schönberg's and Luigi Dallapiccola's compositions and many works of Luigi Nono and Hans Werner Henze are to be understood as engaged, committed art.

An impressive example of what has been said is Schönberg's *Ode to Napoleon Bonaparte* op. 41 of 1942. There is a growing number of indications that the Japanese attack on Pearl Harbor in December of 1941 deeply shocked Schönberg and became the decisive impulse for him to set Lord Byron's ode to music. He designed the work, as he himself explained, as a protest against the crimes of war, against tyranny and against the Nazi ideology.[7] And he thought it a moral duty of the intelligentsia to take a decisive position against tyranny, as Mozart had done in his *Figaro*,

---

5   Ferruccio Busoni, *Entwurf einer neuen Ästhetik der Tonkunst. Mit Anmerkungen von Arnold Schönberg und einem Nachwort von H. H. Stuckenschmidt* (Frankfurt, 1974), 38.

6   Edouard Herriot, *La vie de Beethoven* (Vies des hommes illustres, no. 30) (Paris, 1930), 11.

7   Arnold Schönberg, "How I came to compose the Ode to Napoleon," facsimile, in *Journal of the Arnold Schoenberg Institute*, 2, no. 1 (October 1977), 55–57.

Schiller in *Wilhelm Tell*, Goethe in *Egmont* and Beethoven in the *Eroica* and in *Wellington's Victory*. In 1948, Schönberg wrote to Hans Heinz Stuckenschmidt: "Lord Byron, who had greatly admired Napoleon before, was so disenchanted by a simple resignation that he covers him with the keenest scorn and derision, and I believe I did not miss the mark in my composition."[8] The final section of the dodecaphonic work, marked *Maestoso* and strikingly pervaded by *tonal* formations, serves the glorification of George Washington, the democratic hero and fictive antagonist to Napoleon.[9] The *Ode* is scored for string quartet, a speaker and piano. It was premiered in a version for string orchestra, speaker and piano on November 23, 1944, in New York under the baton of Arthur Rodzinski.

The dislocations that World War II left behind did not leave even the highest ideals untouched. In 1947, five years after the composition of the *Ode to Napoleon*, Thomas Mann completed his novel *Doctor Faustus* in his American exile. There he had his protagonist Adrian Leverkühn proclaim the retraction of the *Ninth Symphony*, the retraction of joy and hope. In one of the final chapters of the novel, the diseased composer makes this crucial confession to his friend Serenus Zeitblom:

> "I have found," he said, "it is not to be."
> "What, Adrian, is not to be?"
> "The good and the noble," he answered, "what people call he human, although it is good and noble. What men have fought and stormed despotic castles for, and what the fulfilled have proclaimed in jubilation, that is not to be. I want to retract it."
> "I do not fully understand you, dear friend. What do you want to retract?"
> "The Ninth Symphony," he replied. And after that came nothing more, however long I waited.[10]

This statement refers not only to the crisis situation of the new art, but also to the end of an entire epoch. Meanwhile, the *Ninth Symphony* is played

---

8 Josef Rufer, *Das Werk Arnold Schönbergs* (Kassel, 1959), 51.

9 Cf. Constantin Floros, "Zum Beethoven-Bild Schönbergs, Bergs und Weberns," in *Beethoven und die Zweite Wiener Schule* (Studien zur Wertungsforschung, vol. 25) (Vienna/Graz, 1992), 8–24; pp. 17–22.

10 Thomas Mann, *Doktor Faustus: Die Entstehung des Doktor Faustus* (Frankfurt, 1967), 634.

again on festive occasions, as though to demonstrate that mankind had regained its faith in its ideals.

What does Beethoven mean for us today? A consensus on this question is probably unattainable: opinions on it diverge too far. While some musicians in Europe, affected with Beethoven fatigue, recommend that Beethoven be registered, as it were, as a historical monument so as to protect his music from excessive wear and tear, the non-European nations have only just discovered Beethoven and draw strength from his music. And whereas some critical-minded intellectuals warn us of idealizing his figure, entire nations frankly confess to an identification with it.

II

"Music is poetry raised to a higher power." Robert Schumann

If one were to conduct an opinion poll about people's conceptions of the function of music, the result might be surprising. For the expectations people connect with music are very different. To some it serves entertainment, should contribute to relaxation and give aesthetic pleasure. To others it is the language of the heart, of feeling and the emotions, is the art of inwardness, the quintessence of the poetic. To some composers, especially today, music is a kind of science – the science of composition. Eduard Hanslick, as we have noted, saw it as "play of moving tonal forms" and prompted a rather one-sidedly formalistic view of music. Certain kinds of music, however, communicate, have a meaning and want to effect something.

Next to works that transmit a public message, there are those whose communication is a "private" one – works that their authors dedicate to friends, sponsors or persons to whom they have a more intimate connection. In many instances, such works contain a "private" message, which initially only the recipient can decode. The recipient's personal relation to the composer, the special knowledge the dedicatee has at his command, put him in a position to decipher the message.

Robert Schumann was probably the chief representative of poetic music in the 19th century. He was well versed in literature and a great admirer of Jean Paul Richter, from who he received some crucial impulses. The highest authority in the aesthetics of both is poetry: the poetic is the prime region of art. Schumann defined music as "poetry [or poesy] raised to a higher power." He never tired of postulating that the composer had to be a "poet" and must strive for a "poetic consciousness." Numerous of his works bear poetic titles, which are intended to direct the listener's imagination in a specific direction.[11]

Whoever aims at a deeper understanding of Schumann's music, as well as that of Hector Berlioz, Franz Liszt, Richard Wagner, Richard Strauss or Gustav Mahler, must not forget that it evinces a close relation to all the intellectual currents of its time. Thus Schumann regarded the traditional barriers between art and politics, music and contemporary events, as razed, and he admitted that many of his own compositions were inspired by extra-musical impulses. On April 13, 1838, he wrote to Clara Wieck:

> I am affected by what passes in the world, politics, literature, people; about everything I think in my own way, which then wants to vent itself, seek a way out, in music. That is also why so many of my compositions are so difficult to understand, because they take off from remote interests, often also significant, because everything remarkable of the present grips me and I then have to express it again musically.[12]

No wonder, then, so many of Schumann's works are replete with extra-musical significance and "private" messages. A large portion of his piano music is written for Clara, applies to her, even when it is not expressly dedicated to her. Schuman's passionate love for Clara, his personal relationship to her, is the subject of many pieces. Schumann himself confessed as much in a letter to his former teacher Heinrich Dorn:

> Certainly much of the struggle Clara cost me may be contained in my music and certainly also been understood by you. She has almost singly instigated the concerto, the sonata, the Davidsbündlertänze, the Kreisleriana and the Novellettes.[13]

Of Schumann's three great piano sonatas, the first in F-sharp Minor is expressly dedicated to Clara Wieck. The third sonata, also called *Concerto without Orchestra*, includes a variations movement on a theme by Clara. Schumann frequently endows his music with extra-musical meaning by

---

11 Cf. chs. X–XII, below.

12 Clara Schumann, ed., *Jugendbriefe von Robert Schumann* (Leipzig, 1910), 282.

13 *Robert Schumanns Briefe*, new series, ed. Friedrich Gustav (Leipzig, 1886), 146 f.

using anagrams and cryptograms, letter notes in diverse groupings, quotations and various kinds of allusions. To cite one example:

The *Phantasie* for piano, op. 17, written in 1836, is one of Schumann's most personal works and is dedicated to Franz Liszt. The three-movement work is headed by a motto with lines of Friedrich Schlegel:

Durch alle Töne tönet	(Through every sound there soundeth
Im bunten Erdenraum	In our earth's motley space
Ein leiser Ton gezogen	A tone softly extended
Für den der heimlich lauschet.	For him who quietly listens.)

In 1838, Schumann wrote to Clara:

> Besides, I have completed a fantasy in three movements, which I had drafted in June of 1836 down to the detail. The first movement is probably the most passionate thing I have ever made – a deep lament about you.

One understands that statement better once one discovers that Schumann in several places in the movement quotes Beethoven's famous song cycle *An die ferne Geliebte* (To the Distant Beloved) op. 98 – significantly the line "Nimm sie hin denn, diese Lieder" (Take them to you, then, these carols).[14]

The more closely one studies the music of the 19th and 20th century, the more often one can discover that many composers wrote works with secret programs. They let themselves be inspired by personal experiences, by visions and philsophical ideas, poems, stories, epics or dramas of world literature, or works of the pictorial arts, based their compositions on programs, but did not divulge these to the public. Many composers have expressed themselves in detail about their extra-musical intentions in letters and conversations, but carefully avoided disclosing anything officially about it. Carl Maria von Weber, Bedřich Smetana, Anton Bruckner, Peter Ilich Tchaikovsky, Gustav Mahler, Ferrruccio Busoni, Arnold Schönberg, Anton Webern, Leoš Janáček, Alban Berg – all of them have written such music. A public sensation some years ago was the discovery that all of Alban Berg's mature works are based on detailed secret programs, some of them so personal that Berg could not bring himself to disclose them.

Both the *Chamber Concerto* and the *Lyric Suite*, as well as the *Violin Concerto*, have biographic references. Thus the *Lyric Suite* tells the story of

---

14 *Jugendbriefe*, 278.

Berg's love for Hanna Fuchs-Robettin, the sister of Franz Werfel and wife of a Prague industrialist, at whose home Berg stayed for several days in May of 1925. The love was as full of pathos as it was mutual, but was hopeless from the start, because Hanna would not think of leaving her children and husband. But Berg's feelings for Hanna plunged him into a severe crisis. For several years love letters traveled from Vienna to Prague, with Theodor Adorno and several friends serving as *postillons d'amour*.

On the outside, the *Lyric Suite* creates the impression of being absolute music. In reality it is based on a secret program. From a semantic analysis produced in the early '70s, I was able to deduce that the six movements tell the story of a love that begins harmlessly and ends tragically with a *liebestod*.[15] A year and a half after the publication of my essay, George Perle made a sensational discovery in the United States: in the estate of Hanna Fuchs-Robettin he found a copy of the first printing of the *Lyric Suite* with hand-written annotations by Alban Berg, which disclose the secret program in considerable detail.[16]

The amount and variety of detail that Berg secreted into the *Lyric Suite* is incredible. The music becomes a secret language that can be fully understood only by the initiated. Tonal ciphers, numbers, quotations, allusions, innuendos – everything has a deeper meaning. Thus the letter notes A and B (= B-flat) stand for Alban Berg, while the tone ciphers H (the German symbol for B natural) and F are the initials of Hanna Fuchs. A dominant role in the construction plan of the work is assigned to the numbers 23 and 20, 23 being Berg's "fatal number," while 10 stands for Hanna (the ten letters of the name Hanna Fuchs). The two numbers determine the tectonics and the agogics, i.e., the dimensions and proportions of the movements and even the metronomic markings.[17]

---

15 Constantin Floros, "Das esoterische Programm der Lyrischen Suite von Alban Bertg. Eine semantische Analyse," *Hamburger Hahrbuch für Musikwissenschaft*, I (1975): 101–145. Cf. Floros, *Alban Berg and Hanna Fuchs. The Story of a Love in Letters*, tr. Ernest Bernhardt-Kabisch (Bloomington: Indiana University Press, 2008).

16 George Perle, "The Secret Program of the *Lyric Suite*," *Newsletter of the Interational Alban Berg Society*, no. 5 (June 1977), 4–12.

17 For a detailed analysis of the *Lyric Suite*, including the sketches to it, see my *Alban Berg. Music as Autobiography*, tr. Ernest Bernhardt-Kabisch (Frankfurt:

Berg works like a medieval cathedral builder, who calculates everything down to the smallest detail. At the same time, however, he endows the music with a maximum of expression. He semanticizes his score by means not only of tonal hieroglyphs and numbers but also of various quotations. Thus he cites Wagner's *Tristan und Isolde*, a work he loved fervently, and Alexander Zemlinsky's *Lyric Symphony*, a cantata after texts of Rabindranath Tagore. In more than twenty places in his quartet, Berg worked in and paraphrased quotations from Zemlinsky's symphony. From that also I concluded that a love poem of Tagore served as a program of three of the *Lyric Suite*'s movements. The poem goes as follows:

You are the evening cloud that drifts along the welkin of my dreams.
I give you color and form with the desires of my love.
You are my own, my own, you who dwell in my unending dreams.
Your feet are rosy red from the blaze of my yearning heart,
You gleaner of my evening songs!
Your lips are bitter-sweet, for they have tasted of the cup of my sorrows.
You are my own, my own, you, image of my lonely dreams.
With the shadow of my passion I darkened your eyes when they plunged into my gaze.
I caught you and wrapped you, beloved, in the net of my music.
You are my own, my own, you, who dwell in my undying dreams! *(tr. E.B.-K.)*

The Adagio appassionato, the fourth movement of the *Lyric Suite*, is based on the idea of a passionate love dialogue, that eventually "ebbs away into the wholly spiritualized, soulful, unearthly." In two places, the viola and later the second violin cite the phrase "You are my own, my own" from the *Lyric Symphony*. Elsewhere, too, Berg supplies much of the thematic substance of the movement from Zemlinsky motifs. At the climax, the initials are united. This Adagio appassionato is among the most expressive movements Berg ever wrote. Hanna Fuchs was Berg's immortal beloved.

Peter Lang, 2014; orig. German publ., 1993), 204–260; and *Alban Berg and Hanna Fuchs: The Story of a Love in Letters*, tr. Ernest Bernhardt-Kabisch (Bloomington: Indiana UP, 2008; orig. German publ. 2001; also French and Spanish translation), which contains a transcription of, and commentary on, Berg's secret letters to Hanna. Further reflections are offered by Hartmut Krones, "Alban Berg, Hanna Fuchs und Charles Baudelaire. Die Konzertarie *Der Wein,*" in *Aria. Eine Festschrift für Wolfgang Ruf*, ed. Wolfgang Hirschmann (Studien und Materialien zur Musikwissenschaft, 65) (Hildesheim/Zurich/New York, 2011), 682–698.

Once one knows the biographic connections, one can understand that Berg kept the program on the *Lyric Suite* a secret.

For similarly personal reasons, Leoš Janáček, too could not disclose the program of his *Second String Quartet*, which originally bore the title "Love Letters." He changed it to *Intimate Letters*, because he did not want to expose his feelings "to the opinion of stupid people" The work of 1928 tells the story of the 74-year-old composer's love for Kamilla Stösslova, a much younger woman.

Janáček's *First String Quartet*, composed within a week's time in 1923, is likewise anything but absolute music. It originated "at the instigation of Leo N. Tolstoy's Kreuzer Sonata," as a note on the title page of the autograph reads. Janáček had an affinity with Russian literature of the 19th century, especially Dostoevsky, Gogol, Lermontov and Tolstoy. As early as 1907, he had planned to write an opera on *Anna Karenina*. In the following year he let himself be inspired by Tolstoy's *Kreuzer Sonata* to write a piano trio. That work is lost, but musical ideas from it eventually made their way into the *First String Quartet*.[18]

That work is undoubtedly based on a detailed program, which the composer, however, did not divulge. But in a letter to his friend Kamilla Stösslova, he did reveal that while composing the work he had in mind "the pitiable woman who gets tortured, beaten and murdered."[19] The quartet thus depicts by musical means a psychodrama, a human tragedy. Janáček took a lively interest in the intonations of the language he studied, collected and made usable for his music.[20] His music is always a speaking one, which naturally also goes for this quartet. The score characteristically includes numerous recitative-like passages and numerous expression marks. Even if we did not have them, we could conclude from the manner of the music that that anxiety and extreme passion, profound melancholy and savagery are the poles of the emotional happening. To cite one example, repeated

---

18 On the genesis of the first string quartet, see Hans Hollander, *Leos Janáček. Leben und Werk* (Zurich, 1964), 181–183.

19 Janáček to Kamilla Stössel, October 14, 1924. See *Leos Janáček in Briefen und Erinnerungen*, ed. Bohumir Stedron (Prague, 1955), 172 f.

20 Leos Janáček, "Sprechmelodien," in *Leos Janáček* (Musik-Konzepte, 7) (Munich, 1979), 42–66.

listening makes clear that the third movement initially bears traits of a love duet: the first violin and the cello play, "con timidezza," a canon in the octave, which time and again is interrupted by brusque interjections from the other two instruments ("fortissimo sul ponticello" [on the bridge]).

*) [befangen jedoch unbeschwert / ligtly, shyly]
[Takt/bar 8–9, Viol. I. ◁ ▷, Vclo ◁ : podle autografu /
nach dem Autograph / according to the manuscript]

The Finale of the *First String Quartet* is linked to the first movement thematically and motivically. The opening motif of the work here recurs in the function of a leitmotif. Initially monodic phrases of the first violin with the telling expression mark "malinconico" are semantically and otherwise significant: profound depression is the initial emotional climate of the movement. The expression marks "come un lamento" and "disperato" more closely characterize the expressive content of the music, which gradually rises to extreme vehemence and closes quasi hymnically: the conclusion is to sound "solemn like an organ."

Janáček's *First String Quartet* makes an emotional-intellectual statement, conveys an emotional as well as a conceptual message. According to the testimony of Josef Suk, Janáček wanted the work to be understood as a moral protest against the despotism of men in their relation to women. Jaroslav Vogel, his major biographer, commented that Janáček here at once interprets and controverts Tolstoy. Whereas the Russian writer ascribes the "most immoral" effect to music in his story. "The Kreuzer Sonata," music in the quartet, we are told, speaks with "heart-wrenching effect as the conscience of humanity."[21] The remark may appear plausible, yet it misses the heart of the matter. For Tolstoy's concern had been to protest precisely against the degradation of women as the "slaves" of men.

From what has been said it should be clear that the idea of a history of art without the artist – a notion that fascinated the sciences of art for a while – is now a thing of the past. There are increasing signs that the endeavor of the aesthetic sciences will in future be directed toward freeing works of art from the isolation into which they had been banished, in order to illumine them in the light of the biographic, intellectual, cultural and social conditions under which they were created. Increasingly, the realization pervades the general consciousness that music does not come about in a vacuum but unfolds in mutual relation with the other spiritual-intellectual currents of the time. With many composers, life and work, biography and art constitute an inseparable unity. Many composers let themselves be inspired in their productions by aesthetic, literary, religious, philosophical ideas and, along with writers, painters, sociologists and politicians, search for new orientations. Common structural analysis therefore does not suffice for the investigation of a work of art. It needs to be complemented and expanded by the approaches of biographic research and inquiries into the genesis of the work. The impulses a musician received in composing a work, the intentions he pursued with it, are equally relevant objects of research as are form and structure. We must not forget that if we want to answer the question whom composers address and what they want to accomplish with their music.[22]

---

21 Jaroslav Vogel, *Leos Janáček. Leben und Werk* (Kassel/Prague, 1958), 387–90; p. 390.

22 I have further developed these reflections on musical semantics in several publications. The latest pertinent one bears the title *Verstehen und Hören. Die Sprache derMusik und ihre Deutung* (Mainz: Schott, 2008).

III. The Fear of Depth

1. Esprit contra Profundity: Mediterranean vs. Germanic Music

"Il faut mediterraniser la musique." Friedrich Nietzsche[1]

In *Beyond Good and Evil* – a publication that won him no new friends – Friedrich Nietzsche sought to demonstrate the cultural superiority of the French to the rest of Europe. As one claim of such superiority he cited the "half-ways successful synthesis of the North and the South in the nature of the French: it preserved them "from the ghastly Northern grey in grey and the sunless conceptual spectrality and anemia" – the German sickness.[2] Elsewhere he sharply criticized the "German profundity," much praised by many as a high virtue, and observed that Germans love clouds and everything that is unclear, emergent, dusky, moist and veiled, feeling whatever is uncertain, unformed, shifting and growing to be "deep."[3]

The antithesis between South and North, between full sun and dusk, between intellectual health and sickness was a topic that occupied Nietzsche ever since his apostasy from Wagner, at the latest. No wonder he, passionate music lover that he was, projected this problem onto the arena of music. Already in *Beyond Good and Evil*, he opposed to German music, as whose summit he regarded the art of Richard Wagner, an "über-German" or "über-European" music, from which he expected the deliverance of music from the North.[4] In *The Case of Wagner*,[5] he took another step: here he played Bizet off against Wagner, enthused unreservedly about *Carmen*, demanded the mediterraneization of music and defined this formulation as the return to nature, to health, serenity, youth and virtue. At the same time, he charged his former friend Wagner with unnaturalness, sickness and decadence.

---

1 Friedrich Nietzsche, *Der Fall Wagner* §3. In *Werke*, ed. Karl Schlechta, vol. 3 (Munich, 1979), 907.
2 Nietzsche, *Jenseits von Gut und Böse* §254. In *Werke*, 3:721–723.
3 Ibid., §244. *Werke*, 3:709–711.
4 Ibid., §255. *Werke*, 3:723.
5 *Der Fall Wagner* §3. *Werke*, 3:907.

When Nietzsche wrote *Beyond Good and Evil*, Wagner's influence had attained its culmination, not only in German, but also in France. The enthusiasm for Wagner's art in France among musicians, poets and writers was indescribable. Critics spoke of a regular Wagner cult. Although the clairvoyant Nietzsche diagnosed a good will in France "to ward off the intellectual Germanization,"[6] he also voiced the prognosis that the more French music learned to shape itself in accordance with the true needs of the *âme moderne*, the more it would *wagnerize*. The history of French music since ca. 1890, can indeed be described also as that of its endeavors to free itself from the immense influence of Wagner.

It is with this background in mind that Claude Debussy's polemical sallies against Christoph Willibald Gluck and Richard Wagner need to be understood – sallies that at the same time were conjurations to recover a sense of the French national heritage. In his late essays and interviews, Debussy, who proudly called himself *musicien français*, appealed to Rameau and Couperin and warned his compatriots again and again of becoming addicted to the magic sorcery of Wagner. "The French like to forget," he noted in 1909, "about clarity and elegance, qualities that correspond to their nature, and let themselves be impressed by the German lengths and depths."[7] An essay of 1915 declares: "We have asked the world to forgive us for our taste, for the light, luminous clarity, and have intoned a chorale in praise of depth."[8] And in a foreword written specifically to the omnibus volume *Pour la Musique Française*, we read: "We have not yet come to that point, we still have to beware, and above all be on our guard against the old reproach of our being 'light,' of having too little depth."[9]

Ferruccio Busoni's *Entwurf einer neuen Ästhetik der Tonkunst* (*Sketch of a New Aesthetic of Music*)[10] has been called a piece of genuine utopia

---

6 *Jenseits von Gut und Böse* §254. Werke, 3:721.
7 Claude Debussy, *Monsieur Croche et autres écrits* ed. François Lesure (Paris, 1971), 280.
8 Ibid., 260.
9 Ibid., 262.
10 Ferruccio Busoni, *Entwurf einer neuen Ästhetik der Tonkunst*, 16 f., 38 f. – The first edition of the *Entwurf* was published in 1907; the second, enlarged edition appeared in Leipzig in 1916.

and at the same time a prophetic anticipation of the Avant-garde. Both judgments are undoubtedly correct. But it seems to have been overlooked that among the leading ideas of the *Entwurf* is Nietzsche's wish dream of an über-German or über-European music. Busoni registers a quiet protest against the hegemony of German music, he wants to point out alternatives to the art of Wagner (the "Germanic giant"), which he regards as no longer *steigerungsfähig*, no longer capable of further development. His discussion of the concept of depth is particularly telling in this respect. The "apostles of the Ninth Symphony," the *Entwurf* states, invented the concept of depth in music. "It still has its full value, especially in Germanic lands." Busoni, however, thinks it necessary to differentiate. There is a depth of feeling and a depth of thought: the latter is literary in nature and cannot be applicable to tones. The depth of feeling, on the other hand, is spiritual and absolutely germane to music. (Even in this conceptual distinction we can recognize the representative of the aesthetics of autonomy.)

About the "apostles of the Ninth Symphony," Busoni says that they had a special, not quite firmly defined estimate of depth in music:

> Depth becomes breadth, and one endeavors to reach it by means of heaviness: it then manifests itself – by process of the association of ideas – in a preference for the "low" registers and, as I was able to observe, also in a reading-into of a second hidden sense, for the most part a literary one.

By "depth of feeling," however, Busoni wants to mean "the exhaustive in feeling": "the complete absorption in a mood." The discussion closes provocatively with the aperçu that there was more depth in the champagne aria of Mozart's *Don Giovanni* than in many a funeral march or nocturne.

It was to be expected that these views would provoke objections. Reactions indeed arose on various sides. Thus Arnold Schönberg remarked in his desk copy of the *Entwurf* that Busoni confused the "deeply felt" with "feeling depth."[11] He conceded that the champagne aria was something "whose utter jolliness comes as much from the depth of human nature as does the exuberance of a profound inwardness." But he submitted that

---

11 Busoni, *Entwurf* (1974), 67.

in general one would have to look for depth more on the side of serious-ness than on that of mirth, and he rather reduced Busoni's reflections to absurdity by pointing out that the Finale of the Ninth Symphony was after all addressed "To Joy."

When he wrote these marginalia in ca. 1917, Schönberg felt as a Ger-man musician. Busoni probably appeared to him like a representative of Romance music. The antagonism between Romanic and Germanic music, in any case, is the idea to which the following judiciously balanced sentence alludes: "But it could also be that just as we supposedly lack the grace and esprit the others have, we have the depth they supposedly lack."

Busoni's *Entwurf* hit Hans Pfitzner in a sensitive spot. He took offense at Busoni's discontent with the present, at his devotion to the idea of progress, and above all at his rather disrespectful remarks about the two German musicians whom Pfitzner admired most of all: Richard Wagner and Robert Schumann. Thoroughly annoyed, Pfitzner wrote the polemic *Futuristenge-fahr* (The Danger of Futurists), which appeared in early 1917. There he expressed his commitment to German music in the sentence: "German music is not just athletics of the brain but also art of the heart." At the same time he criticized Busoni's reflections on the concept of depth. Busoni, he thought, had turned everything topsy-turvy, any spontaneous feeling had to balk at his conceptual definitions. "Why may one call the champagne aria from *Don Giovanni* deep," he asked, "but not a music that disposes one, as it were, to a 'deep mood, or stimulates profound thoughts and contemplations in one?" He would never be able to call the feeling he gets from listening to the champagne aria a deep one, while he would certainly describe the thoughts and feelings the Ninth Symphony, especially the first movement, calls up in him as 'deep.' The whole, he said, was a pointless quibble about words.

What aroused Pfitzner's displeasure was not least Busoni's talk of the "apostles of the Ninth Symphony." With polemical irony, he asked "Who, by the way, are these 'apostles of the IXth Symphony'? Surely, it is to be hoped, all musical, artistic and intellectual people of the entire educated world?! Or does Busoni only mean such as write large symphonic works in which a chorus comes in at the end, like e.g. Gustav Mahler? In which case we would, after all, also have the pleasure of welcoming Ferruccio

Busoni, who has written a major piano concerto with orchestra, in whose fifth movement a chorus is added, among these closer apostles."[12]

2. Music as Expression of the "Complete Human Being"?

> "One can hardly deny that our music in some manner involves the 'purely human' (everything that belongs to it, thus also the 'intellectual')." Gustav Mahler[13]

In the summer of 1904, having completed his Sixth Symphony, Gustav Mahler wrote a letter to his friend Bruno Walter that provides an insight into his conception of music.

> If one wants to make music [it says there], one must not want to paint, poetize or describe. But what one makes music about is nevertheless the complete (that is, feeling, thinking, breathing suffering) human being. There would also not have to be any real objection to a 'program' (though it is not exactly the highest rung of the ladder) – but it is a musician who must be expressing himself in it, not a writer, philosopher, painter (all of them are contained within the musician)."[14]

These sentences reflect impressions Mahler received largely from his reading of Richard Wagner's treatises. Mahler's anthropocentric conception of music is strikingly contiguous to ideas of Wagner. Music, in Mahler's view, addresses itself to, is an expression of, the whole human being.

Mahler's view of music opens an access to his symphonies, which want to be perceived as *lived* music (*erlebte Musik*), as autobiography in musical sounds, and as the expression of a weltanschauung. The programs that Mahler based his first four symphonies on circle about central questions of human existence: questions about existence, eschatological and cosmological questions, the subject of love conceived as *caritas*, and meditations on the life after death. In view of this, it is not surprising that several of his contemporaries spoke of his symphonies as "metaphysical music" and of him as a "symphonizing philosopher."

---

12 Hans Pfitzner, *Futuristengefahr*, first published in 1917 with Süddeutsche Monatshefte. Reprint in Hans Pfitzner, *Gesammelte Schriften*, vol. 1 (Augsburg, 1926),185–223; pp. 203, 212 f.
13 Gustav Mahler to Bruno Walter, Summer 1904, GMB, 293 f.
14 Ibid.

The reputation, to be sure, of having brought music into line with philosophy and, under the influence of Arthur Schopenhauer, having created a metaphysical music, preceded Richard Wagner long before it did Gustav Mahler. It was thus only natural that Claude Debussy took the field precisely against the ideological and philosophical presuppositions of Wagnerian music drama. In an interview from the year 1909, he expressed himself against the linking of (musical) themes and (extra-musical) ideas and commented:

> One combines, one constructs, one contrives themes that are to express ideas; one develops them, modifies them as they encounter other themes expressing other ideas, one practices metaphysics, but one does not make music.[15]

Surprisingly, these reflections largely coincide with thoughts that Busoni set forth in his famous letter to Paul Bekker, the article "Young Classicity" of 1920. Young classicity meant for him, among other things, shedding the sensual, renunciation of subjectivism, recapture of serenity, and above all, absolute music.

> Not profundity and sentiment and metaphysics; but: music as such, distilled, never under the mask of figures and concepts that are borrowed from other areas. Human feeling but not human issues – and that, too, expressed in the dimensions of the artistic.[16]

In these sentences, Busoni declared himself for the aesthetics of autonomy even more emphatically than Eduard Hanslick had done.

Busoni's summons to *young classsicity* was mistakenly identified with the simultaneously spreading Neoclassicism (Busoni protested against that misunderstanding). But his plea for absolute music, that is, for the view "that music is music in and for itself and nothing else," was understood correctly and did not fail to have an effect. Since the 1920s, at the latest, programs were taboo (works like Alban Berg's *Chamber Concerto* and *Lyric Suite*, which were based on suppressed programs, prove it), and attempts to enrich music once again by a literary or philosophical dimension were dismissed as anachronisms.

---

15 Claude Debussy, *Monsieur Croche*, 281.
16 Ferruccio Busoni, *Von der Einheit der Musik. Verstreute Aufzeichnungen* (Berlin, 1922), 275–278.

We have existed in this tradition for decades. While the development of art music during the last 75 years cannot be reduced to a single formula – there have been many changes – the fear of depth has remained constant. Many balk at accepting music as a vehicle of philosophic, literary, religious, political ideas and contents. Music is received as "moving sound forms," as "music in and for itself," according to Hanslick's and Busoni's postulates. Professionals who swear by structural listening find associative listening at least suspect. And to be honest: who today, in listening to the symphonic works of Hector Berlioz, Franz Liszt and Richard Strauss – to name only these three composers – thinks of the program of the *Symphonie fantastique*, of Schiller's *Ideale*, of Lamartine's *Méditations poétiques* or of Nietzsche's *Also sprach Zarathustra*? Who has any interest in Mahler's retracted programs, though they still dictate the structure of the symphonies and the shape of the music? And yet, one will be permitted to ask next, is such a reception adequate, or even correct?

Dreams about falling, Sigmund Freud asserts, are mostly characterized by anxiety – a symptom surely of some repressions.[17] Does our fear of depth in music perhaps signify a fear of our own self, of our own problems and abysses? Busoni's reference to the desideratum of serenity seems to suggest as much.

3. Absurd Music and Music as Message

> "Not to believe in the deeper meaning of things – that is the peculiarity of absurd man." Albert Camus[18]

The development of vocal composition after the Second World War was such that people spoke of *sprachzerfall* – linguistic disintegration – in the New Music. That verdict becomes clearer if one thinks of the area of the so-called *sprachkomposition*,[19] speech composition, that is to say, the various attempts to treat speech as music, to regard it exclusively as phonetic

---

17 Sigmund Freud, *Die Traumdeutung* (Fischer Bücher des Wissens 428/429) (Frankfurt/Hamburg, 1961), 326.
18 Albert Camus, *Le Mythe de Sisyphe, in: Essais,* ed. R. Quilliot (Bibliothèque de la Pléiade, no. 183), Paris 1965, 154.
19 See Wilfried Gruhn, *Musiksprache – Sprachmusik – Textvertonung* (Schriftenreihe zur Musikpädagogik) (Frankfurt, 1978).

material, to destroy its syntactic structure and to largely or wholly disregard its semantic dimension. The dialectics between the phonetics and the semantics of the text, it seems, is a pivot of Avant-garde vocal composition, and much depends on whether a composer is willing to take the "meaning" of the text seriously. Some compositions were downright proud to have "ousted" or "exorcized" all meaning from the textual passages adduced. It can be shown that therein lies a very serious problem.

The idea of speech composition can to some extent be defined as an offshoot of a tendency toward musicalizing language – a tendency that begins with the Romantic poets and that later takes concrete shape among the French Symbolists and the Dadaists. In Mallarmé and in Rimbaud one gets in varying degrees the impression that in their poetry the sound of the words and the magic of the language matter more than the "meaning." The avant-gardist composers of 1950s and 1960s – Karlheinz Stockhausen, Dieter Schnebel, Mauricio Kagel and György Ligeti – picked up those ideas, took a lively interest in linguistics and pursued phonological studies. All of them were fascinated by the idea of employing the sounds of speech as timbres, as sound values.

Some tendencies in speech composition, however, also want to be regarded against the background of the conviction that language has become conventionalized to the extent of rigor mortis and so worn out that it no longer says anything. The dismantling of language thus results logically from a fundamental critique of language, as well as from the admission of being literally speechless.

Of considerable importance, moreover, is the fascination that the philosophy of the absurd has exercised on modern art, modern theater, modern poetry and contemporary music. In a weighty article, Harald Kaufmann called Ligeti's *Aventures* and *Nouvelles aventures* cases of "absurd music" and sought to make clear that the absurdity was to be regarded, not as a leveling but as an intensification and differentiation of the intellectually meaningful.[20]

---

20 Harald Kaufmann, "Ein Fall absurder Musik. Ligetis 'Aventures & Nouvelles Aventures'," in *Spurlinien. Analytische Aufsätze über Sprache und Musik* (Vienna, 1969) 130–158; p. 138.

In reflecting about the aesthetic and philosophical presuppositions of speech composition, one would, finally, also have to refer to the works of Dieter Schnebel – *Glossolalie, Madrasha II* – which are at home in a spiritual realm. The idea they circle about is the synthesis of languages, the realization and simultaneously the abolition of the Babylonian confusion of tongues, the search for a total, universal, global language.

In 1976, Werner Klüppelholz declared the end of speech composition and summed it up as follows:

> To critique this, the human communication, is the real purpose of the musical composition of language. Its arbitrary offenses against syntax and semantics demolish a language whose damaged condition is to be brought to light exactly thereby; artistic defamiliarization of language reflects the alienation of its users from an all-too familiar one, as well as from what it stands for.[21]

Of course, there were also other views. Thus Luigi Nono objected in 1960 in Darmstadt to Karlheinz Stockhausen's interpretation of *Il canto sospeso*, especially to the imputation that Nono in this work had "quite deliberately driven out all meaning from certain textual passages." On this occasion Nono professed emphatically that in his view the word formed a "phonetic-semantic totality," and that the music of all his later choral compositions was to be understood as "composed expression of the word."[22] That was a plea for the conception of music as message.

Nono's plea will not be an isolated one. Every kind of committed music proclaims a message. In this sense, master works like Beethoven's *Ninth Symphony*, his *Fidelio*, the music dramas of Richard Wagner and the symphonies of Bruckner and Mahler cannot be perceived other than as music as message.

The question whether one commits oneself to absurd music (in some respect also to the so-called absolute music) or to the idea of music as message is in the final analysis a question of the "epistemological" and ideological position that each of us decides to occupy. It is really as Albert Camus recognized: the question is whether one believes in the deeper meaning of things or disavows it.

---

21 Werner Klüppelholz, *Sprache als Musik. Studien zur Vokalkomposition seit 1956* (Herrenberg, 1976), 198.

22 Luigi Nono, "Text – Musik – Gesang." In *Texte. Studien zu seiner Musik*, ed. Jürg Stenzl (Zurich/Freiburg, 1975), 41–60; p. 60.

IV. "Relational Magic" in the Music of Wagner's *Ring of the Nibelung*

> "He was a musician as a poet and a poet as a musician."
> Thomas Mann about Wagner

1. On the Function of the Leitmotif

Whoever studies the music in the *Ring of the Nibelung*, indeed in any of Richard Wagner's dramas, may experience something strange: even if one tries hard, one cannot separate the music, even temporarily, from the poetic text and contemplate it as *music as such*. Music in Wagner is so intimately bound up with the text that any attempt to isolate the musical part is bound to fail. By contrast one can experience Wagner's poetry, if need be, separately from the music – quasi as literature. Wagner himself provided a justification for that. Although he had only words of contempt for closet dramas,[1] he often let the texts of his music dramas be printed separately and judged as such.

Music in Wagner attains undreamed-of dimensions: the poetry endows it with *meaning*, with extra-musical semantics. The orchestra has multiple and frequently novel tasks to perform: it illustrates the scenic events, deepens the drama emotionally, and interprets the action psychologically. The music thereby in many ways functions, as it were, like a depth probe of the unconscious, becomes a medium of subtle allusions, recollections and references.

The procedure by which Wagner achieves all this is called *leitmotif* technique – a famous method that has provoked both admiration and ridicule. Its impact on the post-Wagnerian opera and modern literature – think of Thomas Mann, James Joyce or Hans Henny Jahnn – was enormous. Even so, catastrophic misunderstandings still reign about its precise nature. They began, at the latest, when Claude Debussy called the *Ring* a "musical address directory" and charged Wagner with having violated music by the rigid use of the leitmotif technique.[2] Igor Stravinsky and others went

---

1 Richard Wagner, *Das Kunstwerk der Zukunft*, GS, 3:111–113.
2 Claude Debussy, *Monsieur Croche et autres écrits*, 271; cf. ibid., 41, 175.

even farther, comparing the leitmotifs disparagingly to cloakroom tickets,[3] trademarks,[4] or allegorical miniatures.[5]

As clever as these comparisons may appear, they do no justice to the matter. Wagner's method is far more subtle than these characterizations would lead us to think.

It seems as if only Thomas Mann finally discerned Wagner's true intentions. It is in his essays, at any rate, that we find the most profound insights into the nature of the leitmotif. Mann, who confessed to have learned immensely from Wagner, admired him not only as a "passionate theater man," mythmaker and psychologist, but also a great epic poet. The *Ring* in Mann's view is a "scenic epic," a work that owes its grandeur to the "spirit of epic art," and at the same time one in which Wagner's "technique of thematic-motivic texture" achieves its greatest triumphs. The purpose of this technique, Mann says, is to construct ingenious and profound connections and allusions and to spread the "thematic texture" not only across one scene or one drama but across the entire tetralogy. Wagner's relation to music, in Mann's interpretation, was not purely musical but poetic in the sense that it was crucially determined by "the intellectual quality, the symbolism of the music, its signifying appeal, its reminiscence value and "relational magic" (*Beziehungszauber*).[6]

Wagner himself had explained the basic features of his method as early as 1851 in his essay *Eine Mitteilung an meine Freunde* (A Message to my Friends). His elucidations, however, were not always taken adequate notice of. In the essay, he describes how he got away from the traditional operatic forms and came up with formations that were adequate to the nature of his subjects and the mode of representation required by them. In the process he makes quite clear that his leitmotif technique – he himself does not use that term – was primarily a literary one. While working on *Tannhäuser*, and even more markedly on *Lohengrin*, he came to realize that in one of

---

3 Igor Stravinsky, *Musikalische Poetik* (Mainz, 1949), 48.
4 Ernst Bloch, "Paradoxa und Pastorale bei Wagner," in *Zur Philosophie der Musik* (Frankfurt a.M., 1974), 242.
5 Theodor W. Adorno, *Versuch über Wagner* (Berlin/Frankfurt a.M., 1952), 53.
6 Thomas Mann, "Leiden und Größe Richard Wagners" (1933) and "Richard Wagner und der 'Ring des Nibelungen'" (1937), in *Ausgewählte Essays in drei Bänden* (FischerTaschenbuch Verlag No. 1908) (Frankfurt a.M., 1978), 73, 120, 130.

the crucial scenes in the drama no *mood* must be struck "that was not importantly *related* to the moods of the other scenes, so that the development of the moods from each other, and the consistently noticeable perception of this development, inevitably produced the expressive unity of the drama." Corresponding to this state of affairs, the task was to create a "texture" of major musical themes that would extend over the entire drama "in intimate relation to the poetic intention." It is highly instructive that Wagner here speaks of the "texture" or "weave" of his music and of a characteristic "interconnection and ramification of the thematic motifs."[7]

The *Ring* is the first work in which the leitmotif technique is systematically applied. On January 25, 184, Wagner wrote, in a highly important letter to his friend August Röckel, about the composition of the *Rheingold* that it had become "a firm, intricately linked unity": the orchestra, he said, produced hardly a single measure that was not developed from preceding motifs.[8] This statement is not to be dismissed as an exaggeration; the score of the *Rheingold* is indeed distinguished by an admirable thematic economy. Wagner based the tetralogy on a sizable number of leitmotifs, which are exposed, elaborated, altered, regrouped, given new harmonic lights, combined and symphonically developed. Some motifs recur in all four parts of the stage festival cycle, while others are confined to a single drama. There is no consensus as to the total number of motifs. While Hans von Wolzogen (the official Wagner exegete) cites 90 motifs,[9] Arthur Smolian counts 114.[10]

A semantic analysis of the motifs shows that they designate a variety of things: persons, objects feelings, emotion, passions, states of nature, ideas. Corresponding to the tangle of the Nibelung myth, which Wagner shaped into a cosmic tragedy, they comprise the entire universe of being, nearly the entirety of the Teutonic mythology.

---

7 *Eine Mitteilung an meine Freunde* GS, 4:322.
8 Richard Wagner, *Sämtliche Werke*, vol. 29, I. *Dokumente zur Entstehungsgeschichte des Bühnenfestspiels Der Ring des Nibelungen*, ed. Werner Breig und Hartmut Fladt (Mainz, 1976), 94.
9 Hans von Wolzogen, *Führer durch die Musik zu Richard Wagner's Festspiel Der Ring des Nibelungen. Ein thematischer Leitfaden* (Leipzig, n.d.).
10 Arthur Smolian, *Richard Wagner's Bühnenfestspiel Der Ring des Nibelungen. Ein Vademedum* (Meisterführer No. 2) (Berlin, n.d. [1901]).

It can't be denied that Wagner's music has here and there an illustrative, decorative character. Some motifs function as building blocks for the composition of grand natural scenes. They include the billowing waters of the *Rheingold* prelude, the rainbow music in the final *Rheingold* scene, the storm in *Die Walküre*, the forest murmurs in *Siegfried*, and the sunrise in *Götterdämmerung*. Wagner paints with musical means the glow of the Rhine gold, the climbing of Alberich, the ride of the Valkyries, the flickering of the fire.

But one should not overestimate the importance of the descriptive function. Music to Wagner – as to other Romantics – is the language of the soul. According to his dramatic theory, the tonal language is the organ of the "inner feeling of the soul," in contrast to verbal language, the organ of reason.[11] Thus psychic and symbolic qualities always cling to the motifs. The Siegfried motif, for example, symbolizes not only the person of Siegfried but also the idea of heroism, the heroic. Characteristically, the motif sounds repeatedly already in *Die Walküre*, long before Siegfried is born – for the first time when Brünnhilde tells Sieglinde: "the world's most noble of heroes you hold in your nurturing womb!" (*den hehrsten Helden der Welt hegst du, o Weib, im schirmenden Schooß!*)[12] Thus the Siegfried motif is initially an emblem of the as yet unborn "fearlessly freest of heroes,"[13] from whom Wotan and Brünnhilde, each in his and her own way, hope for the redemption of the world.

2. The Categories Presentiment, Realization and Remembrance

Like virtually no other composer of the 19th century, Wagner psychologized and semanticized music. Of great help in more deeply understanding his leitmotif technique are his arguments in his book *Opera and Drama*, specifically in the third part, where he deals in detail with the relation of poetic and musical art. The pivot of his discussion is the relation of verbal and tonal language, of thought and feeling or emotion, of "verse melody" and orchestra. He distinguishes between three stages, states or moments of the dramatic

---

11 *Oper und Drama*, GS, 4:99.
12 *Die Walküre*, Eulenburg-Taschenpartitur (hereafter ETP), 793–795. We always quote hereafter from the five-volumn anniversary edition of the Edition Eulenburg (Nos. 907–910).
13 *Die Walküre*, ETP, 956/957.

expression: *Ahnung* (presentiment), *Vergegenwärtigung* (realization, literally "present-ation" or making present) and *Erinnerung* (remembrance, recollection). Wagner speaks of *Vergegenwärtigung* when the actor/singer communicates a thought and expresses the feeling latent in it via the sung melody (the "verse melody"). If at a later point in the drama the orchestra picks up this melody (i.e., a certain motif), the listener remembers (*erinnert*) that thought, and the music thereby attains an extra-musical significance. In other instances, the orchestra may anticipate a not yet conceptually expressed mood or state of mind. In that case Wagner speaks of *Ahnung* and defines it as "the manifestation of an *unexpressed,* because, in the sense of our verbal language, as yet *inexpressible,* feeling" (italics added).[14] The music of the *Ring* is full of such *Erinnerungen* and *Ahnungen,* remembrances and presentiments or intimations, allusions to past and future incidents. The leitmotif has both a reminding/remembering and a prophetic/predictive function.

Vergegenwärtigung and *Erinnerung* are well illustrated by the example of the motif of the curse. The curse idea is among the motifs that run like a red thread through the entire tetralogy. It is first expressed in the fourth scene of *Das Rheingold.* Wotan and Loge have captured Alberich by cunning. To regain his freedom, Alberich has to give up everything he has: his hoard, his tarn helmet and even his ring. His first act after Loge has unbound him, is therefore to curse the ring: "As by curse I made it mine, so cursed be now this ring" (*Wie durch Fluch er mir geriet, verflucht sei dieser Ring*), he exclaims, with timpani tremolo, to the tune of the curse motif.[15]

---

14 *Oper und Drama,* GS, 4:186–192.
15 *Das Rheingold,* ETP, 564.

Only a little later, we are confronted with a similar situation: to free Freia from her bondage to the giants, the gods must now relinquish the hoard, the tarn helmet and also the ring to the latter. In a quarrel about the ring, Fafner slays his brother Fasolt. As a first *remembrance* of Alberich's curse, the orchestra thereupon intones the curse motif, and Wotan, shaken to the core, comments: "Frightful, now I see, is the curse's force!"[16]

No owner of the ring escapes Alberich's curse: neither Fafner nor even Siegfried. In quarreling about the ring, Gunther is slain, and even Alberich's son Hagen becomes a final victim of his father's curse. Only after the ring has, through Brünnhilde's fiery immolation, returned to the possession of the Rhine Maidens, does the curse lose its power: a fragment of the motif resounds for a last time in the orchestra, and then the curse falls silent forever.[17]

A striking example of the anticipatory use of leitmotifs – what Wagner calls *Ahnung* – occurs in Act II of *Die Walküre*, in the fourth scene, which takes place between Brünnhilde and Siegmund. The scene is ushered in by an orchestral prelude, which consists of three motifs: the motif of fate or the so-called fatal question, the motif of the annunciation of death and a segment of the Valhalla motif. The latter is familiar from *Das Rheingold*. The other two, however, appear here for the first time, so that the listener does not yet know them. Their semantics reveals itself gradually, when the actors begin to sing. Brünnhilde tells Siegmund that he will die in the imminent fight with Hunding and will enter Valhalla. For the musical interpretation of this conceptual content, the first section of the scene is furnished almost exclusively with the three motifs, which stand for fate, the imminence of death and

---

16 *Das Rheingold*, ETP, 654.
17 *Götterdämmerung*, ETP, 1333.

Valhalla. Siegmund's question, "Who are you, say, who so fair and somber appears?" is intoned to the tune of the Annunciation of Death. Brünnhilde's reply, "The death-doomed only I appear to; whoever sees me parts from the light of life" is underscored by the motif of fate.[18] Fate, death and Valhalla (the "Hall of the Slain") here belong together, literally as well as musically, and trigger a chain of associations. And once one has grasped the meaning of the motifs, one also understands the semantics of the orchestral prelude: the listener is to be given a presentiment that Siegmund's fate is sealed, that he will die (see the musical example below).

Perhaps the deepest insight into the nature and the psychological function of the leitmotifs we get from those double-bottomed moments in Wagner when the statement of a character does not appear to agree with that of the orchestra. To explain that situation, Ernst Bloch used the simile of events taking place on two floor levels of a building: in some instances the sung text up above, he says, does not at all speak and act where the leitmotif of the music on the lower level is speaking and acting. As an illustration Bloch also cited an example from the *Walküre*, which, however, belongs to a different category.[19]

18 *Die Walküre*, ETP, 491 ff.
19 Ernst Bloch, *Zur Philosophie der Musik*, 246.

All the more instructive is an example from Act II, scene 2 of *Siegfried*. To teach Siegfried fear, Mime leads him to the cave of Fafner, the giant who has turned himself into a dragon. Mime's emphatic evocation of the dragon's dangerousness makes no impression whatever on the young hero. Naturally, Fafner motifs dominate in the orchestra. But in two places, the motif of the sleeping Brünnhilde crops up – quite unexpectedly, as the Valkyrie, asleep within the sea of flames surrounding her, has no direct connection with the topic of the conversation. A closer scrutiny of the words, however, makes clear that Wagner here performs something like a psychoanalysis of the leitmotif. Mime's words, "When your sight gets blurred, the ground seems to shake, your heart within begins to quake" (*Wenn dein Blick verschwimmt, der Boden dir schwankt, im Busen bang dein Herz erbebt*),[20] refer to the terror the dragon can inspire. In that the orchestra accompanies the word with the motif of Brünnhilde, however, the music beams a light into the unconscious, revealing that Siegfried is afraid only of love.

4. "The Necessity of Doom"

Curse and doom or destruction belong together in the *Ring*. The gods, too, are affected by Alberich's curse. Because they have become unfree, fearful and impotent, they must perish. The idea of the longed-for, even willed end threads the tetralogy like a conceptual leitmotif. Introduced in the *Rheingold*, it is consistently developed in *Die Walküre* and *Siegfried* and is brought to its conclusion in *Götterdämmerung*. Let us trace the chief stages of this development.

The second scene of *Rheingold* commences with an unclouded picture of divine glory. The scene introduces Wotan and Fricka asleep on a mountain height at daybreak, with the gods' new citadel visible in the background. Wotan dreams of honor, "eternal might" and "endless renown." As he awakens, he praises the "resplendent seat" of the castle as a "work ever-lasting." The thought that the magnificent castle has been erected by the giants and that they will demand their pay does not yet trouble him. Wagner underpinned this section logically with the Valhalla motif, which signals

---

20 *Siegfried*, ETP, 547/548.

various aspects of one and the same thing: the divine citadel, the world of the gods, as well as the person of Wotan. The use of the motif is thus quite natural and convincing. What gives us pause is that although nothing is said of the ring in this episode, the orchestra intones the Ring motif (a creepy, minatory counterpart of the Valhalla motif!) simultaneously with Wotan's first words – thus suggesting Wotan's thirst for power.[21]

Sure enough, Wotan comes into possession of the ring by cunning, and under no circumstances wants to part from it when the giants demand it as part of the ransom for Freia. The decisive turn in the dramatic conflict is brought about in the fourth scene by the sudden appearance of Erda. She rises from the depths, discloses her identity as all-knowing seeress and mother of the Norns, warns Wotan of the Ring's curse and the danger lying in wait from Alberich, and prophesies the end of the gods: "All that is ends. A dark day dawns for the gods: you I advise: shun the ring" (*Alles was ist, endet! Ein düstrer Tag dämmert den Göttern : dir rat' ich, meide den Ring!*).[22] In full agreement with the dramatic situation, the music of this section (which has a faint resemblance to the spectral scenes of operatic tradition) is based on the Norn (Erda) motif, the motif of destruction, that of the Twilight of the Gods, the *götterdämmerung*, and the Ring motif. The Norn motif and that of the *götterdämmerung* make their first appearance here; both are indissolubly linked to the idea of doom, of *untergang*.

21 *Das Rheingold*, ETP, 188–190.
22 *Das Rheingold*, ETP, 631–633.

Wagner finished the *Ring* libretto in December of 1852. At this point he had not yet read Arthur Schopenhauer's *chef-d'oeuvre*, *Die Welt als Wille und Vorstellung* (*The World as Will and Idea*). Independently of Schopenhauer, he had already developed a deeply pessimistic weltanschauung. In a letter to Röckel, he commented on the words of Erda just cited by saying: "we must learn to *die*, and to *die* in the fullest sense of the word; the fear of the end is the source of all lovelessness, and it is engendered only where love itself is already fading."[23]

The idea of *untergang*, only hinted at in *Das Rheingold*, is psychologically motivated and broadly developed in *Die Walküre*. Wotan's long narrative in Act II is undoubtedly the most tragic monologue of the tetralogy and one of the most appalling monologues in all of operatic literature: a god expounds why he wishes for self-annihilation. In doing so, Wotan repeatedly refers to Erda and her sayings: he relates how Erda, to whom he descended, warned him of Alberich, his armies and his possible son.

The monologue has two dramatic climaxes. The first is ushered in by Wotan's confession that through contracts/treaties he has become unfree. Fricka now has destroyed his wish dream of creating the free hero working out of his own strength: he has to sacrifice Siegmund, his beloved son, to her legalism. The stage direction at this point reads: Wotan's gestures turn from an expression of direst agony into ones of despair."[24] The curse and the sword motif sound in the orchestra in immediate succession, and

23 *Dokumente zu Der Ring des Nibelungen*, 92.
24 *Die Walküre*, ETP, 403.

then follows the outburst: "Begone, then, imperious pomp, divine splendor's boastful disgrace! Let what I built sink into ruin! I give up my work; I want but one thing still: to end all, to end all!" (*Fahre denn hin herrische Pracht, göttlichen Prunkes prahlende Schmach! Zusammen breche, was ich gebaut! Auf geb ich mein Werk; nur eines will ich noch: das Ende, das Ende!*) Wagner's comment on this passage in the letter to Röckel reads: "Wodan rises to the tragic height of – *willing* his destruction. That is all we have to learn from human history: to *will what is necessary* and to bring it about ourselves."[25]

The second climax is even more appalling. Wotan quotes Erda's saying "When love's benighted foe sires a son in his rage, then the end of the blessed tarries not long," and reveals how Alberich has in fact conceived a son while he, Wotan, did not succeed in creating the longed-for *free* man. Conscious of this failure, he exclaims in loathing and despair: "So take then my blessing, Nibelung son! What wholly disgusts me, to you I bequeath it, the godhead's empty splendor: gorge it in envious greed!"[26]

The leitmotif heard in the orchestra at this point (Hans von Wolzogen labeled it "Blessing on the Nibelung's son") has become famous and is enormously instructive for Wagner's technique. A close look reveals that it is composed of two basic motifs, the Valhalla motif and the Rhine gold motif. Both motifs, however, appear in a minor key and are strangely interlaced. Especially the shape of the Valhalla motif is distorted both rhythmically and harmonically. This modification was intentional: Wagner thus wanted to convey, as he wrote later, "an image of the frightfully darkened soul of the suffering god."[27]

25 *Dokumente*, 92.
26 *Die Walküre*, ETP, 418–421.
27 "Über die Anwendung der Musik auf das Drama," GS, 10:188.

Rheingoldfanfare

Walhallmotiv

die beiden Motive in Veränderung und Verflechtung

The idea of *untergang* is then further developed in Act III of *Siegfried*. At a nocturnal hour, Wotan awakens Erda from deep sleep, longing to know how he can intervene in the cosmic process. But Erda, the "sacredly wisest Vala,"[28] her wisdom at an end, refers him to the Norns and to Brünnhilde. Wotan once more proclaims his will to self-annihilation. But the situation has meanwhile fundamentally changed insofar as the god's former total resignation and embitterment has yielded to a mood of euphoria: whereas in the great monologue in the *Walküre*, Wotan in his rage was willing to leave the rule of the world to the Nibelung's son, he now believes he can perceive the "fearlessly freest of heroes" of his dreams after all in Siegfried and proclaims that he wants to bequeath his legacy to Siegfried and Brünnhilde.

In a letter to King Ludwig II. Of November 6, 1864, Wagner said of this scene:

> It is the most sublime scene of the most tragic of my heroes: Wotan, that is, the all-powerful will to live, has resolved on his self-sacrifice; greater now in renunciation than when he desired, he now feels all-powerful, and he calls out to earthly

---

28 *Die Walküre*, ETP 364.

ur-wisdom, the Nature mother "Erda," who once taught him the fear of the end, that no anxiety could any longer shackle him, since with the same will with which he once only desired life he now wills his end. His end? He knows what Erda's ur-wisdom does not know, that he will live on in Siegfried.[29]

A listener who has the leitmotifs of the first two *Ring* dramas in his ear and knows their semantics can gather from the prelude to the third act – even before the curtain rises – that the next scene will take place between Wotan and Erda, since the music consists almost exclusively of Wotan and Erda motifs.[30] Pertaining to Wotan are the motifs of the *götternot*, gods' distress, and the spear motif, to Erda the motifs of the Norns and of the *götterdämmerung* and the sleep harmonies. In a subtle allusion, the harmonies that characterize the sleep of the all-knowing Erda are the same with which Wotan put Brünnhilde to sleep at the end of the *Walküre*. Equally subtle is the fact that two scenes later another woman – this time Brünnhilde – is awakened – by Siegfried – from deep sleep. The *Ring* is full of such allusions and parallels.

But to return to the Erda scene: its music is developed systematically from older motifs (the only really new one is that of World Heritage, the *Welterbe*), yet it bears its own unmistakable physiognomy. One need not be a Wagnerian to admire Wagner's skill in creating ever new forms from already existing material.

Wotan's hopefulness in the Erda scene springs from his belief that Alberich's curse will not be able to touch Siegfried.[31]Alberich fears exactly the same thing. In Act II of *Götterdämmerung*, he laments to the sleeping Hagen: "Against the fearless hero even my curse will fail" (*An dem furchtlosen Helden erlahmt selbst mein Fluch*).[32] The music of the Norn scene at the beginning of *Götterdämmerung* has it differently and truer: the leitmotifs in the orchestra predict that Siegfried, too, will be destroyed by the curse.

---

29 *Dokumente*, 142.
30 *Siegfried*, ETP, 757 ff.
31 *Siegfried*, ETP, 857/858.
32 *Götterdämmerung*, ETP, 571/572.

According to the Teutonic mythology, the Norns are the goddesses of fate.[33] They administer, foresee, impose and pronounce the destiny that rules even the gods. At the beginning of *Götterdämmerung*, they warp and weave the golden rope, the emblem of the thread of life. They prophesy the end of the gods and the burning of Valhalla.[34] In the orchestra, the motifs of fate, of the annunciation of death and of the twilight of the gods dominate portentously. At the end of the scene, the rope suddenly ruptures. "Eternal knowledge" is at an end; the Norns descend to their mother. Here again the informational content of the music is richer than the textual one. Before the rupture, we twice hear fragments of Siegfried's horn call, which are followed by the curse motif. The sequence foretells musically that Siegfried, too, will succumb to Alberich's curse (see the musical illustration below.)

The conclusion of *Götterdämmerung* contains a crux that has occupied numerous critics and has been interpreted in diverse ways. We know that the tetralogy grew from a one-part drama entitled *Siegfried's Death*, whose text Wagner completed already in 1848. Its conclusion differs in an essential way from the end of the tetralogy in its final version. Brünnhilde returns the ring to the Rhine daughters and ascends the flaming pyre, but there follows no Twilight of the Gods: the gods continue to rule.[35] By contrast, the end of *Götterdämmerung* has Valhalla go up in flames – the gods perish. Brünnhilde here proclaims expressly: "For the end of the gods now is dawning. Thus I throw the blaze into Valhalla's glorious keep" (*Denn der Götter Ende dämmert nun auf. So werf' ich den Brand in Walhalls prangende Burg*).[36]

---

33 Jacob Grimm, *Deutsche Mythologie*, vol 1 (Ullstein Buch No. 35107) (Frankfurt, 1981), 335, 340, 352.
34 *Götterdämmerung*, ETP, 31–39.
35 "Siegfrieds Tod," GS, 2:227.
36 *Götterdämmerung*, ETP, 1298–1301.

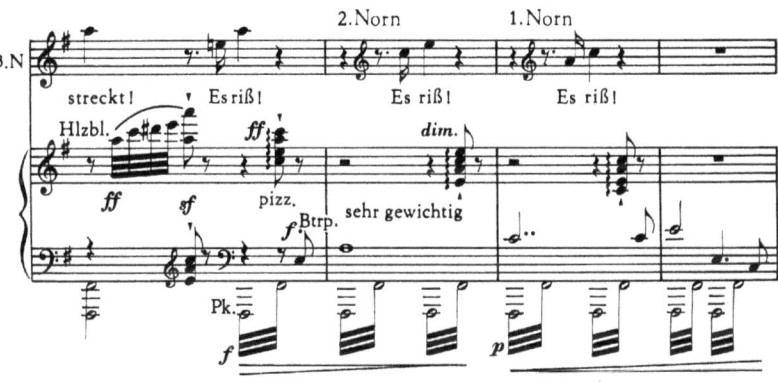

This negative apotheosis has been called Bakunist, imputing an echo of the anarchist and revolutionary ideas of Mikhail Bakunin and of the Dresden uprising of 1849.[37] Wagner himself, in the letter to Röckel, speaks of the "necessity of doom," the *Notwendigkeit des Untergangs* – a necessity growing out of an innermost feeling.[38]

Now it is one of the curiosities of this "stage festival play" that the conclusion of the *Götterdämmerung* has come down to us, in a way, in three versions. The printed edition of the poem contains, besides the one set to music, two additional, uncomposed versions. One of these, which has been called Feuerbachian, culminates in a glorification of love. Brünnhilde proclaims:

Nicht Gut, nicht Gold,	Not goods, not gold,
noch göttliche Pracht;	nor splendor of gods;
nicht Haus, nicht Hof,	not house, not court,
noch herrischer Prunk;	nor arrogant pomp;
nicht trüber Verträge	not turbid treaties'
trügender Bund,	treacherous bond,
nicht heuchelnder Sitte	not sham morality's
hartes Gesetz;	obdurate law;
selig in Lust und Leid	blessed in joy and pain
läßt – die Liebe nur sein.[94]	life can be but through – love.

The other version, inspired by Schopenhauer and by Buddhist ideas, is profoundly pessimistic. Brünnhilde sees the "end of the world" and knows herself redeemed by *rebirth*.

Wagner noted in the printed edition of the poem that he had not set these verses to music because "their gist" was expressed "with greatest certainty already by the impact of the musically sounding drama."[40] Doubt has been cast on the candor and correctness of this statement, but, it seems, unjustly so.

---

37 Hans Mayer, *Richard Wagner in Selbstzeugnissen und Bilddokumenten* (row-ohlts monographien 29) (Hamburg, 1959), 147–150. See also Peter Wapnewski, *Der traurige Gott. Richard Wagner in seinen Helden* (Munich, 1978), 185–197.
38 *Dokumente*, 93.
39 Götterdämmerung, GS, 6:255.
40 GS, 6:256.

The last pages of the score of *Götterdämmerung* pass several key leit-motifs of the tetralogy quasi in review. At the end, often contrapuntally intertwined, we thus hear the Valhalla motif, the Rhine Maidens motif and the motif of Redemption through Love, which has the final say.

Did Wagner with these final symphonic notes not make quite clear how everything was meant? Only a total conflagration may cleanse the world of the curse and misuse of gold. But the only force, in the composer's view, that can make humanity truly free and counteract violence, oppression and the striving for power is love. World-redeeming love: that was Wagner's central theme. All his dramas, from *The Flying Dutchman* all the way to *Parsifal*, are in the final analysis but variations on this theme.

V. Wagner's Idea of a Religion of Art

> "The purification and hallowing of [art] was for him a means of
> purifying and hallowing a corrupt society; he was a cathartic, a
> cleansing being, who wanted to liberate society by means of an
> aesthetic consecration from luxury, lovelessness and the sway
> of money, very close in his social ethos to the Russian epic
> master [Tolstoy]." Thomas Mann about Wagner

1. By Way of Introduction

In no other era of European intellectual history have people thought as
intensively about the affinities between art and religion as they did in the
19th century. It may seem paradoxical, but is nevertheless logical: the century that plunged religion into a deep crisis and opened the doors wide to
atheism was at the same time the age that traced the origins of art back to
religion. The assumption cannot easily be dismissed that many thought
to find in art a substitute for religion – thought that they could satisfy
their spiritual needs by taking refuge in art. It is certain, at any rate, that
the notion of the holiness of art, and especially of music, arose in the
Romantic Movement and rapidly became a topos. To Wilhelm Heinrich
Wackenroder, music was a "holy art."[1] Ludwig Tieck regarded it as "the
ultimate mystery of faith, the mysticism, the wholly revealed religion."[2]
E.T.A. Hoffmann, poet and musician in one, conceived of it as "intimation
of the highest and holiest," as a "cult" whose origin was solely in religion.[3] Georg Wilhelm Friedrich Hegel taught that, objectively speaking,
the beginning of art stood "in closest connection with religion,"[4] and it

---

1 Gerhard Fricke, *Wackenroders Religion der Kunst* (Iserlohn, 1948).

2 In Wilhelm Heirich Wackenroder, *Phantasien über die Kunst für Freunde der
   Kunst* (1799), second section, no. 9: "Symphonien." Quoted from the collected
   works and letters (Heidelberg: Lambert Schneider, 1967), 251.

3 E. T. A. Hoffmann, "Alte und neue Kirchenmusik" (1814), in *Schriften zur
   Musik*, ed. Friedrich Schnapp (Munich: Winkler, n.d.) 212.

4 *Georg Wilhelm Friedrich Hegel, Vorlesungen über die Ästhetik I, Gesamtausgabe* (Frankfurt a.M.: Suhrkamp, 1970), 13:409.

was also Hegel who, in the *Phenomenology of the Spirit*, coined the term *Kunst-Religion*, religion of art.[5]

Its special nimbus, however, the idea obtained only in the second half of the 19th century through the work of Richard Wagner. He not only developed his ideas about the close nexus between art and religion theoretically in 1880, but in 1882, with the premiere of *Parsifal*, a work he called *Bühnenweihfestspiel* – roughly "consecrational stage festival play" – demonstrated to the art world what the religion of art of which he dreamed should look like. It would have been strange indeed if his followers had not celebrated him, more or less secretly, as a religious founder.

Upon first – or once again – delving into Wagner's writings, one cannot but be astonished at the breadth of his subjects. He occupies himself not only with art-theoretical questions, but also with matters of politics, society, economy, science, ethics and religion.[6] His prolixity ceases to be puzzling only once one realizes that his thinking is based on a holistic, universalistic conception, according to which everything is connected with everything else. Wagner was certainly no philosopher, but his endeavor to trace everything back to an *urgrund*, a first cause, a basis of all things, is indeed philosophical. He was fully persuaded that art was closely connected to life; his entire thinking ran contrary to the concept of autonomy, of *l'art pour l'art*.

In 1864, Ludwig II. asked him to indicate whether and to what extent his views about state and religion had changed since his Zurich papers. Wagner thereupon composed a sizable treatise entitled *Über Staat und Religion*, in which he cites the "seriousness" of his artistic striving as the reason for his

---

5   *Phänomenologie des Geistes* (Ullstein Materialien no. 35055) (Frankfurt/Berlin/ Vienna, 1980), 388 f. – Cf. Adolf Nowak, "Wagners Parsifal und die Idee der Kunstrreligion," in Carl Dahlhaus, ed., *Richard Wagner, Werk und Wirkung* (Studien zur Musikgeschichte des 19. Jahrhunderts, vol 26) (Regensburg, 1971), 161–174.

6   Cf. Hugo Dinger, *Richard Wagners geistige Entwickelung* (Leipzig, 1892); Paul Moos, *Richard Wagner als Ästhetiker* (Berlin/Leipzig, 1906); Karl Wilhelm Zinnius, *Die Schriften Richard Wagners in ihrem Verhältnis zur zeitgeschichtlichen Lage* (Heidelberg, 1936): Rainer Franke, *Richard Wagners Zürcher Kunstschriften* (Hamburger Beiträge zur Musikwissenschaft, vol. 26) (Hamburg, 1983).

occupation with questions of politics and religious philosophy. "What I was looking for," he writes, "was really always only my art – an art I took so seriously that I searched and demanded for it a warranting basis in life, in the state, and finally in religion."[7] To fully understand this statement, one should recall that in his Zurich papers he hoped for, and expected, the renewal of art to come from a radical transformation of society and of ethics. He expressed similar ideas thirty years later in his writings about regeneration.

Another basic point, too, deserves our attention. Together with Friedrich Nietzsche, Wagner was one of the sharpest critics of his century.[8] He mordantly criticized everybody and everything: not only the art scene of his time, Giacomo Meyerbeer and the grand opera, but also all the institutions of state and society, the materialism of science, the churches and religions, the age's shallow morals and other matters. As one-sided and subjective as this criticism may seem, one should realize that Wagner also developed alternatives for everything. His notions how the arts and society should look in the future were in part abstruse but almost always also quite concrete. One has to keep this visionary, utopian aspect of his thinking in mind if one wants to do justice to his idea of a religion of art.

2. Art and Religion in Wagner's Zurich Papers

Wagner presented his theory of the *kunstreligion* in a long treatise, which appeared in 1880 in the *Bayreuther Blätter* under the title *Religion und Kunst*.[9] The treatise was written during the relatively long period of four months (March to July 25) of the year 1880 that Wagner spent with his family in Italy. Cosima's diary entries show that Wagner had worked very intensively at this essay.[10] He thought about it a great deal and read Schopenhauer and other works alongside. The treatise meant a great deal to him.

---

7   Richard Wagner, "Über Staat und Religion" (1864), GS, 8:3–29; p. 4.
8   Cf. Kurt Hildenbrandt, *Wagmer und Nietzsche im Kampf gegen das 19. Jahrhundert* (Munich, 1934).
9   "Religion und Kunst," GS, 10:211–253.
10 Cosima Wagner, *Die Tagebücher*, ed. Marin Gregor-Dellin and Dietrich Mack, vol. 3 (1878–1880), 2nd ed. Munich/Zurich, 1982.

An analysis of the individual ideas of this fundamental work reveals that some of them appear already in the Zurich papers written thirty years earlier, albeit partly in different contexts. The comparison shows that Wagner's thinking in some areas is characterized by a remarkable constancy. Some ideas occupied him for decades.

In July of 1849, Wagner wrote the essay "Art and Revolution" while in exile in Zurich. At that point in time he was still inspired by the revolutionary élan, having only recently taken part in the Dresden uprising. His essay concludes with a strange vision, in which Jesus shakes hands with the Greek god Apollo and humanity erects the "altar of the future" to these their "loftiest teachers." Jesus, "who suffered for mankind," had shown, Wagner says, "that we human beings are all equal and brothers." But Apollo would stamp "the great fraternal alliance with the seal of strength and beauty."[11] Although Wagner nowhere speaks of a union of art and religion here, he unmistakably had this holy alliance in mind.

Several months later, Wagner composed his great programmatic treatise *Das Kunstwerk der Zukunft*, The Artwork of the Future,[12] which he dedicated to Ludwig Feuerbach. In it he squares accounts with the art scene of his time, criticizing also the state of the contemporary arts, which, in their isolation, he regards as "unfree" and "hidebound,"[13] The ideal on which he orients himself, and which he opposes to the supposedly degenerate art of his present, is that of Hellenic culture, in which the arts were united. Hellenic art fascinated Wagner also for a different reason: because of the union of art and religion achieved in it. Both the lyric and the dramatic works of art were in Wagner's view "religious acts."[14] Here we also find two conceptions that were characteristic for the later Wagner as well, namely the conviction that art and religion rest on a "common" foundation, and that the religious spirit, the "core" of religion, was actually in better hands in art than in cult.

> Tragedy was thus religious ceremony become *work of art*, next to which the traditionally continued actual religious temple ceremony necessarily lost so much

---

11 "Die Kunst und die Revolution," GS, 3:8–41.
12 *Das Kunstwerk der Zukunft*, GS, 3:42–177.
13 GS, 3:68 f.
14 GS, 3:132.

fervency and truth that it became mindless conventional ritual, whereas its core lived on in the work of art.[15]

Wagner proclaimed Hellenic art to be the "yardstick" for the artwork of the future. The goals he aimed for at this point, however, were "Allmen-schlichkeit" and "Allgemeinsamkeit," all-humanness and all-commonness. Hellenic art, he postulated, had to shed its national character and become un-national, universal, "all-human" art. In the same way, the garment of the specifically Hellenic religion should be widened to become the bond of the "religion of the future," a religion of *allgemeinsamkeit*. The artwork of the future, in turn, would be nothing other than "vividly represented religion" (*lebendig dargestellte Religion*).[16] We can see from all this that the idea of a religion of art preoccupied Wagner already in 1850. Even then he expected salvation to come from this holy alliance, even then he dreamed of a "new religion," which could step into life once the "prevailing religion of egoism" had been expunged.[17]

3. On Wagner's Doctrine of Regeneration

Reading Wagner's later writings for the first time, one might get the impression of having to do less with an artist than with a cultural philosopher and moralist. As important as the idea of the religion of art was to him, the doctrine of the degeneration and regeneration of mankind forms the really great subject of his late writings. He believed unshakably in the "decline" and "degeneracy" of the human race and searched untiringly for the reasons of the evil. Money and property, he thought, had ruined mankind,[18] along with unbridled egotism, the corruption of the blood, the mixing of races, the corrupting influence of Judaism and flesh diet. In *Religion and Art* he speaks as an apostle of peace and vegetarianism, albeit a vegetarianism *sui generis*.

The vegetarian theories Wagner developed, following the writings of Gleïzès,[19] start from the assumption that man originally fed on a vegetarian

---

15 Ibid.
16 GS, 3:63.
17 GS, 3:123.
18 Cosima Wagner on September 29, 1880 (*Tagebücher*, 3:607).
19 See Henri Lichtenberger, *Richard Wagner, der Dichter und Denker*, 2nd ed. (Dresden, 1913), 382 f.

diet and in the course of time became carnivorous. Meat-eating in turn awakened man's "rapacity and blood-thirstiness,[20] turned him into a "predator" dominating the "peaceful world."[21] Wagner had no doubt that carnivorousness, conquest and war were causally connected.

Typical for Wagner is that, not content with having diagnosed the evil, he added concrete therapeutic proposals. He hoped for veritable wonders from a conversion of humanity to plant food. Experiments in American prisons, he maintained, had shown that "by dint of a wisely guided vegetable diet" even the most vicious criminals were transformed "into the gentlest and most honest beings."[22] And if the assumption should prove true that "in Northern climates" the consumption of meat is indispensable, "what would keep us," he continues, from organizing a "rationally managed migration of nations" into countries that thanks to their rank productivity "are capable of feeding the present population of all the continents?"[23]

Wagner sympathized with vegetarians, but criticized that many had no religion[24] and generally found that the modern world in which we lived was "religionless."[25] The "loftiest religions," Christianity and Brahmanism, had both failed, both were in a deep crisis.[26] What humanity needed was a "new," the "true" religion. Only from its soil could arise "the strength for the enactment of the great regeneration."[27]

4. Christianity, Brahmanism and the Critique of Religions

To state it at the outset: the "veritable" religion Wagner had in mind and preached with missionary zeal combines Christian with Buddhist elements, with the synthesis effected under the aegis of Schopenhauer's philosophy and ethics. Schopenhauer's interpretation of Christianity is appropriated wholly by Wagner. Christianity forms the basis of the "new" religion, but

---

20 "Religion und Kunst," GS, 10:230.
21 GS, 10:238.
22 GS, 10:242.
23 Ibid.
24 Cosima Wagner on September 25, 1880 (*Tagebücher* 3:605).
25 "Wollen wir hoffen?", GS, 10:123.
26 GS, 10:223 f.
27 GS, 10:243.

it is an, as it were, cleansed, purified and reformed Christianity, which, moreover, was to absorb certain elements of Buddhism. Wagner was unable to subscribe to any of the existing, purely religious doctrines, having diverse objections to all of them. His religious critique, as can be shown in detail, is based entirely on Schopenhauer and would be unthinkable without the latter.

An essential trait of religion, according to Wagner, is its insistence that the mythic symbols, dogmas and allegories it avails itself of are to be believed as literally "true."[28] It wholly matters to the priests that "the religious allegories" are regarded "as literal truths." Religion, however, becomes "artificial," Wagner says, it lives on only artificially," if it finds itself time and again compelled to shore up and consolidate its dogmatic symbols. Through the growing accumulation of incredible elements, the "true and divine" in it is obscured and its "core" is disfigured. Within the framework of this argument, Wagner could not help including a cut against Catholicism as he speaks of the "theatrical legerdemain," through which "the easily deceived, highly imaginative poor populace," especially in southern countries, is induced "to play frivolous games with the divine."[29]

These ideas reflect impressions Wagner gained from reading Schopenhauer. In the latter's foundational treatise *Über Religion*, we read that Christianity is altogether allegorical in nature.[30] Schopenhauer calls the Christian dogma a sacred "mythos, a vehicle by means of which the populace is taught truths that otherwise would be quite inaccessible to it."[31] This is promptly followed by a decisive statement:

> But the nasty point for all religions always remains that they may not be avowedly allegorical, but only covertly so, and therefore have to present their doctrines in all seriousness as *sensu proprio* true; which, given the essentially required absurdities in them, produces a constant deception and is a great defect. Nay, what is worse, in time it is revealed that they are *sensu proprio* not true: then they perish.[32]

---

28 Gs, 10:211.
29 GS, 10:247 f.
30 Arthur Schopenhauer, "Über Religion" (Parerga und Paralimpomena, II, ch. 15), *Werke* in zehn Bänden (Zurich, 1977), 10:400.
31 Ibid., 10:401.
32 Ibid., 401 f.

Wagner's dependence on Schopenhauer is patent.

To continue with our discussion of Wagner's religious critique: it centers, as was to be expected, in Judaism. Wagner traced the "wreck" of the Christian religion (he deliberately uses the word *Verderb*) to the fact that it drew upon Judaism for the development of its dogmas.[33] Wagner was uncomfortable with the whole Jewish root of Christianity. He was firmly convinced that Christianity and Judaism were two entirely different religions and that Jesus Christ, the "redeemer," had nothing at all to do with Yahweh. He was puzzled by the first Christians' endeavors to derive the descent of the Savior "from the royal house of David."[34] Wagner was intent on simply disregarding the "Old-Testament" roots of Christianity. The doctrine he propagated was that of the Gospels.

For these ideas, too, Wagner is to a large part indebted to Schopenhauer, who had numerous reservations about Judaism and above all about the Old Testament roots of Christianity. Although Schopenhauer felt that "the crude" Jewish dogma had been "sublimated and tacitly allegorized" by Christianity,[35] he saw the crux of the latter in the linking between two such "heterogeneous" doctrines as those of the Old and the New Testament.[36] That, he thought, led to "the absurdities in the dogma."[37]

Schopenhauer's harsh critique of Judaism becomes more comprehensible when one considers his unshakable belief in the doctrine of metempsychosis, the transmigration of souls – a doctrine quite contrary to the Jewish creation story. According to metempsychosis "what a being brings with him at birth, that is, from another world and an earlier life –and thus has as an advantage over others from – is not an alien gift of grace, but the fruit of his own actions performed in that other world"; but the Old Testament teaches "that man is the work of an alien will and is called forth by that will from nothing."[38] For basic reasons Schopenhauer could not agree to the Hebraic doctrine of Creation and opposed it with unusual vehemence.

---

33 GS, 10:232.
34 Ibid.
35 *Werke*, 10:400.
36 Ibid., 401.
37 Ibid.
38 Ibid., 402.

An additional point is also connected to the doctrine of metempsychosis. Schopenhauer deemed it a "cardinal flaw" of Christianity "that it has unnaturally torn man away from the animal world, to which he essentially belongs, and wants to accept him alone, regarding animals downright as things."[39] By contrast, Brahmanism and Buddhism fully acknowledged "the evident relationship" of man and animal nature and through metempsychosis represented man as in close connection with the animal world. In his treatise *Über Religion*, Schopenhauer expressed outrage about the Jewish "conception of nature,"[40] about vivisection and the torture of animals and writes: "The important role that animals play throughout in Brahmanism and Buddhism, compared with their total nullity in Judeo-Christianity, condemns the latter in regard to perfection."[41]

In his late writings, Richard Wagner proves a docile pupil of his mentor Schopenhauer in all of the issues addressed. Wagner, too, invoked the "Brahmanic teaching of the sinfulness of killing what is alive,"[42] he was among the most resolute opponents of vivisection,[43] and he believed firmly in metempsychosis. His views of Christianity, Judaism and Brahmanism are shaped decisively by Schopenhauerian thought.

5. The Affinity of Art with Religion

Wagner's religious critique forms the point of departure and pivot of his reflections about the religion of art. Since even the loftiest religions have fallen into decay, it was the task of art to "salvage" the "core" (the "noblest core"[44]) of religion. The greatest artistic geniuses of the past had solved this problem by idealizing the religious allegories and symbols. To clarify this argument, Wagner discusses the relation of the individual arts to religion.

Of all he arts, the one with the closest affinity to religion, in his opinion, is music. It is "the only art that wholly corresponds to the Christian

---

39 Ibid., 408.
40 Ibid., 411.
41 Ibid., 408.
42 GS, 10:224.
43 Cf. the "Offene Schreiben an Herrn Ernst von Weber," October 1879, GS, 10:194–210.
44 GS, 10:247.

faith"[45] and reveals "with incomparable exactitude" the unique essence of the Christian religion.[46] Especially the symphonic oeuvre of Beethoven is to Wagner the quintessence of religious art. Beethoven's symphonies were to him the "divinest works of musical art," "revelations in sound from the redeeming dream world of purest cognition" and "itself a solemn purifying religious act."[47] If Schiller, in the *Ode to Joy*, exclaims "Ahnest du den Schöpfer, Welt?" ("Dost thou sense thy Maker, world?"), then Beethoven, "the tone-poetic seer," reveals the inexpressible, that is, the certitude "I know that my redeemer liveth!" Wagner almost becomes a poet when he speaks of Beethoven.

As already thirty years before, Wagner firmly believed in 1880 that the deeper truth hidden in religion found a purer and more convincing expression in art than in the cult itself. Aeschylus's *Oresteia* seemed to him more profound than "all the Eleusinian mysteries."[48] Of the miraculous birth of Christ he thought that the immaculate conception of Mary was "horrid" as a dogma but "wondrous" in art, that is, in painting.[49] In general, he held that painting was much more successful than poetry in illustrating "the ideal content of the dogma presented in allegorical terms."[50] Whereas painting was able to make the "allegorical figure" the object of an "idealizing" representation, poetry, had to leave the "conceptual form of the dogma as literally true untouched."[51] In this connection, Wagner indicates that – like Schopenhauer – he was ambivalent in his attitude toward Dante. On the one hand, he acknowledged him as a great poet. On the other hand, he thought Dante had been able to treat "the dogmatic concepts always only according to the ecclesiastical requirement of literal credibility."[52] Wagner was irritated by the "rigid dogma" in the *Divine Comedy*.[53]

---

45 Ibid., 221.
46 Ibid., 222.
47 Ibid., 250 f.
48 Cosima Wagner on May 9, 1880 (*Tagebücher*, 3:526).
49 Ibid.
50 GS, 10:221.
51 Ibid.
52 Ibid., 219.
53 Cosima Wagner on April 27, 1880 (*Tagebücher*, 3:526).

If one translates Wagner's stilted, inflated sentences into sober language, they say that the *kunstreligion* of the future would no longer need the "allegorical trimmings" that have hitherto disfigured the "core" of religion.[54] The artist of the future, the "poetic priest," would lead humanity into a new "reborn" (or "renascent") life and present to it "in an ideal manner every 'simile' of all that is transient" (*in idealer Weise jedes 'Gleichnis' alles Vergänglichen*).[55] The "true art," however, could thrive only on the basis of a "true morality,"[56] could only blossom "in the soil of a new ethical world order."[57] "True" art and "true" religion were "completely *one*."[58] These postulates lead us directly to the central point of the Wagnerian doctrine.

6. The Philosophic and Ethical Bases of the Religion of Art

Ever since Wagner first encountered the philosophy of Arthur Schopenhauer in 1854), he fully identified with it.[59] He professes it in *Religion und Kunst*, though without mentioning Schopenhauer by name (he speaks in general terms of "our philosopher"[60]). In doing so, he manages to make Schopenhauer's metaphysics of the Will the philosophical foundation of his own doctrine of regeneration.

With the bringing forth of Man, Wagner says, the "world-forming" Will had reached its "unconscious aim,"[61] "since in him [Man] it became conscious of itself as *Will*." Man recognizes himself in all the manifestations of this same will, and this ability has endowed him with *Leiden*, suffering or passion. The "blind and only desiring" Will makes itself clearly known only by its anger, the *unwille*, at "what is odious to it as a hindrance or dissatisfaction." That means: the "rage" of the Will expresses its "self-negation." In realizing this situation, Man is thrown upon "the spirit of negation,"

---

54 GS, 10:247 f.
55 GS X, 247. Wagner is paraphrasing the conclusion of Goethe's *Faust II*: "Alles Vergängliche ist nur ein Gleichnis" (All that is transient is but a parable).
56 GS, 10:251.
57 "'Was nützt diese Erkenntnis?' Ein Nachtrag zu: Religion und Kunst," GS, 10:261.
58 GS, 10:251.
59 Cf. Edouard Sans, *Richard Wagner et la pensée schopenhauerienne*, Paris, 1969.
60 GS, 10:245.
61 Ibid., 246.

that is, "the negation of his own will itself." "Compassion, springing from passion/suffering" (*das dem Leiden entkeimende Mitleiden*), however, can help him "to arrive at self-reflection" or self-contemplation.[62] Wagner formulated these thoughts in much simpler terms on April 28, 1880, in a conversation with his wife Cosima, when he said about the two movements of Beethoven's piano sonata in C minor op. 111: "That is my whole doctrine: the first movement is the Will in its pain and heroic desiring, the other the is the assuaged Will, as Man will have it when he has become reasonable."[63]

Wagner expected salvation from the "negation" or at least the "assuaging" of the Will, and he thought – quite in Schopenhauer's sense – one should recognize the degeneracy of the human race as "the stern school of suffering," which the Will "imposed upon itself in its blindness, so as to become seeing." Essentially he is saying: the Will, that is we ourselves, and the experience we have gained from the history of our degeneracy has "established and consolidated a religious consciousness within us." And if a new religion is to be founded, it is only to preserve humanity from a relapse "into the power of the blindly raging Will."[64]

The "true" religion thus presupposes self-abnegation. The ethical implications of this idea, Wagner did not set forth in *Religion und Kunst* but in a supplement to it, the essay *Was nützt diese Erkenntnis?* (Of what Use is this Knowledge?).[65] There he referred expressly to Schopenhauer, praised him as the most important philosopher and ethicist, emphasized "the recognition of a moral significance of the world"[66] as the result of his philosophy, and voiced the recommendation "to make Schopenhauer's philosophy in every respect the basis of all future intellectual and ethical culture." In the process, he fashioned a synthesis of the teachings of the Gospels and Schopenhauer's ethics.

To elucidate: Wagner begins by quoting Schiller's saying about Christianity being the only "aesthetic" religion[67] and declares that in establishing

---

62 Ibid., 244 f.
63 Cosima Wagner on April 28, 1880 (*Tagebücher*, 3:527).
64 GS, 10:245 f.
65 Ibid., 253–263, esp. 257 ff.
66 Schopenhauer, "Über den Willen in der Natur. Hinweisung auf die Ethik," *Werke*, 5:336.
67 GS, 10:258.

the foundation of his ethics he wants to entirely disregard the Ten Commandments of the Mosaic law tables.[68] He exclusively invokes the purely Christian commandment and the three Christian "theological virtues," Faith, Love and Hope, whose sequence he wants, however, to be changed to "Love, Faith and Hope." Love in the Christian definition is the highest commandment to him. With reference to Schopenhauer, he proclaims: "Only the love growing from compassion, and acting compassionately up to the utter breaking of the self-will, is the redeeming Christian Love, in which Faith and Hope are automatically included – Faith as the unfailingly certain consciousness, confirmed by the divinest of examples, of the moral significance of the world, Hope as the beatific knowledge of the impossibility of that consciousness ever being deceived."[69] The connection between this doctrine and Schopenhauer is patent, as Schopenhauer had taught that Love in the sense of *caritas* and *agape* was compassion,[70] and that compassion was the basis of all morality.

From Schopenhauer, incidentally, one can gather additionally that Christianity did not have cardinal virtues but theological ones.[71] He had his own theories about the cardinal virtues. Whereas, according to Plato, there were four cardinal virtues, Justice, Courage, Moderation and Wisdom, Schopenhauer distinguishes only two, "Justice" (*Gerechtigkeit*) and "Charity" (*Menschenliebe*),[72] and he teaches that Justice was "the complete ethical content" of the Old Testament and Charity (Philanthropy) that of the New,[73] with Charity including, according to St. Paul, all of the Christian virtues.

Now it is highly typical of Wagner's thinking that he quietly disregarded "Justice," as being an ethical category of the Old Testament. He concentrated deliberately on the Christian virtues, and he professed frankly not

---

68 Ibid., 259.
69 Ibid., 260.
70 *Die Welt als Wille und Vorstellung* I § 66; *Werke*, 2:464.
71 "Zur Ethik" (*Parerga und Paralipomena* II §110); *Werke*, 9:222.
72 *Über die Grundlage der Moral* §16; *Werke*, 6:252 ff.
73 Ibid., 6:270.

to have been able to find "any trace of a truly Christian idea" in the Ten Commandments of the Mosaic Law.[74]

As for the importance of art for man and the regeneration of humanity: in his chef d'oeuvre, Schopenhauer referred to art as the "faithful mirror of the nature of the world and of life"[75] and also spoke pointedly about the consolation it vouchsafes.[76] In his treatise *Zur Metaphysik des Schönen und Ästhetik* (On the Metaphysics of the Beautiful and Aesthetics), he picks up this train of thought and elaborates it:

> As we know [he writes], the world as Will is the first world (*ordine prior*) and the world as Idea the second (*ordine posterior*). The former is the world of desire and hence of pain and thousand-fold woe. The second, however, is in itself essentially painless: it contains, moreover, a show worth seeing, throughout significant, at the least amusing. In the enjoyment of that consists aesthetic delight.

And in a note he adds:

> The complete sufficiency, the final calming, the truly desirable condition present themselves only in the image, in the painting, in the poem, in music. Admittedly, one could gather a confidence from that that they must exist somewhere after all.[77]

In *Was nützt diese Erkenntnis*, Wagner again stresses the "power" of art for "revelation" and quotes Schopenhauer's footnote as a quintessential statement.[78] From these explanations it emerges again that he ascribed even greater significance to art than Schopenhauer, as he also did not share the latter's pessimism. Whereas Schopenhauer was content to assert that faith was dwindling day by day, Wagner firmly believed in the regeneration of the human race.

---

74 GS, 10:259. Cf. Cosima's note about the "cardinal virtues" on October 21, 1880 (*Tagebücher*, 3:613).
75 *Die Welt als Wille und Vorstellung* I §56; *Werke*, 2:401.
76 Ibid., 1:335.
77 "Zur Metaphysik des Schönen und Ästhetik" (*Parerga und Paralipomena* II §205), *Werke*, 10:458.
78 GS, 10:261 f.

7. *Parsifal*: The Realization of the Idea

The concept of the religion of art is undoubtedly the central one of the late Wagner. It implicitly comprises numerous ideological, ethical, religious, religio-philosophical and art-theoretical ideas, which only careful analysis can identify. Wagner formulated these ideas theoretically in his two essays of the year 1880, the large treatise *Religion und Kunst* and the supplement *Was nützt diese Erkenntnis?* Three years earlier, on April 19, 197, he had completed the text for his "consecrational stage festival play" *Parsifal*. If we now look back from the vantage-point we have gained to *Parsifal* we can without exception find all those ideas already present there. The *Parsifal* poem translates them into cultic and scenic actions, metaphors, allegories, symbols. Cultic Christian ceremonies – communion, foot-washing, baptism – are represented on stage. Central to the poem are the ideas of humanity's degeneracy, its regeneration through love, compassion and self-abnegation, the doctrine of the transmigration of souls (metempsychosis), the prohibition of the killing of animals, and pacifism.[79] Let us consider these ideas more closely.

Amfortas' incurable sickness and the plight of the Grail knights symbolize the degeneracy of the human race. At the beginning of Act Three, as Gurnemanz and Parsifal meet again, the knights are said to be in direst need. Gurnemanz describes their condition in somber hues:

> Since the day of your first sojourn here,
> the mourning then made known to you,
> the dread, grew to extremest need.
> Struggling against his wounds, the torments
> of his soul, Amfortas desires
> in raging desperation now his death.[80]

Since Amfortas cannot bear the sight of the life-giving Grail, the shrine remains closed:

> The holy meal is now denied to us;
> With common food we must be nourished:
> Therefore exhausted is our heroes' might.

---

79 On the following, cf. my article "Studien zur 'Parsifal'-Rezeption," in *Musik-Konzepte 25. Richard Wagner. Parsifal* (May 1982), 14–57.
80 Richard Wagner, *Die Musikdramen*. India paper edition (dtv-bibliothek 6095) (Munich, 1978), 858. We quote the *Parsifal* text hereafter from this edition.

No message comes to us,
No call to holy battles from far places:
Pale and wretched reels about
Despairing, leaderless each fading knight.

Titurel, "whom now the Grail's aspect restored no longer," has died – "a man like others!"

The knights languish in hope for Parsifal, needing the *heil*, the salvation that he brings. They expect the regeneration to come from the "highest" power of compassion and the might of "purest knowledge."[81] The motto of the work, "Knowing [or "wise"] through compassion, the purest fool," is another formulation of Schopenhauer's "All love (*agape, caritas*) is compassion."

The key word in Wagner's ethics, religion of art and redemptive philosophy is *love*. Love forms the quintessence of his entire doctrine. The decay of humanity is owing above all to "lovelessness." In *Was nützt diese Erkenntnis*, Wagner posits the question: "By what is our entire civilization brought to ruin if not by the dearth of love?"[82] This question occupied him already during his years in Zurich, and it largely dictated the conception of the *Ring of the Nibelung*. "The fear of the end," he wrote to August Röckel on January 25, v1854, "is the source of all lovelessness, and it is engendered only where love itself is already fading."[83] The gods in the *Ring* are destroyed because of their quest for power and their "lovelessness." Wagner's conception of love, to be sure, underwent a profound change in the course of time. Whereas in 1854, he held that love in its "fullest reality" was possible only "within sexuality,"[84] he later placed the love of humanity above sexual love. Parsifal's steadfastness in the face of Kundry's seductions symbolizes the victory of *agape* over *eros*. In Schopenhauer's view, compassion, as "true and pure love," ranks above erotic love, which is "self-seeking."[85]

---

81 *Die Musikdramen*, 864.
82 GS, 10;259.
83 Richard Wagner, *Sein Leben in Briefen*, ed. Carl Siegmund Benedict (Leipzig 1913), 178.
84 Ibid., 173.
85 *Die Welt als Wille und Vorstellung* I §67; *Werke*, 2:466.

In the intellectual conception of *Parsifal*, two main components are recognizable: one is the Christian doctrine of the Gospels, the other is the doctrine of Brahmanism and of Buddhism. The synthesis is effected, as already indicated, under the aegis of Schopenhauer's philosophy and ethics. Schopenhauer's doctrine of love as compassion is Christian in origin. Of Buddhist provenance, however, are the doctrine of metempsychosis and the ban on the killing of animals. Kundry, a "wondrous world-demonic woman,"[86] appears in diverse metamorphoses. She has been Herodias and Gundryggia. She lives, as Wagner writes, "an immeasurable life with ever-changing *rebirths*" and seeks the savior" from world to world."[87] The prohibition against the killing of animals is closely connected to metempsychosis. In the precincts of the Grail, no animals may be killed. Parsifal's shooting of the swan is deemed a sacrilege. Consequently, the Grail knights practice vegetarianism. They abstain from meat and live solely on bread and wine.

Of importance is also the idea of pacifism, the condemnation of violence. In Act One, Gurnemanz reproves Parsifal for shooting the swan:

> Unheard-of deed! –
> You could murder, – here, in this sacred wood,
> Whose quiet peace enveloped you?[88]

Another reprimand follows when Parsifal leaps at Kundry in rage and grabs her by the throat. "Lunatic boy! More violence?"[89] In the third act, finally, Gurnemanz admonishes the heavily armed Parsifal that it is not permitted to carry weapons within the precinct of the Grail.[90] In *Religion und Kunst*, Wagner sharply differentiated between culture and civilization, saying that force could civilize but that culture must "spring from the soil of peace."[91]

---

86 Wagner to Mathilde Wesendonck, March 2, 1859.
87 Richard Wagner, *Sämtliche Werke*, vol. 30: *Dokumente zur Entstehung und ersten Aufführung des Bühnenweihfestspiels Parsifal*, ed. Martin Geck and Egon Voss (Mainz, 1970), 72.
88 *Parsifal* in *Die Musikdramen*, 830.
89 Ibid., 832.
90 Ibid., 856.
91 GS, 10:234.

From what has been said it should be clear that Wagner realized his idea of the religion of art already in *Parsifal*. One must ask what might have prompted him to formulate his ideas on the subject also theoretically in two treatises. Wagner did not say anything explicit about his deeper reasons. He told Cosima on April 2, 1880, that with *Religion und Kunst* he planned to wind up his literary oeuvre: "This he still wanted to say, even though he was downright afraid to enter this arena; generally he had a great loathing of authorship."[92] And Cosima noted on June 26, that he was delighted by "the curious connection" between the treatise and *Parsifal*.[93] Although we thus have no concrete knowledge of his intentions, there are good reasons to assume that, being heavily engaged in 1880 in the composition of *Parsifal*, he wanted these late writings to smooth the way for his *Bühenweihfestspiel*. On September 25, 1880, at the latest, at any rate, he made the decision to convert the *Bayreuther Blätter* into a public newspaper.[94] The *Blätter* were to become a medium for the dissemination of his ideas, a propaganda sheet for his regeneration doctrine, vegetarianism, and the religion of art, and a combat organ against vivisection and miscegenation. It is telling that Wagner wrote his last and most controversial essays, *Erkenne dich selbst* (Know thyself) and *Heldentum und Christentum* (Heroism and Christianitty) for the *Bayreuther Blätter*.

8. Art as Substitute for Religion? Wagner as a Religious Founder?

Om July 26, 1882, *Parsifal* had its premiere on the hill in Bayreuth. The extraordinary attention the "consecrational stage festival play" received contributed to the spreading of the notion that Wagner wanted to offer art as a substitute for religion and should be regarded as a religious founder – a notion that provoked enthusiasm and outrage in equal measure. Thus Igor Stravinsky opined as late as 1912: "It would be high time to do away once

---

92 Cosima Wagner, *Tagebücher*, 3:527.
93 Ibid., 554.
94 Ibid., 604.

and for all with the deficient and blasphemous notion of art as religion and the theater as a temple."[95]

In his major treatise of 1880, Wagner himself had emphasized the unity, even the identity, of art and religion, but denied having wanted to found a new religion – such an endeavor he regarded as impossible.[96] Even so there has been no dearth of attempts to develop a practical "religious doctrine" in the Wagnerian sense. Hans von Wolzogen, above all, was active in this direction after Wagner's death. He authored a "Christian instruction in rhymed stories about the "dear savior" and recommended it to "Wagnerian parents" for their children.[97] The piece was to present the adherents of the Bayreuthian weltanschauung with a means of "educating their children to become true Christians." The declared goal of the Wagner movement was a "religious renewal" through art.[98]

Wagner's idea of the religion of art is typical nineteenth century. Rightly to understand it, one has to view it through the spectacles of that century. It is certainly not easy to do justice to the social utopian and cultural philosopher Wagner. The indirect consequences of his anti-Semitic invectives are forever horrible. Yet his writings contain ideas that merit consideration even today. His conviction that humanity needed moral values to rejuvenate itself and his plea for peace are reflections that are still relevant and will remain so as long as the human species exists.

9. Hitler and Wagner

Wagner's anti-Semitism is notorious, and the question to what extent he should be regarded as a forerunner of National Socialism was, and still is, debated vehemently and controversially. As Udo Bermbach has pointed out, during the Third Reich Wagner's work and thinking was regarded as

---

95 Igor Stravinsky, *Leben und Werk – von ihm selbst. Erinnerungen, Musikalische Poetik, Anworten auf 35 Fragen* (Mainz, 1957), 45–47.

96 GS, 10:251.

97 Arthur Seidl, "Bayreuther 'Grals'-Ideal und 'Christenlehre'" (1911), in *Neue Wagneriana. Gesammelte Aufsätze und Studien*, 3 vols. (Regensburg, n.d. [1914]), 2:531–546; pp. 535 f.

98 Ibid., 532.

a systematic anticipation of the Nazi ideology.[99] *Siegfried* was the work Hitler and his circle prized most. Former *Spiegel* editor Rudolf Augstein, however, denied already in 1997 that Wagner's writings and his music were in any way responsible for Hitler's atrocities.[100] There is no question that Hitler admired Wagner and Bayreuth and frequently invoked him. It should be borne in mind, however, that the Nazis did not esteem all of Wagner's dramas to an equal extent.

It is said that Hitler regarded *Parsifal* as something of a crux. Ever since 1934, at the latest, he supposedly endeavored to influence the Bayreuth production of the piece, wanting to strip the work of its supposedly Christian-sacral character. To Saul Friedlander we owe the important realization that for Hitler art became a religion in *Parsifal* – a new religion that was still too Christian for the Nazi leader but that also proclaimed the advent of a holy Arian community.[101]

Had Wagner entertained similar ideas? The music for the work was written partly in Italy, where Wagner was staying with his family in 1879 and 1880, and the treatise *Religion and Art*, which was to pave the way for his final opus, originated there at the same time. The question arises whether *Parsifal* or the treatise contain anything anti-Jewish. The basic thesis of the treatise is that the churches, as well as even the loftiest religions – Christianity and Brahmanism – had failed and that therefore art had to take the place of religion. Apart from the reservations about the "Old Testament root" of Christianity, there is nothing to suggest a critique of Judaism.

As for *Parsifal*, it has repeatedly been asserted that in it Wagner wanted to break a lance for the Arian ideology. There is much to indicate, however, that the new religion of art he had in mind did not admit of any confessional concretization. Wagner preferred to leave many things unsettled. He availed himself of Christian rituals like baptism, communion and foot-washing, used as his central symbol the life-giving Grail reinterpreted as the cup that supposedly contained the blood of Christ, and devoted one scene of the work to a "Good Friday spell." In a conversation with Cosima,

---

99   Udo Bermbach, *Mythos Wagner* (Berlin, 2013), 274.
100   Rudolf Augstein, "Siegfried, Lohengrin, Parsifal," *Der Spiegel*, 30 (1997).
101   Saul Friedländer, "Hitler und Wagner", in Saul Friedländer and Jörn Rüsen, eds., *Richard Wagner im Dritten Reich* (Munich, 2000), 165–178; p. 173.

however, he confessed that in conceiving the work he never thought of the Savior at all.[102] Much is also made of Kundry, the seductress, who at one point is called both Herodias and Gundryggia by her "master," the sorcerer Klingsor. Herodias was the daughter of a Jewish prince; Gundryggia, on the other hand, was a Scandinavian Valkyrie. Wagner called her a "knitter of war" – eternally accursed because she laughed at the crucified Christ. The decisive point about Kundry is her ambivalence. She is both seductress and penitent in one person, and neither simply Jewish nor really Scandinavian, but a deathless sinner roaming the world, like the Flying Dutchman, in search of redemption. Baptized by Parsifal, she is at last redeemed and released into death.

10. The Performance Ban on *Parsifal* since 1939

Udo Bermbach has made important contributions to the reception history of *Parsifal* in the 20th century. According to his account, the work was repeatedly monopolized by theology, its religious content time and again given special prominence. It also received Nazi accents. According to Ludwig Schemann, Wagner created a new path, through art, to religion – to a "true," that is, an "a-Jehovaic," Christianity. Here the Nazis were able to dock on. Interestingly, Hitler and Himmler imagined the SS as a kind of order of Grail knights.[103] Of crucial importance for the reception history of *Parsifal*, however, is that from the beginning of the war in 1939, the "consecrational play" could no longer be performed anywhere in the Third Reich, not even in Bayreuth. Evidently the Nazis were afraid the population might be demoralized by the pacifist tendency of the work. Its religious accents, too, made them uneasy: it had to be reinterpreted in terms of the National-Socialist ideology.

---

102 Cosima Wagner, *Tagebücher*, 2:205.
103 Udo Bermbach, "Liturgietransfer," Friedländer/Rüsen, eds., *Wagner im Dritten Reich*, 40–65; p. 53.

11. Conclusion

How is the late Wagner's turn toward pacifism to be explained? The question is justified, especially when one considers that Wagner had welcomed the Franco-Prussian War of 1870/71 and hailed the victory of the German troops. His nationalistic frame of mind is legendary. He strongly disliked the French, the French *esprit* as well as French music *tout court*. For a time he longed to see the French metropolis go up in flames. So it is all the more surprising that he was later on greatly venerated by personalities like Charles Baudelaire and Stéphane Mallarmé. His attitude toward Otto von Bismarck, the founder of the German Reich, which originally had been a positive one, became in the course of time increasingly critical. During his last years, he came to hate the Iron Chancellor abysmally and extended his hatred to Prussians generally. He found much in Bismarck's politics objectionable and accused him of perpetuating war and plunging people into misery to increase his own power. He once called the Chancellor a "brutal barbarian" and a "boar-hunter," and Wilhelm I. was nothing but a "feeble-minded king" to him – though that did not keep him from composing an "Imperial March" upon the proclamation of Wilhelm as German Emperor.

At this point, new perspectives open for an interpretation of *Parsifal*: the work must certainly be viewed against the background of contemporary socio-political issues. Wagner's insistent demand for disarmament and condemnation of war also relates to the politics of the Iron Chancellor. He pleaded for an ethics of altruism and regarded egotism as the source of all evil.

VI. The *Symphony of a Thousand* as a Message to Humanity

> "Mahler himself regarded his 'Eighth' as the cupola of his entire symphonic oeuvre." Richard Specht (1912)
>
> "His chief work is the abortive, objectively impossible revival of the cultic." Th. W. Adorno (1960)

1. Mahler's "Mass" and "Gift to the Nation"

Gustav Mahler used superlatives and unusual turns of phrase when he spoke of his Eighth Symphony of 1908. He called it his "mass" and "a gift to the whole nation" and thought that all of his previous symphonies had been mere preludes to this one. A close look at these pronouncements can yield much about Mahler's intentions.

Mahler was profoundly religious, yet not really devout in the ordinary sense of the word. He sympathized with the rites of the Catholic Church, loved Gregorian chants and felt drawn to Catholic mysticism. Yet he was trans-confessional in his thinking, and his religiosity bore strongly personal traits. A report by Alfred Roller is illuminating. He says that he once asked Mahler why he did not write any masses. Mahler seemed taken aback. "Do you think that I could do that? Well, why not? But no. It has the Credo in it." And he began to recite the Creed in Latin. "No, I couldn't do that." But after a rehearsal of the Eighth in Munich, Roller continues, remembering their conversation, he cheerfully called out to me: "See, that is my mass."[1]

This utterance should be understood in the sense of the "religion of art," that is, the notion that the churches had failed, that art had to take the place of ritual, and that the work of art was "vividly portrayed religion." Richard Wagner, as we have seen, had propagated these ideas, and Mahler, who profoundly admired Wagner, consciously or unconsciously followed in his footsteps. Like Wagner's *Parsifal*, Mahler's Eighth Symphony is one of the chief monuments of the religion of art.

---

1 Alfred Roller, *Die Bildnisse von Gustav Mahler* (Leipzig/Vienna, 1922), 26.

In a conversation Mahler had with Richard Specht in 1906, he called the Eighth, as noted, "a gift to the whole nation."[2] The majestic word tells us that he was thinking in terms of a bequest, a pronouncement, a message. We cannot help thinking of Richard Wagner again, who on July 10, 1856, wrote to Breitkopf & Härtel about his *Ring of the Nibelung*: "It is the full and sumptuous chef d'oeuvre of my life, and I believe that even in the poem I have given a work to the nation that I can proudly regard as commended to it also for the future."[3] As Wagner did his *Ring*, Mahler regarded his Eighth as his masterpiece.

In the same conversation with Specht, Mahler tried to define the principal difference, in character as well as in form, between the Eighth and the seven preceding symphonies. "All my earlier symphonies," he told Specht, "are but the preludes to this one. The others still have all the subjective tragicalness – this one is a great giver of joy." These remarks suggest that with the Eighth he had a universally valid, "positive," affirmative statement in mind, one to gladden humanity. With the Eighth especially he believed he had created a symphonic work of quasi cosmic dimensions. In August of 1906, he wrote to his friend Willem Mengelberg: "I just finished my 8th. – It is the greatest I have made until now. And so unique in content and form that one can't even write about it. – Imagine that the universe begins to sound and resound. There are no longer human voices, but planets and suns that are revolving."[4]

A further difference between the Eighth and the preceding symphonies is that whereas the latter either are wholly instrumental or include the word only sporadically, the Eighth is based on two texts, the Latin hymn *Veni creator spiritus* and the concluding scene of *Faust II*, which, apart from pre-, inter- and postludes, are sung throughout. Mahler explained this peculiarity in these words:

> But in its form, too, it is something entirely new: can you imagine a symphony that is sung from beginning to end? Until now I have used the word only interpretively,

---

2   Richard Specht, *Gustav Mahler's VIII. Symphonie. Thematische Analyse* (Leipzig/Vienna, 1912), 6; *Gustav Mahler* (Berlin/Leipzig, 1913), 304.
3   Quoted from Joachim Kaiser, ed. *Richard Wagner. Die Musikdramen* (dtv 6095) (Munich, 1978), 512.
4   GMB, 312.

as a foreshortening mood factor, so as to say something that symphonically could have been expressed only in an immense breadth with the kind of curt precision that only the word makes possible. Here, however, the human voice is at the same time instrument; the entire first movement is kept strictly to the symphonic form, while being wholly sung. It is actually strange that no one has had this idea until now – it is, after all, the egg of Columbus, the *symphony as such*, in which the most beautiful instrument in existence is devoted to its destined purpose – and yet not as sound only, since the human voice is at the same time also the medium of the poetic thought.[5]

It can be shown that this "poetic thought," the message of the text, meant a great deal to Mahler.

The Eighth is undoubtedly Mahler's most ambitious work. Corresponding to the magnitude of the intention, the sublimity of the poetic subject, are the monumental shape of the symphony and the gigantic size of the tonal apparatus. The score prescribes two mixed choruses, a boys' chorus, several soloists and a huge orchestra, which includes piano, harmonium, organ and mandolin, among other instruments. At the end of the two parts, besides, four trumpets and three trombones that are positioned in isolation from the orchestra are superadded. The colossal orchestration is symptomatic of the quasi-cosmic intention.

2. Genesis

The Eighth Symphony originated essentially in the summer of 1906 in Maiernigg, specifically during the ten weeks from June 21 to the end of August. Already on June 21, Mahler wrote a letter to his friend Dr. Fritz Löhr with some questions about the Latin Pentecostal hymn *Veni creator spiritus*.

Of special relevance for the origin of the symphony are two program sketches indicating that the Eighth was initially planned in four movements. According to the first sketch, whose text was published by Paul Bekker in 1921,[6] the Pentecost hymn was to be followed by a scherzo as the second movement, an Adagio with the title *Caritas* as the third, and as the finale a hymn on *The Birth of Eros*. The sketch does not say on what sort of text this concluding hymn was to be based. But, as I have argued elsewhere, Mahler

---

5   Richard Specht in No. 150 of the *Tagespost* of June 14, 1914.
6   Paul Bekker, *Gustav Mahlers Sinfonien* (Berlin, 1921), 273, 359.

was probably thinking of the conclusion of the "Classical Walpurgis Night" from Goethe's *Faust II* – a hymnal poem, in which Eros is glorified as the *fons et origo* of all life.[7] This plan was not carried out, because Mahler must have realized that the Christian Pentecost hymn and the thoroughly humanistic tenor of the Classical Walpurgis Night's conclusion clashed fatally, so that the kind of spiritual synthesis he had in mind could not be effected by any artistic means.

This thesis is supported also by the second, probably later, sketch, published in 1933 by Alfred Rosenzweig.[8] Here, too, four movements are planned, with the Pentecost hymn being followed by a second movement entitled *Caritas*, a scherzo called *Christmas Games with the Infant*, and as the finale the hymn *Creation through Eros*. But note the deviations: in contrast to the other sketch, the two middle movements, Adagio and Scherzo, are reversed, the Scherzo has a Christian subject, and the wording of the concluding hymn's title indicates that Mahler now placed the accent not on the *birth* of Eros but on the *creation* by Eros. With this new formulation, a bridge has been thrown to the *creator spiritus* of the Pentecostal hymn.

Instructive for the genesis of the Eighth is also a leaf originally in the possession of Bruno Walter, which is now in the New York Public Library.[9] On one side of the sheet, Mahler, prior to beginning with the composition, wrote out the Latin text of the Pentecostal hymn, while onto the verso he copied two poems from *Des Knaben Wunderhorn*, "Dormi Jesu, mater ridet" (Sleep little Jesus, your mother smiles) and "Steht auf, ihr lieben Kinderlein" (Rise up, you darling little ones). The Latin lullaby is labeled "1st Trio Alto," the German text "2nd Trio Soprano." It is fairly certain that these two poems were meant for the Scherzo of the Eighth, *Christmas Games with the Infant*.

---

7 Floros, *Gustav Mahler*, vol. 1: *Die geistige Welt Gustav Mahlers in systematischer Darstellung* (Wiesbaden, 1977), 130.

8 Alfred Rosenzweig, in *Der Wiener Tag*, No. 3607 (June 4, 1933).

9 Facsimiles in Floros, *Gustav Mahler*, vol. 3 (Wiesbaden, 1985), 355, and in Donald Mitchell, *Gustav Mahler. Songs and Symphonies of Life and Death. Interpretations and Annotations* (London, 1985), 508, 510.

The decisive question we have to ask now, however, is: how did Mahler conceive the idea of combining the Latin Pentecost hymn with the concluding scene of Goethe's *Faust II*?

3. Love as Productive Power: On the Intellectual Conception of the Eighth Symphony

In the above-mentioned conversation with Richard Specht about the just-completed Eighth Symphony, Mahler mentioned that it had long been a desire of his to compose the final scene of Goethe's *Faust II*. Then an old book had by chance recently fallen into his hands, he had opened it to the hymn *Veni creator spiritus*, and all of a sudden the whole had stood before him, not only the first theme, but the entire first movement; and as an "answer" to it he had not been able to find anything more wonderful than Goethe's words in the scene of the Anachoretes.

Mahler was a profound Goethe connoisseur. He reflected at length about *Faust*, and especially about Part Two, before he decided to set the end of it to music. In June of 1909 and June 1910, that is, three, four years after the composition of the Eighth, he wrote three long letters to his wife Alma, which have Goethe, directly or indirectly, as their subject, and which thus present a kind of *ex post facto* interpretation of the Eighth. The central themes around which these letters circle are Goethe's theories of productivity and entelechy, his conception of Love or Eros as productive power, the pyramidal structure of Part Two of *Faust* and the interpretation of the *Chorus Mysticus* that famously concludes the work.

Productivity and entelechy seem to have been closely adjacent in Goethe's intellectual world. Goethe regarded them as higher powers, whose efficacy transcended earthly existence. "Every productivity of the *highest kind*," he said to Eckermann, "every significant aperçu, every invention, every great thought that bears fruit and has consequences is in no one's control and is superior to all earthly power."[10]

The concept of entelechy, of course, goes back to Aristotle and literally means that "which has its *telos*, its end, within itself." Entelechy is thus a

---

10 Johann Peter Eckermann, *Gespräche mit Goethe in den letzten Jahren seines Lebens*, new ed., ed. Fritz Bergemann (Wiesbaden, 1955), 630 f.

goal-oriented activity or force that conditions and determines, as a principle, every development.[11] According to Aristotle, the entelechy of the body, which realizes itself in the body's shape, its changes and activities, is the soul. In Goethe's time, entelechy was generally understood to mean the indestructible principle of life and organization. Goethe himself related the concept to immortality, the continuation of existence after death, and to the soul.[12]

In his letter to Alma of June 27, 1909, Mahler paraphrased Goethe's thoughts about productivity and entelechy like this: "Man – and probably all creatures – are incessantly productive. It happens on all levels, inseparably from the nature of life: if the productive power is exhausted, the entelechy dies, that is, it must obtain another body." By production Mahler here means the ceaseless growth, the restless aspiration, the growth of the soul and the upward-striving of the personality. At the same time, he, the productive artist, goes so far as to say that he thinks little of the so-called human "works." "They are the truly evanescent and mortal; but what man makes of himself – what he becomes by his restless striving and living – that is the lasting." What a man – even an artistically productive one – leaves behind is only "skin, shell, etc."[13]

The eminent Faust commentator Erich Trunz interprets the final scene of Part Two precisely from the aspect of Goethe's vision of entelechy. He writes: "Faust has died. But we encounter him once more. Angels approach bearing 'Faust's immortal part' (in an autograph Goethe wrote 'Faust's entelechy)." "Now, after his death, his entelechy is, more than ever before, only an example of a significant striving human form pure and simple." The images of the final scene show "the destiny of the entelechy after death, a being preserved and simultaneously a dissolution."[14]

Mahler believed unshakably in a continued existence after death and was deeply impressed by Goethe's vision of the spiritual rebirth of Faust.

---

11 Aristoteles, *Hauptwerke*, selected, translated and introduced by Wilhelm Nestle (Kröners Taschenausgabe, vol. 129) (Stuttgart, 1968) x, xxxiii, 131–133, 150–155.

12 Eckermann, *Gespräche* (1955), 347, 374, 629

13 Alma Mahler, *Gustav Mahler. Erinnerungen und Briefe*, 2nd ed. (hereafter AME), (Amsterdam, 1949), 441 f.

14 Erich Trunz, ed., *Goethes Faust* (Hamburg, 1963), 627.

In 1909, he wrote to Bruno Walter: "I see everything in such a new light – am so much in motion I would at times not at all be surprised if I were to notice a new body on me (like Faust in the final scene)."[15]

Modern *Faust* research has recognized that Goethe embodied his vision of the stepped structure of the divine world in the final scene of the tragedy. Vertical motion is particularly characteristic of the imagery of this final scene. The action moves step by step from the lower regions to the upper one. It begins with the Anachoretes and leads via the Patres, the Angels and the Doctor Marianus to the Mater Gloriosa. Mahler had recognized the stepped construction of the final scene – he stretched the arc even farther. He was of the opinion that from scene to scene everything in the Second Part pointed to the *Chorus Mysticus*, "the summit of the gigantic pyramid." Ever more clearly as he approached the end, Goethe, he thought, here gave representation to an "infinite stepladder" of similes or parables: "Faust's passionate search for Helena – ever onward in the Walpurgis Night, from the Homunculus – the as yet non-existent – through the various entelechies of a lower or higher order, represented and expressed ever more consciously and purely, up to the mater gloriosa," whom he calls *expressis verbis* the "personification of the Eternal-Feminine."[16]

To be able to explain the deeper meaning of the *Chorus Mysticus*, however, Mahler constructs a polarity between the "Eternal-Feminine" and an "Eternal- Masculine." The "Eternal Feminine" he took to be "the reposing, the goal"; the "Eternal- Masculine" he defined as an "everlasting yearning, striving, moving toward" that same goal.

The most essential disclosures for a deeper understanding of the Eighth are found in Mahler's letter to Alma of June 1910, the letter in which he expounds his ideas about Eros. Here he again invokes Goethe and his view "that all loving is a begetting, creating; that there is both a physical and a spiritual begetting, which is precisely the effluence of this *Eros*."[17] Mahler compares Socrates with Jesus in this letter, thus brushing aside the temporal and spiritual distance between the Greek and the Christian culture. He does not dispute the contrasts between the two cultures, but sees the common,

---

15 GMB, 351.
16 Letter to Alma, June 1909; AME, 436–438.
17 AME, 456 f.

linking element in the formulation "Eros as the creator of the world." My thesis is that this formula is the very message of the Eighth.

The critic Hans Mayer called Mahler a "magnificent usurper," not only in the musical sphere, but also in the literary one: he related to literature like a naive dilettante, "who in reading stories and novels devours everything that seems to serve the purpose of identification." Mayer questioned that Mahler succeeded in achieving a spiritual unity between the Latin Pentecostal hymn and the final scene of *Faust*.[18] Other commentators, too, have criticized Mahler's procedure and have spoken of an unacceptable syncretism.[19] Numerous arguments can be advanced, however, for the contrary view that Mahler achieved a convincing synthesis.[20]

How did Mahler transform the intellectual conception of the Eighth into music?

4. On the Translation into Music

The more one familiarizes oneself with the Eighth, the clearer it becomes that its two parts strongly contrast in both sound and style. The first part strikes one as an oratorio or a cantata; the second part, on the contrary, approaches the sphere of the music drama and of the redemption mystery. Structure, compositional technique and timbre differ. The first part appears more monumental, compacter, more massive than the second. This strong contrast is dictated by the design and character of the texts. The many-layered, strongly differentiated final scene of *Faust* with its tendency toward mysticism demanded an entirely different musical setting than the quasi archaic, monolithic Latin Pentecostal hymn. Mahler registered the contrast with great sensitiveness.

---

18 Hans Mayer, "Musik und Literatur," in *Gustav Mahler* (Tübingen: Rainer Wunderlich, 1966), 142–156.

19 Karl Blessinger, *Mendelssohn · Meyerbeer · Mahler. Drei Kapitel Judentum in der Musik als Schlüssel zur Musikgeschichte des 19. Jahrhunderts* (Berlin, 1939), 78; Theodor W. Adorno, *Philosophie der Neuen Musik* (Frankfurt a.M., 1958), 24.

20 Floros, *Gustav Mahler*, 1:129–132; 3:213–215.

Richard Specht observed in 1913 that the first part of the Eighth was kept more in the polyphonic style of church music,[21] a remark that points in the right direction. A comparison of mine has shown that in conceiving the first part Mahler also had Bruckner's *Te Deum* in mind.[22] Mahler greatly loved this work, which he had conducted three times with great success in Hamburg. What do the two works have in common? Both are based on sacred texts in Latin; both require a vast ensemble including, besides orchestra and chorus, or choruses, vocal soloists and organ; in both a hymnal, jubilant, "affirmative" tone predominates; and in both more homophonically conceived parts alternate with contrapuntally worked ones. Notably, Bruckner's work culminates in a four-part fugue, which Mahler trumped with an eight-voice double fugue. Traces of subcutaneous relations can be discovered everywhere, motivic reminiscences as well as tectonic analogies.

But to return to the contrasts between the two parts of the Eighth. There can be no crasser one than that between the roaring conclusion of the first part and the shadowlike beginning of the second. The second part differs from the first, for one thing, by the plenitude of vocal solos it contains. The singing of the Pater Ecstaticus and the Pater Profundus is done in a style reminiscent of Wagnerian music drama. The vocals of the Penitent Women, on the other hand, establish a lied-like style, which Mahler was to develop further in the *Lied von der Erde*. But the numerous choruses of Part Two also differ fundamentally in structure and character from those of Part One. Thus the chorus of the holy Anachoretes is to be sung consistently *piano* and *pianissimo*. The impression of pallor this creates was intentional. Several years before Arnold Schönberg, Mahler here already tried out a kind of *sprechgesang*. The choruses of the angels and of the blessed boys are distinguished by a bright tonal character, and the *Chorus Mysticus* commences *ppp* "like a breath" – the concluding crescendo being all the greater for it.

Of the many peculiar opinions in existence, one of the oddest is the assertion that in the Eighth Symphony Mahler paid tribute to the idea of

---

21 Richard Specht, *Gustav Mahler* (Berlin/Leipzig, 1913), 312.
22 Constantin Floros, "Von Mahlers Affinität zu Bruckner," in *Bruckner-Symposion* (Linz, 1986), 109–117.

absolute music.[23] The truth is that, as in all of his vocal works, Mahler reacts sensitively to the text and often to individual poetic nuances in it. He presents a subtle exegesis of the text, interpreting it, making use of the Wagnerian leitmotif technique, of which he had an outstanding command. Especially revealing in this connection are the thematic linkages between the two parts, anticipations of things to come as well as recourses to past elements.[24] Symbolism of tones, keys and instruments constitutes a wide field in the Eighth.

A listener hearing the symphony for the first time might get the impression of a motley variety of thematic characters. But a careful analysis of the score make clear that in this work, as elsewhere, Mahler works economically. From relatively few germ cells he develops motifs and themes and comes up with ever new figures. The variations technique triumphs, the score being a bonanza of the so-called "developing variation." Some variants depart so far from the model that one cannot immediately recognize the derivation.

Two themes are of surpassing importance for the structure of the work. One is the head theme of the symphony, the *Veni* theme, the invocation of the creative spirit. It proves to be the dominant theme of the first part. It appears in its original form, in augmentation, in diminution, in inversion, in *stretto*, and Mahler also treats it contrapuntally, interlaced with other themes. The metamorphoses the *Veni* theme undergoes in the course of the movement are astounding. Its most impressive shape is undoubtedly the one it takes on in the passages *Infirma nostri corporis* (the weakness of our body) at no. 19. Owing to its changed diastematics, dynamics and harmonization, the once so robust *Veni* theme now seems a mere shadow of itself.

The second main theme of the symphony is the *Accende* theme. It is first intoned, by all the soloists, the two mixed choruses and the boys' choir, in the development of the first movement, at no. 38/39, in the grandiose passage marked "with sudden upswing," to the words *Accende lumen*

---

23 Stefan Strohm, "Die Idee der absoluten Musik als ihr (ausgesprochenes) Programm. Zum unterlegten Text der Mahlerschen Achten," in *Schütz-Jahrbuch 1982/1983*, 73–91.

24 Floros, *Gustav Mahler*, 3:228.

sensibus / Infunde amorem cordibus (Kindle your light for our senses / Pour you love into our hearts); and it is picked up again at the end of the movement, at no. 91, by the separately placed trumpets and trombones and the boys' choir, to the words *Gloria in saeculorum saecula Patri*. This theme, to which Mahler attached the semantics of a love theme, then becomes the leading theme of the second part, where it appears time and again in countless variants. This thematic linkage between the two parts of the Eighth is of programmatic significance. A hitherto unpublished letter by Anton von Webern to Arnold Schönberg of September 12, 1910, contains a vital clue. During a rehearsal for the premiere of the symphony, Mahler, according to Webern, said about the passage *Accende lumen sensibus* that it was the pivot of the entire work: from it a bridge led to the conclusion of *Faust*.

The leading idea of the concluding scene of *Faust* is that of love. As a red thread it extends through the entire scene. As Erich Trunz remarked, Goethe lets the literary leitmotif of love sound ever more strongly:[25] thus at the beginning *Heiliger Liebeshort* (Holy hoard of love, l. 11853), then *Ewiger Liebe Kern* (Eternal love's core, l. 11865), *allmächtige Liebe* (omnipotent love, l. 11872), *Liebesboten* (love's envoys or couriers, l. 11882), and so on in numerous variations, culminating in words like *Ewigen Liebens Offenbarung, die zur Seligkeit entfaltet* (Eternal loving's revelation that to blessedness unfolds, l. 11882), *Und hat an ihm die Liebe gar von oben teilgenommen* (and if love has attended him, moreover, from above, ll. 11938 f.) and *heilige Liebeslust* (holy love lust, l. 12003). After the angels have declared about man's twofold nature that "eternal love alone can separate it" (*Die ewige Liebe nur vermags zu scheiden*, ll. 11964 f.), the latter appears in the form of the *Mater Gloriosa*.

Mahler was fully aware of these concatenations and thus in the second part gave the lead to Love. Meanwhile the *Veni* theme – the major theme in the first part – retreats in the second. It is intimated once by the horns in mm. 563–566 and a second time by the trumpets and horns in mm. 1228–1231, but then is intoned again only at the end of the symphony. The relation of the two main themes to each other, their character, the way

---

25 Trunz, ed., *Goethes Faust*, 637.

they are treated – all of this evokes the impression that the *Veni* theme personifies the male principle and the love theme the female. *The creator spiritus*, the shaping spirit, the process of striving very likely represented the masculine principle for Mahler; the power of love, on the other hand, which emanates from the Mater Gloriosa, symbolizes the Eternal-Feminine. Thus the dialectic of the Eternal-Masculine and the Eternal-Feminine finds its embodiment also in Mahler's music.

The subject of world-redeeming Love was central for Mahler. He had made it his theme already in the Finale of his Third Symphony. In the autograph, the movement bears the poetic-programmatic heading *Was mir die Liebe erzählt*, "What Love tells me." By love he meant there not earthly but eternal love, as he expressly stated in a letter to Hermann Behn.[26]

Mahler frequently regretted not being understood as a symphonist. Time and again he had the painful experience of his intentions being misconceived by both the public and the critics. It may very well be that in the Eighth, which is almost throughout sung, he resorted to texts to give transparency by means of the word to a process otherwise difficult to comprehend. The message he wanted to proclaim was the message of creativity though love. He hoped with this work to conquer the hearts of all listeners at one blow. "After the first theme there will not be a single antagonist in the hall," he remarked to Specht; "it must bowl everyone over."[27] The sensational success of the Munich premiere on September 12, 1910, is the handsomest proof that his wish was fulfilled.

---

26 *Gustav Mahler. Unbekannte Briefe*, ed. Herta Blaukopf (Vienna/Hamburg, 1983), 24.
27 Specht, *Gustav Mahler* (1913), 315.

GUSTAV MAHLER, Eighth Symphony
Autograph of the first page of the score of Part Two
First publication, by permission of
The Bavarian State Library, Munich

The second part of the Eighth opens with a metamorphosis of the love theme that now seems altogether shadowy and quasi riven (dissolved into its motivic segments). The notably spare compositional texture and sound symbolizes the solitary wilderness of the Anachoretes scene.

The Love theme of the Eighth Symphony
Several manifestations, segments and variants
(Mahler treats the theme frequently according to the method of the *developing variation*)

II. Teil, T. 704–711

II. Teil, T. 780–783 [Erscheinung der Mater gloriosa]

Äußerst langsam. Adagissimo

97

VII. Basics of Program Music

> "There is hardly another topic in music that can claim the
> advantage of actuality in the same measure as the so-called
> program music." Rudolf Louis (1902)[1]

> "For it cannot be denied that the symphonic poem is in favor
> with the 'public'." W. Lubosch (1902)[2]

1. Introduction

When Rudolf Louis and W. Lubosch formulated the above remarks, program music had reached, and already almost passed, its last great heyday: the chief tone poems of Richard Strauss had already been composed and performed. The attention these works received sparked a renewed lively discussion about the nature, peculiarity and justification of program music – a discussion that was among the most topical subjects of contemporary musical scholarship and journalism. Between 1900 and 1908, several books and countless essays about program music appeared. Many felt called upon to express themselves on the issue, and all did it with vehement engagement, pro and con. Oddly enough, the only German-language history of program music was written by an opponent of the genre.[3]

After World War I, program music became unfashionable and even discredited. Beginning in the 'twenties, the ideal of *absolute* music grew prevalent almost everywhere: Eduard Hanslick's rigorous aesthetics of autonomy experienced a posthumous triumph. Although a few noted composers continued to write program music – frequently with secret programs – the issue was essentially closed: many regarded the genre as outdated, as a typical product of the 19th century and moreover a synonym for inferior music. Under the circumstances, critical interest in the genre inevitably waned.

---

1 Rudolf Louis, "Franz Liszt und das Problem der Programmusik," *Die Musik*, 1:17 (1902), 1527–1543; p. 1527.
2 W. Lubosch, "Zur Ästhetik der symphonischen Dichtung," *Die Musik*, 2:4 (1902), 243–249; 2:5 (1902), 330–335; p. 244.
3 Otto Klauwell, *Geschichte der Programmusik von ihren Anfängen bis zur Gegenwart* (Leipzig, 1910).

The fact that that interest now appears to reawaken is largely due to two reasons. For one thing, semiotic approaches are increasingly taken notice of in musicology as elsewhere – never have questions about the "meaning" and the understanding of music been asked as insistently as since the 1970s[4] – and for another, quite a few composers in our time continue to test the possibilities of representation through music.

It is no exaggeration to say that confusion reigns about the nature of program music. Not only is there no universally accepted definition, it is often impossible to mediate between contrary conceptions. The term is used in the most varied senses, and definitional criteria, too, vary greatly. While some authors limit the term too narrowly, others define it very widely. Elsa Bienenfeld, for example, took program music to mean "the representation of a single (specific) process through acoustic impulses that imitate solely the particular instance in question"[5] – meaning merely a form of tone painting. Frederick Niecks, on the other hand, included in it both the imitative representation of acoustic models (e.g., nature sounds, battle din) and the rendering of visual impressions (light, shadow and color effects), as well as the expression of psychic states and even the mediation of ideas ("soul painting" and "body painting").[6]

Such definitional diversity results at times in paradoxical, even grotesque situations, as when one and the same work – for example, Beethoven's piano sonata *Les Adieux* op. 81a – is included under the rubric of program music by some but not by others, or when it is asserted in all seriousness that Smetana's symphonic poems could actually not be ranked with program music!

The questions that have been, and still are, central to the discussion of program music are: what is program music? What is its relation to tone painting and to *absolute* music? What does the word "program" mean, and what must a program consist of? Should one take it to mean a mere

4   Cf. Peter Faltin and Hans-Peter Reinecke, eds., *Musik und Verstehen. Aufsätze zur semiotischen Theorie, Ästhetik und Soziologie der musikalischen Rezeption* (Cologne, 1973).
5   Elsa Bienenfeld, "Über ein bestimmtes Problem der Programmusik (Darstellung von Schlachten)", *ZIMG*, 8 (1906/1907), 163–174; p- 164.
6   Frederick Niecks, *Programme Music in the Last Four Centuries. A Contribution to the History of Musical Expression* (London, n.d. [1907]), 1–6.

extra-musical heading or a detailed subject? Finally, Can one speak of program music only if the subject has produced a new musical form?

Let us pursue these questions.

2. "Characteristic" Music and "Painting Symphonies" (*symphonies à programmes*)

Whence did the newer program music take originate? To answer this question succinctly, one does not have to go back to Clément Jannequin and Greek antiquity (the Pythian nomos of Sakadas). One might rather refer to Froberger, Frescobaldi, Johann Kuhnau (*Biblische Historien*), Johann Sebastian Bach (*Capriccio sopra la lontananza del suo fratello dilettissimo*) and François Couperin (*Le Parnasse ou l'Apothéose de Corelli* and *L'Apothéose de Lully*) – i.e., exclusively to works of instrumental music. The beginnings of program music in the historical sense of the term, however, occurred in the last third of the 18th century in France.

At that time it was becoming customary to perform *symphonies à programmes*, that is, symphonies for which concert bills with details about the works performed were handed out. Berlioz' teacher, François Lesueur did so, and we learn that in the 1790s such programs were distributed for symphonies by Dittersdorf and Rosetti.[7] From there there is obviously a direct connection to Berlioz, who had the program of his *Symphonie fantastique* published in the Parisian paper *Le Figaro* on May 21, 1830, as a way of announcing the planned (but then canceled) premiere of the work.

An article published in 1800 in the *Allgemeine musikalische Zeitung* about the "Current State of Music in Paris" provides some essential information about the early practice of program music. The Paris correspondent of the paper reports there about certain "painting symphonies" (*symphonies à programme*) and states that Dittersdorf and Rosetti had been the first to try such compositions "in which the composer resolves not only on a fixed but always also on a picturesque purpose." Such symphonies, he adds, represented a kind of dramatic action, which the listener could follow

---

7   According to Hugo Goldschmidt, *Die Musikästhetik des 18. Jahrhunderts und ihre Beziehungen zu seinem Kunstschaffen* (Zurich/Leipzig, 1915), 250.

"with the bill in hand."[8] The works to which the reporter refers are Carl Ditters von Dittersdorf's symphonies after Ovid's *Metamorphoses* (three of these symphonies appeared in print before 1800 in Vienna and Paris[9]) and a "historical or painting symphony" *Calypso et Télémaque* by Francesco Antonio Rosetti (alias Franz Anton Rösler), first performed in Paris in 1791.[10]

In Germany the genre of the *symphonies à programmes* was not very well known around 1800. Friedrich Rochlitz, the editor of the *Allgemeine musikalische Zeitung*, felt compelled to comment about the Paris correspondent's report:

> *Symphonies à programmes* – so far as we know, we do not as yet have a generally accepted coinage for this compositional genre in the German language. If the above term is unacceptable, one could call it *historical,* which, however, might delimit it too narrowly and make things even harder for an advocate than they will be under any circumstances.

In 1835, Robert Schumann published his famous review of the *Symphonie fantastique* in the *Neue Zeitschrift für Musik*. He there addressed Berlioz' program in detail, censures its particularity, and comments:

> However, Berlioz wrote initially for his French audience, whom one can little impress with ethereal modesty. I can imagine them following the music "with playbill in hand" and applauding their compatriot, who came up with such good likenesses for everything; the music by itself does not matter to them.[11]

Even as late as 1838, the *symphonies à programmes* did not have a particularly high reputation in Germany. Thus Gustav Schilling could write about them in vol. 6 of his *Encyclopädie*:

---

8   *Allgemeine musikalische Zeitung*, 2 (Leipzig, 1800), 745 ff.
9   Karlheinz Schlager, ed., *Einzeldrucke vor 1800* (RISM A/I/12) (Kassel, etc., 1972), 424.
10 Horace Fitzpatrick, article "Anton Rösler," in MGG, 1 (1963) col. 619–624; col. 621. It is to be noted in this connection that as early as 1777 Ignazio Raimondi performed a long symphony in Amsterdam entitled *Les aventures de Télémaque*, a symphony about the story of Telemachus and Calypso. See Wilhelm August Ambros, *Die Grenzen der Musik und Poesie. Eine Studie zur Ästhetik der Tonkunst* (Leipzig, 1855), 138.
11 Robert Schumann, *Gesammelte Schriften über Musik und Musiker* (hereafter GS), 5th ed., ed. Martin Kreisig, 2 vols. (Leipzig, 1914), 1:83 f.

By *symphonies à programmes* (there is as yet no German name for them) is meant symphonies whose purpose is to describe certain external, especially historical, events by the sole means of musical tones without the aid of poetry. It goes without saying that such a representation can be achieved only by the lowest sort of *tone painting* (q.v.), and we therefore must observe to our delight that this genre of symphony has not yet been able to meet with any particular acclaim. Dittersdorf and Rosetti wrote such *symph. à programme*. The former wrote, e.g., the *Four Ages, Fall of Phaeton* etc.' the latter *Telemach*. Haydn's *Seven Words*, too, must be counted among them.[12]

In the fourth volume of the *Encyclopädie*, incidentally, under the key word *malende* [painting] *Sinfonien*, we find a cross-reference to *symphonies à programme*.[13]

From all this it appears that the terms *program music* and *program symphony* entered German musical terminology only in the 1850s – at the latest after the appearance of Franz Liszt's fundamental treatise about *Berlioz und seine Harold-Symphonie* of 1855.[14]

The expression "program music" (*musique à programme*) thus seems originally to have been confined to the French-speaking region. A related term, however, was widely used throughout the Europe of the late 18th century: the expression "characteristic music" (*musique characteristique*).[15] In numerous prints and manuscripts from the time around 1800 we find the designations *characteristic* symphonies, overtures, sonatas and pieces.

A hitherto little noticed definition of the designation "characteristic symphony" is given in the piano exercise manual of Daniel Türk of 1789.

---

12 Gustav Schilling, *Encyclopädie der gesammten musikalischen Wissenschaften*, 6 vols. (Stuttgart, 1835–1838), 6:551.

13 Ibid., 4:503.

14 Franz Liszt, "Berlioz und seine Harold-Symphonie" (1855), in *Gesammelte Schriften*, ed. Lina Ramann (hereafter GS), 6 vols. (Leipzig, 1880–1883), 4:3–102. August Wilhelm Ambros, incidentally, speaks about "Programmen-Musik" in his book *Die Grenzen der Musik und Poesie* of 1855 (see note 10 above). We should also note in this connection that while the word *program*, meaning a subject for a musical composition, became familiar in Germany, as we have shown, only around 1855, it was current in Italy already at the beginning of the 19th century. See Giuseppe Carpani, *Le Haydine ovvero Lettere su la vita e le opere del celebre maestro Giuseppe Haydn* (Milano, 1812), 69 ff.

15 *Musique caractéristique* was the title of a work by Muzio Clementi published by Artaria in Vienna. See RISM A/I/2, p. 159.

> Characteristic symphonies [Türk says] one could chiefly call those symphonies that are designed as openers for operas etc. in lieu of the usual overtures. This nomenclature, however, befits the symphony only if the character of the following opera is generally represented in it, or if the composer has expressed an immediately preceding action in the symphony.[16]

Happily, Ludwig van Beethoven's original designations of some of his works provide us with concrete examples for a fuller understanding of these *caracteristica*: Beethoven regarded the *Sinfonia pastorale* op. 68 as a *sinfonia caracteristica*; he labeled the first *Leonore* overture op. 138 (1805) "characteristic overture"; he called the piano sonata "Les Adieux" op. 81a expressly a "great characteristic sonata"; and he took *Marcia sulla morte d'un Eroe* in the piano sonata in A-flat Major op. 26 to be a *pezzo caracteristico*, i.e., a character piece , as is evident from the Berlin sketchbook Landsberg 7.[17] From this it appears that in the late 18th and early 19th century characteristic music was taken to mean compositions that bore extra-musical titles, or sometimes works written for specific occasions.

What, then, is characteristic music's relation to program music? It is not easy to differentiate the terms precisely. Certainly there were many points of contact between the two areas; numerous observations even suggest that the two terms were frequently used synonymously. To illustrate:

1. Various sonatas of definitely programmatic character by Johann Ludwig Dussek and Johann Baptiste Vanhal are expressly called characteristic sonatas in individual prints from the time around 1800. All of them are works that refer to specific contemporary events. Among them we find sonatsas on regular naval battles on the occasion of the defeat of the great Dutch fleet by Admiral Duncan von October 2, 1797, and of the Battle of Abukir (Battle of the Nile) of August 1 to 3, 1798.[18] In like manner, Vanhal used the "Celebration of the return of our all-beloved

---

16 Daniel Gottlob Türk, *Klavierschule, oder Anweisungen zum Klavierspielen für Lehrer und Lernende* (Leipz/Halle, 1789), 392 (Documenta musicologica, 1:xxiii, facsimile reprint, ed. Erwin Jacobi (Kassel etc., 1962).

17 For details, see my *Beethoven's Eroica. Thematic Studies*, tr. Ernest Bernhardt-Kabisch (Frankfurt: Peter Lang, 2013; orig. German ed. 1978), 79–81. See also F. E., Kirby, "Beethoven's Pastoral Symphony as a *Sinfonia caracteristica*," *MQ*, 56 (1970): 605–623.

18 RISM A/I/2, pp. 476, 496; RISM A/I/9, pp. 51 f.

monarch Francis I on November 29, 1809" as an occasion for the composition of a characteristic sonata.

2. The Paris correspondent of the *Allgemeine musikalische Zeitung* cites Dittersdorf's symphonies as models of the novel *symphonies à programmes*. Dittersdorf himself describes his twelve symphonies after Ovid's *Metamorphoses* as "charakterisierte Sinfonien."[19]

3. Türk distinguishes between two kinds of characteristic symphonies: those in which "the *character* of the following opera is generally represented," and those in which "a specific immediately preceding action" is expressed in the symphony. We recall that the Paris correspondent of the *Allgemeine musikalische Zeitung* thought that the *symphonies à programmes* represented "a kind of dramatic action." In both instances, the subjects of the sonatas are thus "actions."

4. Beethoven called the *Pastoral Symphony*, as already noted, *sinfonia caracteristica*. The term *symphonie à programme* was probably not known to him. The *Pastoral* is nevertheless a program symphony for two reasons: for one thing, because the titles of the five movements were stated on the concert bill of the first performance of December 22, 1808;[20] and secondly, because these headings, when taken together, form a fairly detailed program that can be perceived as a progressive action: *jolly gathering of the rustics – thunderstorm – herdsmen's song. Glad, thankful feelings after the storm.*

Before 1800, we might add, works with extra-musical subjects were also presented with other designations. Thus a sonata by Johann Ludwig Dussek, whose theme is the fate of Queen Marie Antoinette from her arrest to her death, is classified as *musique allégorique* in a Dutch printing.[21] Similarly, a piano sonata in E-flat Major by Dussek bears the addition *intitulée Les Adieux* in a Parisian printing.[22] One automatically thinks of Beethoven's sonata of the same title, as well as of the score copy of the Third Symphony

---

19 Carl Ditters von Dittersdorf, *Lebensbeschreibung seinem Sohn in die Feder diktiert*, 1st ed. (Leipzig, 1801); reprint (Munich, 1967), 221.

20 George Grove, *Beethoven und seine neun Symphonien*, German adaptation by Max Hehemann (London, n.d. [1906]), 174 f.

21 RISM A/I/2, p. 490.

22 Ibid., 492.

dated August 1804, bearing the significant notation *Sinfonia grande intitolate Bonaparte.*[23]

But let us stay with the *Les Adieux* sonata for another moment. The work demonstrates impressively that what matters most in *characteristic* music is evidently the depiction of states of feeling. The three movements of the sonata trace three stages of an emotional process: the *Adagio-cum-Allegro* the parting, the *Andante espressivo* the absence, and the *Vivacissimo*, finally, the reunion. The sonata first appeared in July of 1811.[24] It must have enormously impressed Carl Maria von Weber: his plan for a piano concerto in F Minor exhibits the same basic "programmatic pattern.' In March of 1815, Weber told Friedrich Rochlitz that in conceiving the work, a "kind of story" had "really strangely" come spontaneously to underlie the whole in him, "according to whose thread the pieces line up and receive their character, and do it so detailed and quasi dramatically" that he would see himself forced to give them the following titles: "Allegro, parting; Adagio, lament; Finale, highest anguish, consolation, reunion, rejoicing."[25] That became the well-known Concert Piece (FWJ No. 282).

The piano sonata in G Minor op. 50 No. 3 of Muzio Clementi, written in 1821, is modelled according to a different but likewise tripartite "program pattern." It bears the title *Didone abbandonata* and the subtitle *Scena tragica*. The headings of the movements are *Introduzione. Largo patetico e sostenuto – Allegro, ma con espressione – Adagio dolente – Allegro agitato, e con disperazione*. The movements feature several expression marks – *diliberando e meditando, lamentando, languente, con furia, con passione* – which point directly toward Franz Liszt. Paul Mies is right in thinking that the three movements reflect Dido's inward experience,

23 Floros, *Beethoven's Eroica*, 6.

24 Georg Kinsky, and Hans Halm, *Das Werk Beethovens. Thematisch-bibliographisches Verzeichnis seiner sämtlichen vollendeten Kompositionen* (Munich/Duisburg, 1955), 217.

25 Max Maria von Weber, *Carl Maria von Weber. Ein Lebensbild*, 3 vols. (Leipzig, 1864–1866), 1:478 f., 2:311 f. – Friedrich Wilhelm Jähns, *Carl Maria von Weber in seinen Werken. Chronologisch-thematisches Verzeichnis seiner sämmtlichen Compositionen* (Berlin, 1871). Reprint (Berlin-Lichterfelde, 1967), 337–339.

"which rises from mournful love to vehement anguish and despair."[26] Friedrich Rochlitz ranked this sonata as belonging to the genre of characteristic music. In a longish review of 1822,[27] he observed: "The third sonata is also *characteristic* in the special sense in which the French, so far as we know, first used this epithet by, as it were, linking it to something *historical*."[28]

3. Tone Painting and "Narration of Inner Processes"

> "Every painting in instrumental music, if pushed too far,
> loses." Ludwig van Beethoven[29]

One of the most disastrous misunderstandings about program music is its confusion with tone painting. Many people, when program music is mentioned, think primarily or preponderantly of the imitation of acoustic and visual sense impressions, of storms, thunder, rain, the evocation of still or flowing waters, sunrises, light and shadow, the clatter of horse hooves, the din of battle, etc. Already around 1860, the heyday of program music, these notions evidently circulated widely. Richard Pohl, one of the most committed champions of the New German school, felt compelled to point out that although tone painting (a species) was program music, program music (the higher generic term) was by no means already tone painting.[30] Albert Wellek similarly stated a hundred years later that tone painting was an artistic *technique*, while program music was an artistic *genre*, and he

---

26 Paul Mies, Preface to the Henle-Verlag edition of the sonata (Munich/Duisburg, n.d. [1957]).

27 Friedrich Rochlitz in *Allgemeine musikalische Zeitung*, No. 39 (Leiptig, 1822). Reprinted in Arnold Schering, *Beethoven und die Dichtung. Mit einer Einleitung zur Geschichte und Ästhetik der Beethovendeutung* (Neue deutsche Forschungen, vol. 77) (Berlin, 1936), 573–575.

28 A kind of interpretation of the sonata is also contained in a review that appeared in 1822 in the *Quarterly Musical Magazine and Review*. See Leon Plantinga, *Clementi. His Life and Music* (London, 1977), 263 f.

29 Berlin, Foundation Preußischer Kulturbesitz, bundle Landsberg 10, p. 161. See Dagmar Weise, *Beethoven. Ein Skizzenbuch zur Pastoralsymphonie op. 68 und zu den Trios op. 70, 1 and 2* (Veröffentlichungen des Beethovenhauses in Bonn, new series, vol. 13 (Bonn, 1961) pt. 1:17.

30 Richard Pohl, "Liszts Faust-Symphonie" (1862), in *Gesammelte Schriften über Musik und Musiker*, vol. 2 (Leipzig, 1883), 269.

added that one could love and cultivate tone painting and yet reject program music out of hand – though the reverse case was unthinkable.[31]

Certainly program music constitutes a wide area comprising a considerable diversity.[32] Let us first of all consider the history of the genre around 1800.

The aesthetics of music of the late 18th and early 19th century clearly distinguished between tone painting and the "expression of feelings," between "picturesque music" and "music of the soul,"[33] and the characteristic music of the time was conversant with both. In 1780, the art philosopher Johann Jacob Engel postulated that a musician should "always rather paint feelings than objects of feelings."[34] Beethoven may have known Engel's book *Über die musikalische Malerey*. His much-quoted maxim about the *Pastoral Symphony*, "More expression of feelings than painting," in any case, is conspicuously close to Engel's ideas. The saying by no means signifies, though, that Beethoven altogether dispensed with tone painting in the *Pastoral*; it should rather be understood as a caveat against too much tone painting. That is the meaning of Beethoven's less well-known notation, which we used as a motto for this section: "Every painting in instrumental music loses if pushed too far."

In a meritorious study, Adolf Sandberger has expressed the view that in the *Pastoral Symphony* Beethoven not only used the traditional means of tonal painting but intensified them.[35] I can only concur. The sketchbooks alone make it very clear that Beethoven in conceiving the work let himself be guided by tone-painterly intentions. Thus in the sketches for the fourth movement, the keywords lighting, storm, rain and thunder appear. The

---

31 Albert Wellek *Musikpsychologie und Musikästhetik. Grundriß der systematischen Musikwissenschaft* (Frankfurt, 1963), 219.

32 On the concept of tone painting, see above all Paul Mies, "Über die Tonmalerei," *Zeitschrift für Ästhetik und allgemeine Kunstwissenschaft*, 7 (1912), 397–450, 578–618; Ludwig Misch, "Die Mittel derTonmalerei," in *Neue Beethoven-Studien und andere Themen* (Munich/Duisburg, 1967), 201–206.

33 Adolph Bernhard Marx, *Über Tonmalerei in der Tonkunst. Ein Maigruß an die Kunstphilosophen* (Berlin, 1928), 46 ff.

34 Johann Jacob Engel, *Über die musikalische Malerey* (Berlin, 1780), 25.

35 Adolf Sandberger "'Mehr Ausdruck der Empfindung als Malerei'" (1820), in *Ausgewählte Aufsätze zur Musikgeschichte*; vol. 2 (Munich, 1924), 201–212; p. 212.

movement marks the culmination of a long tradition of tempest presentations – a tradition that can be traced back all the way to the beginning of the 17th century.[36] The *Scene at the Brook* contains not only the famous "bird concert" at the end (which prompted Parisian concert impresarios to add the phrase *langages des oiseaux* to the original title of the movement[37]) but also all kinds of other stylized avian voices belonging to the picturesque props of the nature idyll. (Stylized bird voices also play a role in the head movement of the *Pastoral*.[38]) Beethoven has moreover "painted" with every means of the pastoral genre: sustained notes (musette basses), alphorn calls and, not least, Lydian turns (paganisms) frequently determine the scene of the movement.[39]

Perhaps one will most nearly do justice to the *Pastoral* by seeing it as an ideal synthesis of "tone-painting" music and "music of the soul." Nature imitation attains such a high degree of stylization and sublimation in this work that the acoustic prototypes are often hardly recognizable and noticeable as such any longer. That may explain why the identification of the redbreast motifs and above all of the warble of the yellow hammer in the *Scene at the Brook* presented some difficulties.[40] (In 1823, Beethoven told Schindler that the birds, among them the gold hammers, had "mitkomponiert," helped with the composing of the *Scene at the Brook*.[41]); and it may similarly explain why Beethoven's original notations of the "murmuring of the brooks" (in a sketchbook from 1803) differs so consider ably from the "murmuring" figure of the strings in the *Scene at the Brook*. From this

---

36 Sandberger, "Zu den geschichtlichen Voraussetzungen der Pastoralsinfonie," ibid., 154–200; pp. 166 ff.
37 Grove, *Beethoven und seine neun Symphonien* (1906), 193.
38 See, e.g., the turn figures of the flutes in mm. 46–52 and the cuckoo calls in mm. 187–190 and 233–236.
39 See Floros, *Gustav Mahler*, vol. 2: *Mahler and the Symphony of the 19th Century*, 111 f.
40 Robert Lach, "Die Vogelstimmen in Beethovens Werken" in *Neues Beethoven Jahrbuch*, 2 (1925), 7–22., esp. pp. 13–17. And cf. Willi Kahl, "Zu Beethovens Naturauffassung," in *Beethoven und die Gegenwart. Ludwig Schiedermair zum 60. Geburtstag* (Berlin/Bonn, 1937), 220–265; pp. 233 f.
41 Anton Schindler, *Biographie von Ludwig van Beethoven*, 3rd ed. (Münster, 1860), 1:153–155.

Gustav Nottebohm drew the logical conclusion that Beethoven did not proceed simply "realistically" in composing this scene.[42]

With the *Pastoral Symphony*, Beethoven showed program music a new way, which later composers were to pursue. In his major successors, in any case, we rarely find purely picturesque, purely descriptive music: "soul-painting" always predominates. Even Hector Berlioz, who is said to have had a weakness for tone painting, was first and foremost a "soul painter." Although the program of the *Symphonie fantastique*, which is located on a dreamlike, almost surrealistic level, may evoke the impression of depicting also external happenings, what mattered to Berlioz, as it did to Beethoven, was the "expression of feelings." The heading of the first movement, *Reveries. Passions*, is symptomatic. Pure tone painting, like the warbling of nightingale and quail in the *Scène aux champs*,[43] the distant thunder (four timpani) in the same movement, and the drum roll after the execution in the *Marche au supplice,* are the exceptions to the rule. Berlioz' innovation consists above all in having *psychologized* symphonic music. Through the introduction and leitmotif-like recurrence of the *idée fixe* he opened a portentous symbolic dimension to program music, which later composers would no longer want to dispense with.

Even more prominently than in Berlioz, "soul painting" comes to the fore in Franz Liszt's symphonic oeuvre. His conception of program music is miles apart from the trite illustrations undertaken by some of the 18th-century composers. For by program music Liszt understood, not the depiction of external realities, but a "sequence of states of mind" and the "narration of inner events" (see ch. X, below). Berlioz' conception of program music was modeled on the drama, Liszt's, on the other hand, on the epic, more precisely on the modern "philosophical epopee," by which he meant high- and highest-ranking literary works like Byron's *Manfred* and Goethe's *Faust*.

Even so, we should not get the impression that Liszt dispenses with tone painting altogether. Illustrative elements can be found in his works as well. Thus the symphonic poem *Les Préludes*, after Lamartine's *Méditations poetiques*, contain a storm scene (*Allegro ma non troppo* and *Allegro*

---

42 Gustav Nottebohm, *Zweite Beethoveniana* (Leipzig, 1887), 375 f.
43 See Floros, *Gustav Mahler, 2: Mahler and the Symphony*, 158 n. 32.

tempestoso) notable for its many coloristic elements, chains of chromatically sequenced seventh chords, tremolos, crescendos and stringendos, timpani rolls, etc. However, the tempest here does not have the semantics of a thunderstorm, a natural catastrophe, but is of metaphoric significance. As the program explains, what is meant is an existential storm that destroys the "first delights of happiness" and its "sweet illusions." The action thus attains in fact a "symbolic sheen" here.

As sparsely as Liszt deals with descriptive tone *painting*, the means of tone *symbolism* he deploys extensively. His instrumental music is located in a highly significative tone-symbolic sphere, whose exploration only started in the last thirty years or so. Liszt's tone symbols include intervals (e.g., the tritone/*diabolus in musica*), motifs (like the "tonal symbol of the cross"), themes, chorales and other character pieces (marches, waltzes, etc.), rhythms (leitrhythms), chords (leitchords) and instrumental colors or timbres, with idiophonic sound symbols (e.g., bells, tamtam) playing a material role. In the development of the world of tone symbols Liszt went as far as hardly any other composer before him (except for Richard Wagner).

In a study published in 1903, Max Vancsa distinguished between two directions in the program music of the 19th century: a "realistic and an "idealistic" one. The realistic direction, he thought, confined itself to the detailed musical illustration of a given program "that in most cases is already marked externally by its depicting events, whether from nature, history or human life." This direction, he thought, presented itself essentially as a continuation of the original naïve programmatic music and was often identical with tone painting. The idealistic direction, on the other hand, took the program merely as a "basis for moods and ideas"; it did not want to exhibit the individual process to the ear but merely to find a commensurate musical expression for its "ideal content.'[44] Vancsa regarded Richard Strauss as the leading representative of this idealistic direction in program music!

---

44 Max Vancsa, "Zur Geschichte der Programmusik," *Die Musik*, 2:23 (1903), 323–343; 2:24 (1903) , 403–418; pp. 413 ff.

4. New Formal Concepts and Supposed Formlessness

> "I merely ask leave to determine the form by the content...."
>
> Franz Liszt (1856)[45]

In no other area of music does the question as to the relation between *form* and *content* arise as imperiously as it does in program music. To what extent does the subject of a given work determine its musical form? Is it true that program music violates the logic of music, or is it rather that it has brought forth new concepts of form? These questions inevitably arise when one reads the literature.

Otto Klauwell takes program music to be a "species of music" that, not content with specifically musical effects, undertakes to make extra-musical, inner or outer, events the object of representation. The decisive criterion for judging program music is, according to Klauwell, whether and how the program has affected the shaping of the music. In this respect, three categories of cases are to be distinguished in his opinion, which he defines as follows:

1. The program has had no influence on the form of the music, either because it was too general in its tenor to warrant certain formal peculiarities or because it was, as it were, tailor-made for a specific preexistent form. Examples: Beethoven's Pastoral Symphony and Saint-Saëns' *Dance of Death*.
2. The program has led to a specific new form, which, although not measurable by an existing yardstick, is nonetheless constructed according to musical logic and does not require the program for a musical understanding. Example: the Prelude to *Lohengrin* (whose program can be read up on in vol. 5 of R. Wagner's writings), as well as diverse of the smaller movements in the symphonies of Berlioz.
3. The constant concern with the program and its particulars has resulted in a musical piece that, incomprehensible in purely musical terms, is like an insoluble riddle whose solution is therefore included in the program. Enjoyment of such a piece is not an immediate one but can be gained only by constant comparison with the program. Examples: The Mountain Symphony by Liszt and R. Strauss' *Don Quixote*.[46]

The comments Klauwell adds to these categories are highly questionable. Thus he thinks that the first category should not even be included in the

---

45 Liszt to Louis Köhler, July 9, 1856. *Franz Liszt's Briefe*, 8 vols., ed. La Mara, (Leipzig, 1893–1905), 1: 225; hereafter FLB.
46 Klauwell, *Geschichte der Programmusik* (1910), v/vi.

genre; in the second category he perceives "the only possible solution to the program-music program and one that is also unquestionably fruitful for the continued development of musical art"; whereas the third category, the only one that he accepts as actual program music "in the strict sense of the term," is also one he thinks he must protest against.

These specifications, willful, arbitrary and subjective as they are, can obviously not do justice to the matter. How questionable Klauwell's procedure is becomes evident at the latest when one considers that he is not willing to accept Beethoven's *Pastoral Symphony* or Haydn's *The Savior's Seven Words on the Cross* as program music – works that not only have extra-musical titles but also are based on programs that clearly exhibit a progressive action of sorts. And who could agree with Klauwell's view that there is nothing in the *Pastoral* "that could not also occur in a piece belonging to absolute music without seeming in any way peculiar, let alone enigmatic"?[47]

In diametric opposition to this claim it can be argued that countless details in the musical shape of the *Pastoral* are programmatically conditioned and must remain altogether incomprehensible without knowledge of the program. To elaborate:

As a rule, a symphony in Beethoven's time consisted of four movements. By contrast, the *Pastoral* is composed of five movements, of which the last three merge into each other *attacca*. Just as unusual is the fact that in the scherzo-like third movement the Trio is replaced by a rustic dance – an extraordinarily robust allegro in two-fourth time!

A further irregularity: the form of both the first and the slow movement of the *Pastoral* is that of the sonata; the finale represents a mixture of rondo, sonata movement and variations form, all of which is certainly not unusual. The thunderstorm movement, on the other hand, is distinguished by a remarkably bold and free design, for which no parallels from the realm of absolute music can be adduced. Viewed from a distance, the movement appears like a gigantic crescendo-decrescendo arc, with the crescendo developing in several stages.

---

47 Ibid., 76 f., 83 f.

Again, the disposition of means is in the service of the programmatic intention in the *Pastoral*. Besides strings, the orchestration of the first two movements calls merely for flutes, oboes, clarinets, bassoons and horns. The trumpets are added only in the third movement, while timpani, trombones and piccolo flute are saved for the fourth movement, in some respects the climax of the entire symphony. Equally symptomatic is the fact that Beethoven uses dissonances very sparingly in the first three movements, only to deploy them all the more excessively in the thunderstorm section!

Finally, one can really grasp Beethoven's humor in the *Pastoral* – for example, the premature entrance of the oboe in the third movement, m. 91, followed by the rather unmotivated burlesque figure of the bassoonist – only after having taken cognizance of Anton Schindler's detailed report, according to which Beethoven had sought to "copy" the ineptness of Austrian village musicians in the third movement.[48]

What has been said should make clear that, contrary to Klauwell's opinion, the program of the *Pastoral* contributed decisively to the shaping of the music. It is certainly out of the question that, as Klauwell asserts, "it was, as it were, tailor-made for a specific preexistent form." Admittedly, to be sure, there are works of program music that do not depart overly much from the traditional canon of forms. Klawell's view that one can speak of program music really only where the program has resulted in a specific novel form cannot be maintained in this rigorous formulation. Even so, one has to concede that his thesis reflects certain ideas of Franz Liszt. To explain:

Central to Liszt's thinking during the Weimar years (1848–1861) was the form-content problem. Liszt was fully persuaded that in the New Music he championed the content, that is, the poetic idea, had to determine the form. As early as December 2, 1852, he called this question, in a letter to Wilhelm von Lenz, the "axis of criticisms and the aesthetics of music." There he proposed to divide Beethoven's oeuvre into two categories:

> a first one, in which the traditional and adapted form embraces and guides the master's idea; and a second one, in which, the idea, expanding, breaks up, recreates and newly shapes the form and the style according to its requirements and inspirations.[49]

---

48 Schindler, *Biographie*, 1:155–157.
49 *FLB*, 1:124.

In his treatise about *Berlioz und seine Harold-Symphonie* of 1855, Liszt made no bones about his conviction that the traditional forms were exhausted. New ideas, he postulated, needed new forms, and he argued that Berlioz did not cultivate form for the sake of form but regarded form as having "a reality secondary to content."[50] Several pages later, he makes a fundamental distinction between absolute music and program music.

> In the so-called classical music, the recurrence and thematic development of the themes is determined by formal rules, which are regarded as irrevocable, even though composers had no other prescription for them but their own imagination and they themselves made the formal arrangements that one now wants to set up as laws.

In program music, on the other hand, recurrence, change, alteration and modulation of motifs were conditioned by their relation to a "poetic idea." Here, one theme did not call forth another "by formal law," here the motifs were not the results of stereotypical approximations or contrasts of tonal colors; neither did the timbre condition the grouping of ideas. All exclusively musical considerations – although by no means disregarded – were subordinated to the "action of the given subject." Action and subject of the new symphonic genre thus demanded "an interest superior to the technical treatment of the musical matter."[51]

Ultimately these arguments signify that the programmatic idea can lead to an astonishing variety of new formal conceptions. Since each work must be based on an unmistakable subject, and since the composer must seek to lend to his composition a form that is commensurate with the subject and at the same time freed from all schematic constraints, the result will be a wealth of original formations.

With these principles, Liszt made himself the co-founder of what was subsequently called "heteronomy aesthetics" in music,[52] and it deserves to be emphasized that he always kept to these principles in his symphonic work. His two program symphonies, the *Faust* and the *Dante* symphony, and his thirteen symphonic poems reveal indeed new formal conceptions,

---

50 Franz Liszt, GS, 4:59–61.
51 Ibid., 69.
52 The terms *Autonomie-* and *Heteronomieästhetik* were coined by Felix M. Gatz, *Musik-Ästhetik in ihren Hauptrichtungen* (Stuttgart, 1929).

overall as well as in detail: the musical shape in all its dimensions is dictated by the subject. Liszt strove for thematic unification of his symphonic works and developed several methods for this purpose, of which the techniques of *derivation* and of *intensified recurrence* are especially important.[53] The term derivation signifies the technique of deriving several – if not all – themes of a work from a core motif by means of diastematic, rhythmic and harmonic variation. Especially impressive examples of this are the symphonic poems *Tasso* and *Les Préludes*. "Intensified recurrence" (*gesteigerte Wiederkehr*) – the coinage is Liszt's – means the procedure of synthesizing the themes and motifs of a composition at the end in significantly intensifies form (*steigerung*). The symphonic poem *Die Ideale* (The Ideals) may be cited as a prime instance.

Considering the originality of Liszt's conceptions, one can understand why they were sneered at, attacked and almost always totally misunderstood by his antagonists. Eduard Hanslick accused him not only of formlessness but also of a lack of "musical cash of his own,"[54] Otto Klauwell spoke of his "sapping all hitherto form,"[55] and Willibald Nagel felt called upon to criticize his "neglect of all musicological laws.[56] Only much later – after program music had lost its topicality – it began to be recognized that programs in music can be fully warranted. The only condition that Reinhardt Raffalt attached to this conclusion was that the program had to subordinate itself to the "autonomy of the musical" to the extent that its "foreign content" could be supported by the "inner musical" life of the work without an aesthetic breach.[57]

The reproaches cited, of course, are each and all groundless and unjust to the matter. The aesthetic of Liszt's and Richard Strauss' program music

53 See Floros, *Mahler and the Symphony*, 45–50 and ch. XV, below.
54 Eduard Hanslick, *Fünf Jahre Musik [1891–1895] (Der Modernen Oper VII. Teil)* (Berlin, 1896), 265.
55 Klauwell, *Geschichte der Programmusik*, 368.
56 Wilibald Nagel, *Wesen und Bedeutung derProgramm-Musik* (Musikalisches Magazin, No. 42) (Langensalza, 1912), 44.
57 Reinhardt Raffalt, *Über die Problematik der Programm-Musik. Ein Versuch ihres Aufweises an der Pastoral-Symphonie von Beethoven, der Berg-Symphonie von Liszt und der Alpensinfonie von Strauss* (diss.) (Tübingen/Passau, 1949), 80.

is based, as I have argued elsewhere,[58] on the following, fully legitimate train of thought: the *poetic idea* (the subject), as the "foreign content" of a composition, shapes the musical content, that is to say, the musical themes in the widest sense and, moreover, also determines its representation, i.e., the musical form.

This axiom, of course, does not mean that every program-bound composition is *a priori* logical as music: the program alone obviously does not vouch for the quality of the music. Schumann's maxim, formulated in 1843, "Above all, let me hear that you have made beautiful music, then your program shall be pleasing to me as well,"[59] holds true for all program music. And no one will want to maintain that there are no shallow works within the genre (as there are also within absolute music). Whoever immerses himself into the works of Berlioz, Liszt and Strauss, however – to mention only those three – will have to concede that these masters always knew how to harmonize the demands of the program with the demands of musical form and musical logic.

5. Mere Title Headings vs. Detailed Programs

> "'The earlier programs,' we hear it being said, "'were kept terse.'"
> Liszt (1855)[60]

> "More exhaustive and detailed programs, such as, e.g., Berlioz still
> used at times, with Liszt have become progressively rarer and
> today have disappeared almost entirely." R. Louis (1902)[61]

There is evidently not a single point in the discussion about program music that has not been controversial. How does a program have to be constituted so that one can speak of program music? On this question, too, opinions are divided. To some a mere titular heading suffices, while others demand a comprehensive, detailed program fixed in every particular.

Liszt was among the exponents of the first view. Program music to him meant any kind of music bearing an extra-musical heading. In his Berlioz treatise, he includes in the genre, i.a., chansons by Jannequin (16th c.), pieces

---

58 Floros, *Mahler and the Symphony*, 39 f.
59 Robert Schumann, GS, 2:129.
60 Liszt, GS, 4:23.
61 *Die Musik*, 1:17 (1902), 1542

by Froberger, Kuhnau's *Biblische Historien* (1700), Couperin's *Pièces de Clavecin* (1713), and J. S. Bach's *Capriccio*. Beethoven's *Eroica* and *Pastoral Symphony*, his piano sonata *Les Adieux* and the *Heilige Dankgesang eines Genesenen* (Sacred Song of Thanksgiving of a Convalescent) are obviously program music for him, and the same is true of such of Schumann's pieces as bear characteristic titles. The only condition Liszt makes is that there must be no misuse of programs, in other words, program or title can be justified only "when they are a poetic necessity, an inseparable part of the whole and indispensable to its comprehension."[62]

In contrast to Liszt, Richard Hohenemser distinguishes two categories of program music: The first is based on a "detailed" program, where the music is linked "step by step" to a specific "train of thought" that is "fixed, or at least fixable, in words"; in the second, the program is merely a title prefixed to the musical piece, with the "detail of the execution" being entirely left up to the music. As an example of the first category, Hohenemser cites Beethoven's *Battle of Vittoria*, while he exemplifies the second category with works of Schumann like the *Carnaval*, the *Novelleten*, the *Children's Scenes*, the *Forest Scenes*, the *Gesänge der Frühe* (Morning Songs), as well as pieces with individual titles like *Das bittende Kind* (The Beseeching Child), *Aufschwung* (Uplift), *Grillen* (Crotchets), etc.[63] For entirely implausible reasons, Hohenemser denies aesthetic justification to the first category, whereas he regards the second as justified. His argument is grounded in a psychology of perception: pieces that are based on a specific extra-musical train of thought, he says, distract from the music; at the same time, the music prevents any concentration on the train of thought. A mere title heading, on the other hand, puts the listener into a certain mood (an "overall state of mind") that is kindred to the mood content of the art work to be absorbed.[64]

---

62 Liszt, GS, 4:21–28.

63 Richard Hohenemser, "Über die Programmusik," SIMG, 1 (1899–1900), 307–324; p. 319.

64 Albert Wellek (1963, p. 221), who distinguishes between "title music or music under a motto" and music with a detailed program, also thinks that a work programmed in detail could be "an aesthetically nonsensical concern."

M.-D. Calvocoressi takes an altogether different standpoint. To him not all music that has a mere theme is necessarily program music. True program music must have a precise and complex subject (*une donnée non seulement précise mais complexe*) and one that successively expresses specific and diverse things. A true program, he thinks, consists in an assertion composed of facts, actions or consecutive states (*un énoncé de faits, d'actions ou d'états consécutifs*), though not necessarily objective (material) givens. Calvocoressi illustrates his theses with several examples. Thus to him the head movement of Beethoven's piano sonata *Les Adieux*, unlike the beginning of Bach's *Capriccio*, is *not* program music, and similarly Liszt's *Hamlet,* a symphonic poem that supposedly merely evokes the character of the hero, should not be called program music, in contrast to, say, Glasunov's *Stenka Rasin* (1885), a work in which episodes of a detailed narrative are traced.[65]

Calvocoressi's criterion for determining the concept of program music is thus the presence of a detailed program that must also dictate the musical form. Obviously, however, this definition is too narrow, sweeping and therefore unacceptable. To be specific:

Liszt's symphonic poem *Hamlet* is not program music according to Calvocoressi because the work dispenses with the tracing of a story and only evokes the character of the hero. His reason, however, does not correspond to the facts: he evidently overlooked that the symphonic poem, like Shakespeare's drama, closes with music resembling a funeral march and, besides, contains numerous allusions to scenes of the drama;[66] Liszt himself indicated in the score that the calm middle movement gestures toward the figure of Ophelia.

There are, besides, probably very few prominent overtures (to plays) that are without any reference to events in the drama but are exclusively to be regarded as character portraits. The following example is instructive: Beethoven's *Egmont* overture (op 84) consists of three parts: a slow introduction (*Sostenuto ma non troppo*) , a sonata movement (*Allegro*) and a lively concluding part (*Allegro con brio*) in F Major, whose substance is

---

65 M.-D. Calvocoressi, "Esquisse d'une esthétique de la musique à programme," SIMG, 9 (1907/1908), 424–438. – On Glasunov's *Stenka Rasin*, see Klauwell, *Geschichte*, 347–352.
66 Floros, *Mahler and the Symphony*, 210–213.

borrowed from the "victory symphony" (no. 9 of the music to *Egmont*).[67] In sketches to the overture, Beethoven formulated the leading idea of the work by saying "The main point is that the Dutch defeat the Spanish in the end."[68] That means that the overture does not just sketch a character portrait of Egmont but also makes reference to diverse points in Goethe's drama; its subject is thus, in Calvocoressi's own terms, both precise and complex.

No one is likely to doubt today that Liszt's *Hamlet* is program music. And what about the numerous other overtures to stage plays? Are works like Beethoven's overtures to *Egmont* and to *Coriolanus*, Mendelssohn's overture to *A Midsummer Night's Dream*, Schumann's overture to *Hermann und Dorothea*, Pfitzner's overtures to *Das Käthchen von Heilbronn* not program music?

The distinction between music with a detailed program and music with a mere title heading is in reality smaller than it seems. There is a difference of degree between Berlioz' *Symphonie fantastique* and the program of Beethoven's *Pastoral Syhmphony*, but not one of kind: both denote a sequence of images and mental states, and both works at bottom belong to the genre of *seelenmalerei*, of mind-painting. Liszt often dispensed with detailed programs and contented himself with mere titles – as, e.g., in the *Faust* symphony. And Schumann, who had some reservations about Berlioz' direction, nevertheless wrote works that undoubtedly have strong affinities with program music. Thus the *Papillons* op. 2 are demonstrably written under the impression of several passage in the penultimate chapter of Jean Paul's novel *Flegeljahre* (The Awkward Age). Schumann himself never tired of referring to the significance of the autobiographic element in his early work, and it was he also who called his *Carnaval* op.9 a sequence of "little scenes" (*scènes mignonnes*). The kinship of several of his piano works with program music is so manifest that Hermann Abert felt compelled to attest

67 Kinsky/Halm, *Das Werk Beethovens* (1955), 225–232.
68 Kestner Museum Hannover, collection Culemann, no. 95, fol. 1r. Facsimile in Adolf Fecker, *Die Entstehung von Beethovens Musik zu Goethes Trauerspiel Egmont* (Hamburger Beiträge zur Musikwissenschaft, vol 18) (Hamburg, 1978), plate I.

"program character" to them.[69] (His feeling obliged to add that this "program character" did not rob the works "of their lasting value" is probably a concession to those contemporaries who looked down with disdain on the genre of program music.)

In the more recent literature one occasionally encounters the view that the term program music signified any music that has an (extra-musical) subject, regardless of whether what is involved is a mere title heading or a detailed program. Horst Berner, for example, takes program music to mean "music about whose content or subject the composer provides information in a program, that is, fixed in writing, either as a brief heading, as a title, or as a more extensive synopsis of the 'content' of the work as a whole or also of individual parts ('movements')."[70]

By this definition, all of Schumann's pieces bearing brief titles would have to be accounted program music. What is decisive for Berner is that the program, whatever its form, must be "fixed in writing." Wolfgang Stockmeier similarly proposes to assign the term program music to all music "that has a concrete extra-musical title and thus takes its bearings from an extra-musical model, regardless whether action, situation, image, idea, or whatever."[71]

These definitions have two advantages: for one thing they live up to the original meaning of the modifier (προγράφειν in Greek meaning something like prewriting, designating in advance), and for another they are in harmony with Franz Liszt's conception of program music.

---

69 Hermann Abert, *Robert Schumann* (Berühmte Musiker, vol 15), 4th ed. (Berlin, 1920), 61.

70 Horst Berner, "Untersuchungen zur Begriffsbestimmung und zu einigen Fragen der Rezeption von Programmusik. Ein Beitrag zur Musikerziehung und zur musikalischen Populärwissenschaft" (diss., typescr.) (Leipzig, 1964), 209.

71 Wolfgang Stockmeier, "Die Programmusik," *Das Musikwerk*, no. 36 (Cologne, 1970), 6.

VIII. The Discomfort with Program Music

"Nothing – for its manifestation in life, mind you – is less absolute than music, and the defenders of absolute music evidently do not know what they mean."
Richard Wagner (1857)[1]

The instrumental music of the 19th century is certainly among the most intensively researched areas of more recent music history. That may be partly the reason why the image we have of it in many ways exhibits altogether fixed contours. A closer study of the literature may reveal that most of the views and judgments in this research area can be reduced to three basic perceptions.

The first of these comes down to the realization that a sharp line of demarcation is to be drawn between autonomously conceived and heteronomously produced works.[2] Heteronomously devised work means exclusively or primarily program music. In the common view, the antithesis between *absolute music* and program music largely determines the development of instrumental music after 1850.

The second perception concretizes itself in the notion that in several areas autonomous creation is more or less the norm. Here one thinks of the instrumental concerto, which by its nature and history largely meets a formalistic definition of music (music as play of "moving tonal forms" or "forms moving in sound"), as well as of the genre of chamber music, often regarded as the prime example of instrumental music, one that is as sophisticated as it is *pure*. In the symphonic area, to be sure, the polarity between the symphony as a genre of *absolute* music and the genres of symphonic *program* music is made much of. But even here program music is accorded a more exterritorial status.

The third perception is the frequently, though not always, conceded conviction that autonomous creation is to be valued more highly than music prompted by something extra-musical. Typically, highly esteemed composers are classified as "absolute musicians," irrespective of

---

1   Richard Wagner, "Über Franz Liszts symphonische Dichtungen" (1857), GS, 5:191.
2   Hans Conradin, *Ist die Musik heteronom oder autonom?* (diss) (Zurich, 1940).

extra-musical elements in their work. Program music, on the other hand, is often viewed as a maybe interesting but nevertheless problematic and sometimes also as an inferior species. A number of critics do not deny having their doubts about the purely musical qualities and *raison d'être* of this kind of music.

The evidence one can adduce to substantiate what has been outlined is gigantic. We will limit ourselves to a few instances.

We know of several composers who were not "program musicians" à la Berlioz, Liszt and Richard Strauss that they nevertheless wrote poetically inspired compositions or even regular program music. Even so, many critics insist that the total output of these composers is to be regarded as autonomously conceived music.

Thus there seems to have been a consensus since 1930 that the instrumental works of Beethoven – apart from very few exceptions – have nothing in common with poetically inspired or program music. The views of Walter Riezler are typical. In deliberate contrast to Paul Bekker, Alfred Heuß and Arnold Schering, who had interpreted Beethoven as an "ideational musician," Riezler, in 1936, thought that he could classify Beethoven's entire instrumental works as absolute music. By the same token he played down the significance of the poetic and programmatic titles of many of Beethoven's works and even went so far as to insist perversely that knowing the titles of the piano sonata *Les Adieux* op. 81a yielded no "deeper understanding of the sonata as music."[3]

Robert Schumann was the most committed pioneer of poetically inspired music. Numerous of his compositions were prompted by pictures and/or literary impressions. Nevertheless he is frequently regarded, since ca. 1850, as an opponent of program music and a representative of autonomously conceived creation.[4]

---

3   Walter Riezler, *Beethoven* (Berlin/Zurich, 1936). Part II: "Beethoven und die absolute Musik," 67–120; p. 88.

4   [4] Theodor Uhlig, "Rezension der Lieder und Gesänge Schumanns op. 98," *NZfM*, 35 (1851 II), 219–221; p.221.

Johannes Brahms believed in Schumann's aesthetics of the "poetic" in music creation.[5] He furnished some of his pieces with characteristic titles and gave explanations of "content" to several works. In spite of that, he is accounted, at least since Julius Spengel,[6] as a prototype of the "absolute musician," the autonomously creating artist.

Anton Bruckner, according to the testimony of his pupil Rudolf Louis, esteemed program music "as something, as it were, nobler and more elevated, or at least more interesting, than absolute music."[7] He delivered programmatic explanations to the Fourth and Eighth symphony, whose authenticity is beyond question.[8] Nevertheless his symphonic music is widely deemed a model of autonomously conceived music.[9] Peter Raabe proclaimed him in 1944 to be the absolutest "of all absolute musicians."[10]

Gustav Mahler commenced his compositional career demonstrably as a program musician. His first four symphonies are based on authentic programs. A semantic analysis reveals that Mahler's programmatic ideas largely determined the structure of the compositions.[11] In disregard of that, Mahler's entire symphonic oeuvre is declared to be music *an sich*. Richard Specht's claim of 1905 that "among all symphonists of the new century, Gustav Mahler is perhaps above all an absolute musician and fanatical

---

5   In a conversation with Richard Heuberger in May of 1878, Brahms tirelessly emphasized that the technical questions of composition he discussed with Heuberger "had nothing in common with the poetic essence of musical creation." See Heuberger, *Erinnerungen an Johannes Brahms*, ed. Kurt Hofmann (Tutzing, 1971), 14/15.

6   Julius Spengel, *Johannes Brahms. Charakterstudie* (Hamburg, 1898), 35: "It can even be said that no composer after Beethoven made music so utterly without any 'program' as did Brahms."

7   Rudolf Louis, *Anton Bruckner* (Munich/Leipzig, 1905), 208 f.

8   Cf. Floros, *Brahms and Bruckner as Artistic Antipodes. Studies in Musical Semantics* tr. Ernest Bernhardt-Kabisch (Frankfurt, 2015; German orig. 1980).

9   Thus Werner F. Korte, *Bruckner und Brahms. Die spätromantische Lösung der autonomen Konzeption* (Tutzing, 1963).

10 Peter Raabe, *Wege zu Bruckner* (Deutsche Musikbücherei, vol. 19) (Regensburg, 1944), 181.

11 Floros, *Die geistige Welt Gustav Mahlers in systematischer Darstellung* (Wiedbaden, 1977); *Mahler and the Symphony of the 19th Century*.

opponent of any and all programs"[12] extends like a red thread through the literature to this day.

Even more telling (and also more dubious) is the tendency of several critics to regard and analyze program-bound works by acknowledged "program musicians" in separation from the programs as *Musik an sich*. The relevance of the program to the structure of the composition, in other words, the formative "power" of the program, is relativized, called in question or even negated outright.

This tendency characterizes, for example, the otherwise sterling Liszt monograph of Peter Raabe, who lets no opportunity go by without referring to the supposed "preponderance of the musical over the poetic" in Liszt; who in several cases misconceived Liszt's programmatic "keywords" in the autographs of several compositions as "instructions to the musician"; and who holds the view that in works whose program Liszt did not communicate, for example the symphonic poem *Hamlet*, it would be altogether senseless to attempt an interpretation.[13]

In a similar tendency, independent of Raabe, Joseph Heinrichs[14] and Joachim Bergfeld[15] have sought to explain Liszt's formal and technical innovations in terms of music's inherent, autonomous laws. Both emphasize the musical logic of Liszt's forms and deny that programmatic aspects might have significantly affected the formal structure.

Wilhelm Mohr made similar statements about the symphonic poems of César Franck. Franck, he insisted, was "by nature and above all an absolute musician"; his music lived in accordance with its inherent laws, never by extra-musical influences;" his four symphonies were "ever music of intrinsic power, intrinsic law."[16]

---

12 Richard Specht, *Gustav Mahler* (Moderne Essays, ed. Hans Landsberg, no. 52) (Berlin, 1905), 16, 31 f.

13 Peter Raabe, *Liszts Schaffen* (Stuttgart, 1931, Tutzing, 1968), 54 f., 94–96, 99 f., 107 f., 228, 302. See my commentaries in *Mahler and the Symphony*, 47–50, 98, 273–275.

14 Joseph Heinrichs, *Über den Sinn der Lisztschen Programmusik* (diss.) (Bonn/Kempen, 1929).

15 Joachim Bergfeld, *Die formale Struktur der "Symphonischen Dichtungen" Franz Liszts* (diss.) (Berlin/Eisenach: Verlag Philipp Kühner , 1931).

16 Wilhelm Mohr, *Cäsar Franck. Ein deutscher Musiker* (Stuttgart, 1942), 171 f.

These examples may have made clear that many critics – but also many musicians and music lovers – confront program music and, by the same token, any kind of non-autonomously conceived musical creation with many reservations. In no other artistic area are so many prejudices and misconceptions widely held as in program music. One feels tempted to speak of a discomfort with any kind of music that does not correspond to the common notions about the "purity" of musical art. In seeking to determine the reasons for this state of affairs, one has to consider a number of things.

1. Many of the prejudices about program music can be explained in terms of the developmental history of the genre and the changes in musico-aesthetic thought. The second half of the 19th century was, as we know, the heyday of programmatic music. Since 1850, and especially since the proclamation of the New German School of 1859, Berlioz and Liszt found followers in nearly every European country.[17] Program music was praised by its apologists as the only timely kind of instrumental music. To its opponents, on the other hand, it was a sphere of activity for charlatans, a "fraud" and the undoing of young composers. Thus Eduard Hanslick wrote in 1892 in a review of Richard Strauss' *Don Juan*: "The calamity is that most of our young composers think in an alien language – philosophy, poetry, painting – and only then translate their thinking into their native language – music."[18]

After the deaths of Wagner (1883), Liszt (1886) and Bruckner (1896), the quarrel, carried on with extreme vehemence, about the alternative "absolute music" vs. "program music" entered a critical phase; around the turn of the century, it was decided in favor of *absolute music*. The symphonic poem went out of fashion, the aesthetics of autonomy propagated by Hanslick prevailed, that of heteronomy lost ground. Intimidated by the growing influence of the opponents of program music, composers who had originally declared for program music, distanced themselves from it – frequently only

---

17 See Franz Brendel, *Geschichte der Musik in Italien, Deutschland und Frankreich. Von den ersten christlichen Zeiten bis zur Gegenwart*, 4th, 6th ed. (Leipzig, 1867, 1878), 575–595; Felix Weingartner, *Die Symphonik nach Beethoven*, 3rd ed. (Leipzig, 1909), 100–102; R. W. S. Mendl, "The Art of the Symphonic Poem," *The Musical Quarterly*, 18 (1932), 443–462.
18 Eduard Hanslick, *Fünf Jahre Musik*, 181.

pro forma. Gustav Mahler and Felix von Weingartner issued corresponding public declarations, retracted the programs of their works, or kept silent about them.[19]

After 1820, in line with the spread of an anti-Romantic mentality, the one-time ideal of a poetization of instrumental music, as a typically 19th-century phenomenon, was declared an anachronism. In many places, the term program music became synonymous with obsolete, "inferior" or even "bad" music. Thus we can understand the tendency among many critics after 1920 to cleanse the works of Beethoven, Schumann, Bruckner and Mahler of the taint of the programmatic and to look at the program music of Liszt, regardless of its programs, as *Musik an sich*!

2. Numerous prejudices against program music can be traced all the way back to the early 19th century. They spring from one-sided notions about the nature of music and from misconceptions about the intentions of the program musicians. Of primary significance for this is the early Romantic (*frühromantische*) belief that the "unique inner nature of tonal art" (such the title of one of Wackenroder's *Phantasien*) revealed itself in "pure" (or "purely") instrumental music, which, in contrast to vocal music, expressed "indeterminate feelings." This idea, which already E. T. A. Hoffmann formulated unequivocally,[20] became, with minor modifications, the cardinal principle of the aesthetics of autonomy: *pure* instrumental music is, for Eduard Hanslick[21] as well as for Hugo Riemann[22] (and many others), the

---

19 See my *Die geistige Welt Gustav Mahlers*, 30–33.

20 Thus E. T. A. Hoffmann wrote already in 1819 in a review of Beethoven's Fifth Symphony: How little was this unique quality of the music recognized by those instrumental composers who tried to represent those determinable feelings, or even events, and thus to treat the art that is directly opposed to the plastic arts in a plastic manner! Dittersdorf's symphonies of this kind, as well as all the newer *Batailles des trois Empereurs* etc. are, as ludicrous aberrations, to be punished by total oblivion." Quoted from E. T. A. Hoffmann, *Schriften zur Musik/Nachlese*, ed. Friedrich Schnapp (Munich: Winkler, 1963), 34.

21 Eduard Hanslick, *Vom Musikalisch-Schönen. Ein Beitrag zur Revision der Äs-thetik der Tonkunst* (1854), 12th ed. (Leipzig, 1918), 33/34: "What instrumental music cannot do must never be said to be possible in music, because only it is the pure, absolute musical art."

22 Hugo Riemann, "Das formale Element in der Musik": "Neither song nor the program symphony, but only the absolute music can inform us about the nature

norm by which every musico-aesthetic argument has to orientate itself. The rejection of program, and of any sort of "poetically" inspired, music follows logically from that. Program music meant to August Wilhelm Ambros a transgression of the limits of musical art.[23]

3. Not the least source of the growth and dissemination of some of the prejudices about program music was surely Schumann's famous review of Berlioz' *Symphonie fantastique*. Schumann there expressed some reservations about Berlioz' programmatic direction and, while dispensing with detailed explanations, advanced the following theses: first, that the composer must not "gag" (not "roughly lead") the imagination of the listener by means of detailed programs; secondly, that the artist had the right and the duty to conceal occasion and process of his creation from the prying eyes of the public; and thirdly, that what mattered in judging a program-bound composition was "whether the music is something substantial in itself also without text and elucidation, and, above all, if spirit dwells within it."[24]

Schumann's recension – similarly to E. T. A. Hoffmann's review of Beethoven's Fifth Symphony – had a strong opinion-forming impact on music journalism in the German-speaking region. His statements, however, have been frequently misunderstood and misconstrued. Thus apologists for absolute music declared him a key witness against heteronomy aesthetics and, frequently with reference to him, propagated the rather one-sided view that musical study should be exclusively text-based (work-based), that the genetic history of musical works was not necessarily of any interest, and that the influence of extra-musical elements on the genesis and shaping of a composition was wholly irrelevant to the understanding of its structure.

These and similar views were due to a misunderstanding of Schumann's observations, which are much more enigmatic than they appear to be. To understand them correctly one should not look at them in isolation but must

---

of music itself; only by itself will it be able to unfold its powers freely and without hindrance." Quoted from Hugo Riemann, *Präludien und Studien. Gesammelte Aufsätze zur Ästhetik, Theorie und Geschichte der Musik* (Leipzig, n.d. [1895]), 1:43.

23 August Wilhelm Ambros, *Die Grenzen der Musik und Poesie*, 178/179.
24 Robert Schumann, GS, 1: 69–90, esp. 83–85.

analyze Schumann's overall aesthetics, which is anything but an aesthetics of autonomy!

What has been set forth may have made clear that the "accepted" image of 19th-century instrumental music is in essential points in need of elucidation and revision. For that it is necessary to analyze the views of leading composers about fundamental questions of musical creation (for music historiography, the aesthetics of composers is more instructive than the aesthetics of the theorists!), and, in analyzing their works, to include semantic aspects more strongly than has hitherto been done. The following investigations start out from the thesis that the instrumental music of the 19th century is more closely related to all areas of intellectual life, especially to literature and philosophy, than is commonly supposed.

IX. "Tone Poets" and "Specific Musicians": 19th-Century Composer Types

> "The greatest good and the only useful one is education."
> Friedrich Schlegel (1800)[1]

> "He who understands Shakespeare and Jean Paul will compose differently than one who has gotten his wisdom solely from Marpurg etc." Robert Schumann (1842)[2]

1. Art-Theoretical Presuppositions

The close relation of 19th-century music to the intellectual, literary, philosophical and political currents of the age manifests itself, to begin with, in the emergence of a new type of artist, who appears on the scene around 1800 and who is composer, poet, critic and aesthetician in personal union. E. T. A. Hoffmann, Carl Maria von Weber, Robert Schumann, Hector Berlioz, Franz Liszt, Richard Wagner, Peter Cornelius, Hugo Wolf, Claude Debussy, Richard Strauss and Hans Pfitzner are the most prominent representatives of this type. They all had strong literary interests, most of them felt themselves to be "tone poets," and nearly all of them published criticism, elucidated their works, authored treatises on art theory and aesthetics, wrote stories, novellas, poems of various kinds and even novels, and in many cases also created or adapted the texts they set to music. Except for the Middle Ages, the 19th century has the largest number of critic-composers and poet-composers in music history.[3]

Naturally this situation has to be viewed against an art-theoretical background. It is very closely related to a "modern" theory of art and education, a theory that rests above all on the following core ideas:

---

1 *Athenäum*, 3 (1800), fragment no. 37.
2 Schumann in an 1842 review of piano works by Stephen Heller, GS, 2:115. – Friedrich Wilhelm Marpurg (1718–1795) was an 18th-century German musicologist.
3 On the diversity of talents of several composers of the 19th century and questions of their social background, see the remarks of Alfred Einstein, *Music in the Romantic Era* (New York, 1947), 25–30.

1. The reflection that, in principle, the fine arts all have the same aesthetics, that music and poetry, in particular, grow from a single root and should mutually permeate each other, that there is a unity between musical and poetic creation, and, finally, that the perfect poetico-musical work of art presupposes one and the same creator, an artist, in other words, who is a poet-composer;
2. the idea that music should be liberated from its relatively isolated position in the system of the arts and should participate in the spiritual and intellectual currents of the day;
3. the notion that art criticism is something that belongs in the hands of the artist.

Let us scrutinize these propositions more closely.

1. The poetics or art theory of Romanticism is generally known to have been a philosophic theory of *poiesis* (ποίησις). As such, its object is what all the arts and all artistic creations have in common.[4] In the framework of this theory, what matters is not so much to draw the lines of division between the individual arts as precisely as possible as it is to search out the affinities between them. It is against this background that Friedrich Schlegel's paradoxical-seeming "metonymic" definitions of the arts have to be understood, such as his views that poetry is "a spiritual music" and, conversely, that many musical compositions are "merely translations of poems into the language of music."[5]

These ideas exerted a considerable influence on aesthetic thought in the first third of the 19th century. There were, to be sure, writers on music who frowned upon them. Thus in 1826, Hans Georg Nägeli said about the new aesthetics (as whose central idea he expressly cites the proposition that "what held good for poetry" should "also be good for sculpture

---

4 August Wilhelm Schlegel, *Vorlesungen über schöne Literatur und Kunst*, pt. I: "Die Kunstlehre" (1801/02).

5 *Athenäum*, 1 (1798), fragments nos. 325 and 392. The poetization of music and musicalization of poetry are among the leading ideas of the Romantic Movement. See the fundamental essay by Walter Wiora, "Die Musik im Weltbild der deutschen Romantik", in *Beiträge zur Geschichte der Musikanschauung im 19. Jahrhundert*, ed. Walter Salmen (Studien zur Musikgeschichte des 19. Jahrhunderts, vol.1) (Regensburg, 1965), 11–50; p. 21.

and music") that "a sober connoisseur" would rarely "derive anything conducive to a special insight" from it, wherefore many renowned composers had also "not taken the least notice" of it.[6] The writings of Robert Schumann, nevertheless, document that the new ideas did, after all, fall on fertile soil. Thus Schumann even before 1833 formulated the apothegm: "The aesthetics of one art is that of the others; only the material is different" (GS I, 26).[7]

Of major significance for the development of the "new" music in the first third of the century was the notion that music and poetry – the "most Romantic" arts – were closely related. In the "far-away realm" of art, as E.T. A. Hoffmann put it already in 1813, "the poet and the musician are the most intimately related members of *one* church: for the secret of the word and of the tone is one and the same, which the loftiest consecration has disclosed to them."[8] In logical consequence, Hoffmann adds to this idea the downright Wagnerian postulate that in a "true" opera, the music had to spring "immediately from the poetry as the necessary product of the latter."

But the notion of the close relationship between music and poetry also decisively influenced the development of pure instrumental music: since the death of Beethoven, at the latest, we encounter with increasing frequency instrumental compositions said *expressis verbis* to have been inspired by poems, as well as works based on explicit programs. And it is highly

---

6 Hans Georg Nägeli, *Vorlesungen über Musik mit Berücksichtigung der Dilettanten* (Stuttgart/Tübingen; 1826), 24/25.

7 As early as 1830, Schumann wrote in his travel log: "The rules of *one* art apply to all. That's why I often read Winkelmann." Quoted from Georg Eismann, ed. Robert Schumann. *Tagebücher, vol. I [1827–1838]* (Leipzig, 1971), 314. Nothing marks the diametric contrast between Schumann's and Hanslick's aesthetics as clearly as Hanslick's "maxim that the laws of beauty of each art are inseparable from the peculiarities if its materials, its technique" (*Vom Musikalisch-Schönen*, ch. I, p. 3).

8 E. T. A. Hoffmann "Der Dichter und der Komponist." Quoted from Hoffmann's *Serapions-Brüder* (Munich: Winkler, 1963), 83. Cf. Schumann's youthful essay, "Über die innige Verwandtschaft der Poesie und Tonkunst," which circles about the idea that the poetic and the musical art have the same origin and the same effect (GS, 2:173–175).

symptomatic of instrumental music's strong orientation towards poetry that at the same time the terms tone poet and tone poem start to be fashionable.[9]

2. Owing to the spread of the Romantic theory of art, music experienced an enormous upgrading in the first half of the 19th century. Whereas Immanuel Kant in 1790 had still assigned it the lowest rank among the arts,[10] Friedrich Schlegel esteemed it the highest of all the arts, E. T. A. Hoffmann as the most Romantic, and Arthur Schopenhauer even as the very "image of the Will." Even so, in the view of many philosophers and intellectuals, it ranked lower than painting and especially poetry. Many thought that musicians were below the contemporary level of educational refinement.

Robert Schumann and Franz Liszt were among the first composers to emphatically require an all-round education (*Bildung*) of musicians. A comparison of their respective formulations of this demand makes clear that they were guided by different aims.

Schumann was profoundly convinced that a right comprehension of much of the newer music required a large measure of universal education. He believed that in many of the works of Beethoven, Schubert, Berlioz and Stephen Heller extra-musical themes were expressed, and concluded logically that a mere musical training and experience was insufficient for a

---

9 Both terms are encountered repeatedly in E. T. A. Hoffmann's tale "Über einen Ausspruch Sacchinis und über den sogenannten Effekt in der Musik," which first appeared in June of 1815 in the fourth volume of the *Fantasiestücke in Callots Manier*. The corresponding French terms, *poète musicien* and *poème musical*, occur in Berlioz' Beethoven articles from the 1830s. See Hector Berlioz, *A travers chants*, ed. Léon Guichard (Paris, 1971), 54, 71. Beginning in 1830, Carl Löwe termed several of his program-bound piano works *Tondichtungen*, including *Mazeppa* op. 27 (1830), *Der barmherzige Bruder* op. 28 (1830), and *Le Printemps* op. 47 (1835). See Schumann, GS, 1:91/92, and Klauwell, *Geschichte der Programmusik*, 187–192. Schumann, too, was in the habit since the 1830s of calling pieces he particularly liked *poems*. Thus he thought that the first of Chopin's twelve *Etudes* op. 25 was "a poem more than an etude" (GS, 1:255). Of Sterndale Bennett's impromptus he spoke as of "veritable poems" (GS, 1:368), and to Clara he wrote on April 13, 1838, that the word "poems" was in his opinion "very noble and fitting for musical compositions" (*Jugendbriefe*, ed. Clara Schumann, 281). – On the prehistory of Liszt's coinage *poème symphonique*, see my remarks in *Mahler und die Symphonik*, 24n.10.

10 Immanuel Kant, *Kritik der Urteilskraft* § 53: "thus music ranks lowest among the fine arts, inasmuch as it merely plays with feelings."

right understanding of these works. Thus he wrote about Berlioz' *Symphonie fantastique* that the "proper place" of the work within the history of the arts could be determined "even now" only by a person who was "not only a philosophically educated musician but also an intimate connoisseur of the history of the other arts," wo had "pondered the significance and interlinkage of its manifestations and the deeper meaning of its succession" (GS II, 215).About Beethoven's last quartets he thought that to understand them one needed "more than just the desire to listen": "the most receptive, most open music lover will come away untouched by them if he does not bring to them a deep knowledge of Beethoven's character and of his later mode of expression generally" (II, 420). And about the music of Stephen Heller he opined: "To understand, to love it surely takes more than a mere dilettante's, even a musician's education. From that playful humor speaks more than mere musical experience" (II, 115).[11]

Liszt, in turn, fought for the legitimation of program music, partly because of his conviction – a "motive" hitherto wholly ignored – that only by being poeticized and given a literary dimension could instrumental music take part in the intellectual currents of the day and would thereby gain in esteem in the cognizance of the educated! In his detailed review of Adolph Bernard Marx's *Die Musik des neunzehnten Jahrhunderts und ihre Pflege* (The Music of the Nineteenth Century and its Cultivation), he speaks expressly of the necessity of "refuting judgments such as Hegel was still able to pronounce when he confessed 'never to have met any musicians who were not badly lacking in *ideas*.'"[12] And he argues that the great word of *Zukunftsmusik* – "Music of the future" – could become reality only once the insight had gained currency that for a musician, whether "virtuoso or composer, a workman-like skill no longer sufficed," because it would then be a question

---

11 Cf. also Schumann's essay "The Comic in Music" (GS, 1:112).

12 Liszt here evidently refers to the following statement in Hegel's aesthetics: "because of this emptiness of matter, we not only see the gift of composition frequently develop already at the tenderest age, but gifted composers often remain all their life the most unconscious, substance-less persons." See Georg Wilhelm Friedrich Hegel, *Vorlesungen über die Ästhetik III* (Werke in zwanzig Bänden, vol. 15) (Frankfurt: Suhrkamp, 1970), 217.

that to become a musician, a man should above all educate his intellect, that he learn to think, to judge, in a word, that he have ideas so as to cause the strings of his lyre to coincide with the pitch of the times, so as to group the declarations of his art into images that are connected with each other by a poetic and philosophic thread.

Liszt thought that music would "command the respect" of its critics only "once the pupil will have learned from his teacher that in the nineteenth century *to become a proper musician one first had to be an eminent human being.*"[13]

3. The Romantics, foremost Friedrich Schlegel, developed altogether new conceptions about the nature of art criticism. They distinguished between *Charakteristik*, i.e. "non-poetic" criticism, and *poetische Kritik*, in which the difference between poesy and criticism is abolished, called for a poetic criticism, and advocated the idea that such *poetic criticism* should be solely the business of "poets and artists."[14]

It deserves to be underscored that these ideas influenced E. T. A. Hoffmann and later, via the latter's work as a music critic, Carl Maria von Weber, Schumann, Wagner and Liszt. Hoffmann's critiques set out from the axioms that criticism should be practiced only by those with the proper calling, that it was to be a service to art, that it presupposed a more than ordinary intuition or empathy, and that, because of the high rank it needed to demonstrate, it had to become itself a work of art.[15] Liszt went still a step further when, in a letter to George Sand of January 1837, he voiced the conviction "that about works of art a kind of philosophic criticism has to develop, which no one knows better how to practice than the artist himself" (GS II, 131).

---

13 Franz Liszt, GS, 5:183–217, esp. 201–205.

14 Walter Benjamin, *Der Begriff der Kunstkritik in der deutschen Romantik*, ed. Hermann Schweppenhäuser (suhrkamp taschenbuch wissenschaft 4) (Frankfurt, 1973), 63–65.

15 Arnold Schering, "Aus der Geschichte der musikalischen Kritik in Deutschland," *JbP*, 35 (1928), 9–23; p. 17; Paul Greeff, *E. T. A. Hoffmann als Musiker und Musikschriftsteller* (Cologne/Krefeld, 1948), 110–116.

2. Composers and Fractions

The composer of diverse talents and universal education is undoubtedly a phenomenon that distinguishes the 19th century to an exceptional degree and one that highlights the contrast to the 18th century. But the unique dynamics that characterizes the German music history of the 19th century results to a large extent from the fact that the type of musician outlined stands in an antagonistic relation to the older, still existing composer type. Any discussion about issues of 19th-century musical historiography must keep in mind that simultaneously with the "progressive"-minded tone poets, countless conservative composers were at work, who were equipped with a solid training in music theory and compositional technique and who reflected about specific questions of musical creation, but who were not willing to transgress the narrower limits of musical art, were not prepared to comply with the demands of the new aesthetics , and who therefore confronted the "progressive" tendencies of the time with skepticism or even open hostility. It is only logical that this constellation would favor the formation of musical fractions at loggerheads with one another.

In speaking of rivalling parties in German music history of the 19th century, one thinks primarily, or even exclusively, of the antagonism between the New German School of Liszt and Wagner and the conservative "opposition" around Brahms and Hanslick.[16] There can be no doubt that the conflict between these parties played an important role in the development of German music in the last third of the 19th century. But the polarization of musical life, the division of composers into fractions did not commence only in 1859 with the "proclamation" of the New German School but had already taken place several decades earlier.

It is clear from Robert Schumann's articles that already the 1830s distinguished three groups of composers in Germany: the progressive, the moderate and the reactionary, or, in Schumann's terminology, the *Romantics*, the *Moderns* and the *Classics*. Thus Schumann writes already in 1836:

---

16 Karl Gustav Fellerer, *Der Akademismus in der deutschen Musik des 19. Jahrhunderts* (Rheinisch-Westfälische Akademie der Wissenschaften. Geisteswissenschaften. Vorträge G212) (Opladen, 1976).

The present is characterized by its fractions. Like the political scene, the musical can be divided into Liberals, Moderates and Reactionaries, or into Romantics, Moderns and Classics. On the right sit the old, the counterpointers, the anti-chromatics, on the left the young, the Phrygian caps, the form-despisers, the genius-flaunters, among whom the Beethoveners stand out as a class of their own. In the *juste-milieu*, both young and old vacillate in a medley. Most of the day's products are included there, the creatures of the moment, created and again annihilated by it.[17]

There were two key points on which the parties begged to differ: the conception of music as a specific or else a poetic art and the relation to tradition. While the progressives, whom Schumann calls, not without irony, Romantics, form-despisers and genius-flaunters (*Genialitätsfreche*) wanted to escape from the traditional canon of forms, championed the right to (tone-)poetic freedom, and invoked Beethoven, especially the late Beethoven, the reactionaries (the "classics," "counterpointers," and "anti-chromatics") disparaged every innovation as an offense against the norms of hallowed tradition.[18] One should note that in the 'thirties and 'forties the "Romantics" still constituted a heterodox minority.[19] The composers whom Schumann enumerated include Chopin, Berlioz, Stephen Heller, Mendelssohn, Ferdinand Hiller, William Sterndale Bennett, Adolf Henselt and, of course, Schumann himself.

---

17 Schumann, GS, 1:144/145.

18 It is noteworthy that Schumann used all of the terms mentioned already before 1836. Thus in his humorous essay "Der Psychometer" he speaks of "Classicists," "Juste-Milieuists" and "Romantics" (GS, 1:103). There are ironic aphorisms about "counterpointers" and "antichromatics" already in the "Denk- und Dichtbüchlein" (GS, !:22). There is ironic talk of *Genialitätsfrechheit* (genial cheek) and *Verachtung aller geachteter Formen* (disrespect for all respected forms) in the essay "Die Davidsbündler" (The David's League), which appeared anonymously in December of 1833 in the journal *Der Komet*. See F. Gustav Jansen, *Die Davidsbündler. Aus Robert Schumann's Sturm- und Drangperiode* (Leipzig, 1883), 15. We can also gather something about Schumann's notion of the "form despisers" and "cheeky geniuses" fom the following passage from his 1842 review of a quartet by Hermann Hirschbach (GS, 2:74): We can see, he [Hirschbach] wants to be called a poet, everywhere he wants to evade the stereotypical forms; Beethoven's last quartets are to him only the beginnings of a new poetic era, in which he wants to work on; Haydn and Mozart date far back to him. "

19 See Leon B. Plantinga, "Schumann's View of 'Romantic'," *MQ*, 52 (1966), 221–232.

In the late 'forties and early 'fifties, the ideological dispute between the parties entered a crucial phase. The old war between the adherents of progress and the "reactionaries" flared up anew in the quarrel about the alternative of absolute vs. program music. The writings of Peter Cornelius, Franz Liszt and August Wilhelm Ambros document that even before 1855 the question whether a composer should – in modern terminology – create autonomously or be guided in his work by extra-musical – poetic, literary, philosophic – ideas had become the cardinal issue of aesthetics.

Thus Cornelius, in his review of a "Symphony of Praise" by Richard Würst, wrote already in 1854:

> Even today, this question divides the musical world into two factions. To one, music is a fanciful play with tones according to rules of euphony and aesthetic laws that are derived from the specifically musical works of Haydn, Mozart and Beethoven (to the extent that he followed in their track), such as: unity in variety, clarity and measure in forms and means, etc. According to this view, music should achieve its effects through itself without any mediating associations; it should lift the soul from its narrow existence to ideal heights and with its tonal waves, as it were, wash every mold and rubbish of life from it.
>
> The other party regards the music come down to it from the great masters as a poetically developed language in which it wants to speak and to represent; it sees in it a created world, in which the human being, the poetic thought, is now to walk. It takes Beethoven at his word, not only where he sought to inwardly vivify the classic form by means of a certain poetic thought, and where he did not do that, yet at least broke through the rigid classic form in an organic, developmental process; it goes even further: it wants to determine the particular form out of the poetic thought – only the latter is to lend it its authorization.[20]

In 1855, Liszt, in his great Berlioz essay,[21] made a principal distinction between two types of composers: the "mere musician" or "specific symphonist"

---

20 *NZfM* 1854, no. 24 (Dec. 8). – Quoted from Peter Cornelius, *Aufsätze über Musik und Kunst*, ed. Edgar Istel (Leipzig, 1904), 41–46.

21 Franz Liszt, "Berlioz und seine 'Harold-Symphonie'" (1855), GS, 4:47–50. Liszt conceived the plan of writing the article in April of 1851. See *FLB*, 4:87. The manuscript of the original French version was complete by early July of 1854 (see *FLB*, 1:161). The German translation was made by Richard Pohl. The essay first appeared in 1855 in the *NZfM*. Peter Cornelius is likely to have known the article in manuscript form when he wrote his essay.

and the "tone poet" or "poetic symphonist."[22] The mere musician," he explained, works "according to certain traditional rules" and therefore can only rarely arrive "at new and bold, unusual and intricate" tonal combinations. He places value and emphasis only on the "formal shaping of the material" and does not have the ability to "wrest new formulations from it and breathe new energies into it." The "poetic symphonist," on the other hand is, according to Liszt, called upon to enrich and enlarge the form. For he uses it as a "means of expression," as a "language," which he can shape "according to the needs of the [extra-musical] ideas to be expressed," and he regards it as his task to "reproduce" an "image clearly present to his mind, a sequence of mental-emotional states that reside unequivocally and determinedly in his consciousness," with "equal clarity" with the aid of a program.

August Wilhelm Ambros, finally, professed in the Preface to his important aesthetic text *Die Grenzen der Musik und Poesie* (The Limits of Music and Poetry) that he wrote his treatise with a view to the critical situation of contemporary music. "Let no one fail to realize," he wrote emphatically, "that we have reached a disquieting point with our musical art. Hardly anyone knows any longer what he should and should not, can and cannot, do." Of the "active musical artists" a part, "by far the smaller one, has taken refuge in older views and forms" and there cultivates "its modest field according to the principles of the so-called 'classical' period." The larger part, however – "and above all the more gifted" – no longer knows "what to do with all its ideas." And at issue are not musical ideas – "those are not exactly abundant" – but poetic, philosophic, political ones, etc. To clarify this point of view, Ambros seeks to explain the fundamental difference between the "intellectual musicians" (*Bildungsmusiker*) of his time and the older composers.

> Compared with the musicians as they were still fifty years ago, we now occupy a nearly opposite standpoint. Back then the composer knew most exactly everything that specifically belonged to his art – his thorough-bass, his theories of chords,

---

22 The expression "specific musician" in distinction from the term "tone poet"occurs also in writings by Ambros (1855) and Hans von Bülow (1856). Richard Pohl (*Briefe aus Weimar über Kunst und Künstler der Gegenwart*) distinguishes between the "specific-technical musician" and the "artistic-poetic musician." See R. Pohl, *Hektor Berlioz. Studien und Erinnerungen* (Leipzig, 1884), 109.

harmony and imitation, simple and double counterpoint, etc. Apart from that he had a far-flung *venia ignorantiae* – he did not have to concern himself with anything else. If one reads the letters of the young Mozart from Italy, one will notice that he was solely interested in the singing and dancing signore and signori – the Coliseum and the Vatican with all that it contains he seems hardly to have noticed. Today, the composer reads his Shakespeare and Sophocles in the original language and knows them half by heart, he has studied Humboldt's cosmos as thoroughly as the historical works of Niebuhr or Ranke, he knows the operations of the dialectical process according to Hegel as precisely as, or rather even more precisely than, the correct way of countering a fugal theme, – in Italy, if he has time and money for a journey thither, he does not concern himself with the opera (something one can hardly take ill of him), but instead, when in Rome, pays his respects every Thursday to the Jupiter of Otricoli and the Jupiter Verospi and what their names all are, he dreams away his *villegiatura* with the enjoyment of Nature and the folk life in Aricia, etc. In short, one could almost call such a gentleman "Sir Microcosm." He knows all kinds of things, except perhaps not quite so much of whatever pertains to the strict discipline of his chosen art. If then understandably his compositions exhibit a critical lack of development, if harmonies and rhythms occur that the most tolerant of ears has to repudiate, the freedom of the genius is insisted upon, nay, the very blunders may be said to conceal profound thoughts. The composers want to import their great wealth of extra-musical ideas into the music, force things upon it for which it has no language. So, for example, we may get instrumental movements that paint the geological state of the planet during the Lias or Keuper period (*L'avant homme* by Felicien David) or something else that without added marginal glosses no person would look for in it. Music has become a willing and nimble servant, who, since the *impossible* is desired of her, makes a concerted effort to produce at least the *unusual*.[23]

Ambros' humorous delineation fails to do justice to the historical reality in two points:

1. Our discussion has shown that composers of a versatile education first appeared not around 1850 but in several instances much sooner. We should remember that already Beethoven saw himself as a tone poet,[24]

---

23 Ambros, *Die Grenzen der Musik und Poesie*, ii/iii. – The ironic phrase „Herr Mikrokosmus" is a quote from Goethe's *Faust I*, l. 1802.
24 Especially indicative is Beethoven's well-known sentence in the letter to Nanette Streicher of July 30, 1817, "when you stray through the secretive fir forests, think that Beethoven has often poetized [*gedichtet*] or, as one says, composed there," and the title of the *Ouverture zur Namensfeier* op. 115 in the original edition of 1825: *Große Ouverture in C-dur gedichtet [...] von Lud. Van Beethoven.*

that he had active literary interests and a predilection for Homer, Shakespeare, Goethe and Schiller,[25] and that he exhibited a lively concern for the political events of his time.[26]

2. Ambros does not conceal the fact that he did not rate the technical ability of many of the contemporary composers very highly. His remarks about Berlioz' *Roméo et Juliette* – he calls that important work a "rather monstrous tragelaph"[27] – make clear, however, that he was trapped in his views about the limits of music and was not equal to the innovative boldness of many works.

3. Schumann, Liszt and Wagner as All-Round Educated Musicians

Ambros clearly missed the salient point: that the composers of universal education he describes were not trying to make up for any technical ability by their "great wealth of extra-musical ideas," but rather to liberate music from its isolation and have it take part in the intellectual currents of the time. That is why they took an interest in political, social, religious, philosophic questions and sought for a new orientation in concert with poets, men of letters, philosophers and sociologists.

Robert Schumann, for example, who in the later party conflict was frequently classified as a conservative – Felix Draeseke remarked of him that he was a genius who ended as a mere talent[28] – may be called a typical representative of the "literary musician": he had a close relation to literature,[29] he was active as a journalist, he had erected his aesthetics on

25 See Arnold Schering, *Beethoven und die Dichtung. Mit einer Einleitung zur Geschichte und Ästhetik der Beethovendeutung* (Berlin, 1936), 61–63

26 See above all Arnold Schmitz, *Das romantische Beethovenbild. Darstellung und Kritik* (Berlin/Bonn, 1927), *passim*, esp. chs. 3–6; and Constantin Floros, *Beethoven's Eroica.*

27 *Die Grenzen der Musik und Poesie*, 163. – A tragelaph is a legendary cross of a goat and a stag.

28 Hans von Bülow, *Adolf Jensen* (1863). Quoted from Hans von Bülow, *Ausgewählte Schriften, 1850–1892* (Leipzig, 1911), 2nd section, p. 37.

29 Regrettably, only few of Schumann's numerous belletristic works (poems, stories, fragments of novels and dramas) have hitherto been published. See the youthful poems included by Martin Kreisig in GS, 2:190–200, and Schumann's

the basis of the Romantic theory of art, and he frequently let himself be inspired in his instrumental compositions by literary works.

The following passage from a letter of Schumann's to Clara Wieck is instructive in several respects, for it documents, for one thing, that by 1838, Schumann regarded the traditional barriers between art and politics, music and current events as having broken down; secondly, that many of his compositions were prompted by extra-musical impulses; and, thirdly, that Schumann himself cited this fact as the reason why many of his works were regarded as so hard to understand:

> Everything that happens in the world affects me: politics, literature, people; everything I think about in my way, which then wants to vent itself, seek a way out, in music. That is also why my compositions are so hard to understand, because they start from remote interests, often also significant, because everything remarkable of our time grips me, and I then have to restate it musically.[30]

Franz Liszt, too, was the epitome of a "literary musician." The many hundreds of letters he left behind testify to a stunning familiarity with world literature and a profound learning, which today one would be able to expect at best from a professor of comparative literature. Liszt was fully at home in French, English, Italian and German literature,[31] and he engaged in regular literary studies by, for example, perusing writings and commentaries about Goethe and Dante.[32]

No less avid was his interest in political, philosophic, social and religious questions. Especially during his years of residence in France, he wrestled with the most diverse of theories, and he let himself be thrilled by such contrary directions that Heinrich Heine perceived signs of fickleness in Liszt's intellectual restlessness and in 1837 wrote the following about him in the tenth of his *Briefe über die französische Bühne* (Letters on the French Stage):

Moscow poems published by Georg Eismann in *BzMw*, 1 (1959), as well as the list of the "literary works" in vol. 1 of the *Tagebücher* (1971), 480/481.

30 *Jugendbriefe*, 282.

31 On Liszt's education and intellectual world, see my *Mahler and the Symphony*, chs. 10 and 21. For Liszt's relation to French literature, see Léon Guichard, "Liszt et la littérature française," *RMI*, 56 (1970), 3–34.

32 Liszt read Goethe studies by Hermann Hettner (1821–1882) and Adolf Stahr. See his letter to Stahr of May 26, 1851 (*FLB*, 8:87).

He is a man of eccentric but noble character, unselfish and without guile. His intellectual tendencies are most remarkable, he has a great gift for speculation, and more even than in the concerns of his art he is interested in the investigations of the various schools of thought that are occupied with solutions to the great questions embracing heaven and earth. For a long time he was fervent about the beautiful world view of the Saint-Simonians, later on he was befogged by the spiritualistic, or rather vaporistic, ideas of Ballanche, now he enthuses about the republican-catholic doctrines of a Lamennais, who has planted the Jacobin liberty cap onto the Cross ... Heaven only knows in what intellectual stable he will find his next hobby-horse. But what always remains praiseworthy is his relentless thirsting for light and divinity: it testifies to his sense for the sacred, the religious.[33]

Liszt must have been taken aback by these statements, since in a long letter to Heine of April 15, 1838, he took issue with the individual reproaches in a rather ironic manner. The following passage, which contains the quintessence of his apology, illuminates his frame of mind and simultaneously casts a side-light onto the historical situation generally:

O my friend, let us have no accusation of changeability, no countercharges: the century is sick, we all are sick with it. And look you, the poor musician has still the least heavy responsibility; for he who wields neither saber nor quill may without compunction give himself up to his intellectual curiosity and turn to every side where he thinks he can discern some light.[34]

What Liszt says here about himself applies *mutatis mutandis* also to Wagner. The young Wagner, we know, let himself be influenced by republican, socialist and revolutionary ideas; he was friends with poets of the Young Germany, established contacts with Bakunin, studied Feuerbach, Stirner and Proudhon, came under the influence of Schopenhauer in 1854, and in his last years turned toward Christian and Buddhist ideas. For this as for other reasons Hans Mayer called him an "intellectual fellow-traveler," who

---

33 Heinrich Heine, „Über die französische Bühne. Vertraute Briefe an August Lewald." Quoted from Heine, *Sämtliche Schriften in zwölf Bänden*, ed. Klaus Briegleb (Munich/Vienna, 1976), 5:351. The letters first appeared in 1837 in the *Allgemeine Theater-Revue*, ed. August Lewald, 3rd year (Stuttgart/Tübingen, 1837), 155–248.
34 Liszt, "Essays und Reisebriefe eines Baccalaureus der Tonkunst," GS, 2:197–203; p. 201.

not always knew how to distinguish clearly between his own and adopted ideas.[35]

The reproach is unfair, however: for one thing, because the intellectual development Wagner underwent is in line with the times – in a sense it mirrors the changes in European thinking between 1830 and 1890;[36] and for another, because Wagner, though well-read in philosophy, was an artist and not a philosopher. Unity and logical consistency of a system of thought, however, is something one can require only of a philosopher.

Finally, a few remarks about the principles of the New German School. In the summation that concludes his *Geschichte der Musik*, Franz Brendel expressed the view that the movement called forth by the New German School had brought about a "new beginning." As the main elements of the new consciousness imparted by the activities of Liszt and Wagner he listed the following:

1. the fulfillment of the demand for a higher education "from all disciples who join this movement"; he regarded it as especially significant in this respect "that almost all members of the new school are also active literarily" and that they also "more extensively participate in criticism, in contrast to the fatuous prejudice of earlier times, which advised the musician to stay away from all literary, and especially all critical endeavors";
2. the realization "that only a new intellectual content entitled one to compose, the recognition that musical creation is now pointless if it does not have a higher intellectual endowment for its background";
3. the acknowledgment of the demand "that from now on the endeavor of our art must be aimed at studying the past and its masterpieces but not to imitate them slavishly. Because forms incessantly change and vanish in the changing and vanishing of time";

---

35 Hans Mayer, *Richard Wagner in Selbstzeugnissen* (1959), 7, 59, 80.
36 See Hugo Dinger, *Richard Wagners geistige Entwickelung* (Leipzig, 1892). On Schopenhauer's influenceon Wagner, see Edouard Sans, *Richard Wagner et la pensée schopenhauerienne* (Paris, 1969). On the changes in European thought in the second half of the 19th century, particularly the critique of materialism, see my account in *Die geistige Welt Gustav Mahlers*, 100–103.

4. the striving of all adherents of the new school "to lift music out of the position in which it was no more than a higher kind of luxury article";

5. "the elevated position of the artists of the new school vis-à-vis the public, the elimination of that slavish dependency, into which particularly the virtuosi had plunged the artist."[37]

Franz Brendel and the followers of the New German School may have regarded these five maxims as the chief articles of a new art-philosophic creed. Our investigation will surely have shown, however, that these principles derive from ideas that the early 19th century had already developed.

---

37 Franz Brendel, *Geschichte der Musik in Italien, Deutschland und Frankreich*, 618–621.

X. Music and Poetry: The Views of Schumann, Wagner and Liszt

"Poesy is the only *other* world in this one." Jean Paul (1804/1813)[1]

"Music is the higher power of poesy." Robert Schumann (1828)[2]

"... la poésie, qui est l'essence de tout art ..." Franz Liszt (1860)[3]

The conception that music and poetry, the "most Romantic" arts, are closely related is fundamental to Romantic art theory. It appears in the Schlegel Brothers, In Jean Paul, in E. T. A. Hoffmann and others and follows logically from the maxim that poesy is the quintessence of every art. "Most compositions," Friedrich Schlegel deemed already in 1797, "are only translations of poesy into music,"[4] and Jean Paul defined music as "Romantic poetry through the ear."[5] Poetry/poesy here does not signify the poetic art in the narrower sense of the term but the world of the poetic in general – a "higher" world, which, according to E. T. A Hoffmann and Jean Paul, stands in dualistic opposition to the "prosaic world" of the everyday[6] – in short, "the only *other* world in this one."

These ideas, formulated already around 1800, impacted the musical aesthetics of the 19th century decisively, and they also directed the thinking of many leading composers. The ideal of a union, or even fusion, of music

---

1   Jean Paul, *Vorschule der Ästhetik*, program 1 §1. Quoted from Jean Paul, *Werke in zwölf Bänden*, ed. Norbert Miller (Munich/Vienna: Carl Hanser, 1975), 9:30.
2   Schumann, "Hottentottiana" (July, 1828), *Tagebücher* (1971), 96.
3   Liszt to Agnes Street-Klindworth, July 25, 1860; FLB, 3:125.
4   Friedrich Schlegel, *Literary Notebooks 1797–1801*, ed. Hans Eichner (London, 1957), 118 (fragment no. 1117).
5   *Jean Paul, Kleine Nachschule zur ästhetischen Vorschule* (1825), program 5, §7 (*Werke*, 9:466): "Each poetic genre has its corresponding likenesses in the body that activate us. Thus music, e.g., is romantic poetry through the ear." According to Wolfgang Boetticher, *Robert Schumann. Einführung in Persönlichkeit und Werk* (Berlin, 1941), 353, Schumann underlined these sentences in his copy of the *Vorschule*.
6   Cf. Karl Ludwig Schneider, "Künstlerliebe und Philistertum im Werke. E. T. A. Hoffmanns," in *Die deutsche Romantik*, ed. Hans Steffen, 2nd ed. (Göttingen, 1970), 200–218.

and poetry is a prime idea that a number of composers tried to realize in various ways, and one that fostered diverse "solutions": in Schumann it led to the poetization of music (principally instrumental music), in Wagner to the creation of the *gesamtkunstwerk*, in Liszt to the development of a certain species of program music. Let us take a closer look at each of these three "solutions."

1. Schumann's Ideal of a "Poetic Music"

Robert Schumann's art-theoretical views were, as we know, heavily influenced by ideas of Jean Paul.[7] The highest authority in the aesthetics of both men is poesy: the poetic – for Schumann the "ideal world"[8] – is the region of art as such. Schumann defines music as "the higher power of poesy" or better "poesy raised to the higher power." He never tires of postulating in his letters and writings that the composer has to be a "poet"[9] and should strive for a "poetic consciousness (*dichterisches Bewusstsein*).[10] In his writings he often uses the words *poetic* and *the poetic* and repeatedly distinguishes the "poetic" from the "theoretic" and the "virtuosic" side of music (GS I, 44; II, 70).

The question what Schumann meant by the expression of "the poetic" in music has hitherto received only marginal attention.[11] If one pursues it in a systematic way, one finds that Schumann often uses the word in connection with partly synonymous or semasiologically related terms. An analysis of the individual "equations" and correspondences yields the following picture:

1. "Poetic music" can be defined, negatively, as the opposite of all music that merely aims at "increasing external virtuosity" (I, 38) and only wants

---

7   See Hans Kötz, *Der Einfluß Jean Pauls auf Robert Schumann* (Weimar, 1933); Robert L. Jacobs, "Schumann und Jean Paul," *ML*, 30 (1949), 250–258.
8   Schumann, "Das Leben des Dichters," speech given September 12, 1827: "The poet lives in the ideal world and works for the real one" (GS, 2:183).
9   Schumann to Clara Wieck, January 24, 1839. *Jugendbriefe*, 283.
10 To Clara, April 13, 1838. *Jugendbriefe*, 283.
11 See above all Arnold Schmitz, "Die ästhetischen Anschauungen Robert Schumanns in ihren Beziehungen zur romantischen Literatur," *ZfMw*, 3 (1920–21), 111–118; Wolfgang Boetticher, *Schumann* (1941), 106n.5; Thomas Alan Brown, *The Aesthetics of Robert Schumann* (New York, 1968), 24–28.

to be sound play. In a review of lieder by Robert Franz dated 1843, Schumann tried to explain the genesis of the "Romantic School" and its ideal of "poetic music" as follows:

> We know that during the years 1830–1834 a reaction against the reigning taste set in. The struggle was basically not an arduous one; it was against the dominance of empty phrases that pervaded nearly all genres, above all piano music – Weber, Loewe et al. excepted. The first attack also issued from piano music; instead of passage pieces, more thoughtful constructions appeared, and the influence especially of two masters showed itself in them: Beethoven's and Bach's (II, 147).

Beethoven, in Schumann's perception, was "an enemy of everything mechanical," his oeuvre seemed to him as the prototype of a "purely poetic creation" (I, 215). One of the aims of Schumann's founding of the *Neue Zeitschrift für Musik* was to "prepare for, to help accelerate, a new poetic era" (I, 38).

2. "Poetic music" is above all romantic music. The ancestor of Romanticism, according to Schumann, is Johann Sebastian Bach; Beethoven and Schubert are genuine Romantics[12] and pioneers of the "Romantic School" that began to unfold after 1830. In the "highest kind" of music, "such as Bach and Beethoven gave to us in individual creations," Schumann thought he could discern "poetic depth and novelty everywhere, in the detail as in the whole" (I, 343). "The deeply combinatory, poetic and humorous of the newer music, however," he wrote to his friend Dr. Gustav A. Keferstein on January 31, 1840, "has its origin mostly in Bach: Mendelssohn, Bennett, Chopin, Hiller, all the so-called Romantics (I always mean the German ones) are far closer to Bach in their music than to Mozart...."[13] Typical for

---

12 „A trait of Beethovenesque romanticism, which one could call the provencealic one, was developed in his uniquely personal spirit into virtuosity by Franz Schubert" (1:42). "... and over the whole a romanticism poured out, such as one knows it from elsewhere already in Franz Schubert" (1:463).

13 *Robert Schumanns Briefe*, new series, ed. F. Gustav Jansen, 151. On the term *das Tiefkombinatorische* (the "deep-combinatory"), cf. Friedrich Schlegel, "Lessings Geist aus seinen Schriften" (1804), part 2: "Vom kombinatorischen Geist," in *Kritische Schriften*, ed. Wolfdietrich Rasch (Munich, 1971), 421–428. On the semantics of the term *das Humoristische*, see the remarks by Boetticher, *Schumann* (1941), 237–240, 251. – It is typical of Schumann that, in contrast to many of his contemporaries (see GS, 2:425/426, 433, 442), he does not distinguish between *Romantik* and *Neuromantik*. (In GS, 2:249/250, he distances himself

the synonymity of the terms *Romantic* and *poetic* is also this sentence from a letter to Clara of January 24, 1839: "But the Romantic is not in the figures and forms; it will be in them anyway, if the composer is only a poet."[14]

3. "Poetic music" for Schumann, as for Hegel,[15] is "language of the soul" (I, 344). A music "that only sounds and has no language nor sign for "states of the soul" or "states of mind" (*Seelenzustände*) would, according to Florestan, be "a small art" (I, 22). Schumann sees the "poetic" in music in the manifestation of "rare," "nobler" and "secret" "states of mind" (I, 343). Predominance of the "idea," "basic poetic material" and the "nobler states of mind" are contrary to "formalism, the rule of fashion and philistinism" (I, 179). Titles are justified and necessary especially in case of "secret states of mind": "There are secret states of mind, where a hint in words from the composer can lead to a quicker understanding and is to be gratefully accepted" (II, 24.

4. "Poetic" is contiguous to "characteristic music" to the extent that the latter, too, "represents" *seelenszustände*. In Schumann's definition, "a composition has musical *character* if a mentality predominantly expresses itself in it, obtrudes itself to such an extent that no other interpretation is possible. [...] Characteristic music differs from the picturesque in that it represents states of mind, while the latter represents states of existence; for the most part we find both of them mixed together" (II, 207). But the terms "poetic music" and "characteristic music" are not synonymous. The specific difference seems to be that what matters in "poetic music" is the conveyance of "rare states of mind."[16]

---

from the "materialism" of the "French Neoromantics.") Evidently there was no principal difference in his view between Beethoven's romanticism and that of his contemporaries, whom he championed.

14 *Jugendbriefe*, 298.
15 Hegel, *Ästhetik III*, 185: "Only the poetic in music, the soul's language ...] – the free sounding of the soul in the field of music is what becomes melody." Hegel's lectures on aesthetics first appeared in 1835.
16 About a trio by J. Rosenhain, which he regards as the work of a "richly talented" but not yet independent composer (1:168), Schumann typically writes: "Admittedly we do not, in the trio, come upon any *rare condition*, no grandly original style, but always upon the generally valid and genuinely human; it is a model study after the best masters: everywhere love for the chosen art, talent, even solemnity."

Regardless of this difference, however, there are many points of contact between these two "kinds." Thus many pieces whose *poetic* qualities Schumann praises belong to the "characteristic" genre.[17] No less symptomatic is the fact that Schumann repeatedly uses the words "character piece" and "poetic" conjointly. About Ferdinand Hiller's *Etüden* op. 15, for example, he opines that the composer was evidently more concerned to produce "character pieces and to lend wings to the poetic sense than to train a mechanical pianism" (I, 49). And most of Bach's fugues are in his view "character pieces of the highest kind, in part truly poetic creations, each of which demands its own particular expression, its own special lights and shades" (I, 354).

5. "Poetic music" must always be imaginative and able to stir the imagination of the listener. These principles Schumann borrowed from the aesthetics of Jean Paul, for whom imagination is the highest of the "poetic powers."[18] Eusebius' wish "that the silver thread of imagination should always wind about the chain of the rules" (I, 20) recurs repeatedly in Schuman's reviews as a standard of criticism.[19] Thus Florestan criticizes that in spite of their formal perfection, J. N. Hummel's *Etüden* op. 125 lack the most important quality "throughout": "the charm of imagination." Moscheles' *Etüden*, on the other hand, are said to be "interesting character pieces that would also occupy the imagination" (I, 12).[20] Schumann praises WilhelmTaubert's *Erinnerungen an Schottland* (Recollections of Scotland) op. 30, because he sees in them "original scenes and genre pictures, all of them captivating and entertaining the imagination most winsomely" (I, 41). About a work (op. 16) of his favorite composer Sterndale Bennett he writes: "From Bennett's unique harmonic turns, too, we can guess the

---

17 This is the case, for example, with Wilhelm Taubert's *Impromptus caractéristiques* oeuvre 14 and with Ignaz Moscheles' *Chakteristische Studien für das Pianoforte* op 95. See GS, 1:191, 362.

18 Jean Paul, *Vorschule der Ästhetik*, program 2, 47 ff.

19 Cf., e.g., this sentence from a letter to Clara of August 28, 1835 (*Jugendbriefe*, 266): "And if it is true that the greatest music is that in which the Faustian mantle of the imagination wraps itself around sturdy forms, then our journey is a good one."

20 In the manuscript of the review, "the imagination" is followed by the crossed-out apposition "the first element of all art" (GS, 2:369)

poet. The character of the first three sections is preponderantly lyrical, the last one rises dramatically and excites the imagination most strongly: musicians, painters and poets will all find matter here" (I, 418). About Berlioz' Overture to *Waverly* Schumann thinks that it would be easy for him to describe it, "whether in a poetic way by reproducing the pictures it variously prompted in me, or by analyzing the mechanism in the work" (I, 422/423). Kalkbrenner's *Etüden*, on the other hand, made him "truly melancholy," as they consist of pieces that exhibit "nothing but dry formulas" and lack imagination (I, 437). We should add that in many cases (though not always!) Schumann thought headings permissible as guideposts for the listener's imagination (II, 104).

6. "Poetic music," as an art of "poetic freedom," has to be original, new and fanciful. Especially during his early years, Schumann was firmly convinced that music like no other art developed with "great speed" into the "higher poetic freedom" (I, 10; II, 369), and that Beethoven "reached poetic freedom via years of study" (I, 17). Schumann understood poetic freedom to mean liberation from rigid schemes, a renewal of form and expression. He thought these qualities also distinguished the best work of those composers whom he regarded in large measure as Romantics. Thus he wrote about the *Three Impromptus* op. 7 of Stephen Heller that their forms were "new, imaginative and free" (I, 250). He praised Chopin's *Masureks* op. 30 for almost every one having "some poetic feature, something new in form or expression" ((I, 371). And the freedom with which Berlioz treated meter and rhythm in the *Symphonie fantastique* made it appear to him as if music wanted "to incline again towards its very beginnings, when it was not yet pressed by the heavy weight of the beat, and elevate itself independently to unbound speech, to a higher poetic punctuation (as in the choruses of Greek drama, in the language of the Bible, in the prose of Jean Paul)" (I, 74).[21]

7. "Poetic music," according to Schumann, leads to the "spirit realm of art" (I, 343), into the world of dreams, exerting its "full force" where "it plays over into the supersensory, into the spirit realm" (I, 362). It is clear that in entertaining these ideas Schumann was wholly under the spell of

---

21 Of his own *Studien nach Capricen von Paganini* op. 3 (1832), Schumann writes in the preface: "Poetic liberties suit no genre of musical composition so well as they do the Caprice."

E. T. A. Hoffmann, whose review of Beethoven's Fifth Symphony antici-
pates in a nutshell some essential elements of Schopenhauer's metaphysics
of music. "Music" (i. e., instrumental music), Hoffmann wrote in 1810,
"unlocks an unknown world to man; a world that has nothing in common
with the external world of the senses that surrounds him, and where he
leaves all conceptually determined feelings behind to abandon himself to
the inexpressible." And Beethoven's Fifth, which unfolds his Romanticism
more "than any other work of his," sweeps the listener "irresistibly" into
the "wondrous spirit realm of the infinite."[22]

8. Poems can inspire the composition of "poetic music," and conversely,
"poetic music" can inspire the writing of "poetry." Schumann formulated
this thought most concisely in 1835 in a review of the eight *Minnelieder für
das Pianoforte* op. 16 by WilhelmTaubert.[23] To elucidate the specific difference between these *Minnelieder* (which were inspired by poems of Heinrich
Heine – the texts precede each piece) and Mendelssohn's *Songs without
Words*, Schumann wrote: "For they differ from those of Mendelssohn in
that they are prompted by poems, whereas the latter are perhaps meant to
stimulate the writing of poems" (I, 100).[24]

2. Wagner's Ideal of a Union of the "Purely Human Art Forms" in the Drama

The idea of a union of music and poesy is central also to Wagner's theory
of art. But Wagner drew entirely different conclusions from it than did

---

22 E. T. A. Hoffmann, *Schriften zur Musik*, ed. Schnapp (1963), 34, 37. See on this
Ernst Lichterhahn, "Über einen Ausspruch Hoffmanns und über das Roman-
tische in der Musik," in *Musik und Geschichte. Leo Schrade zum sechzigsten
Geburtstag* (Cologne, 1963), 178–198.

23 On Taubert's Minnelieder, see Elfriede Glusman, "Taubert and Mendelssohn:
Opposing Attitudes toward Poetry and Music," *MQ*, 57 (1971), 628–635.

24 We might mention in this connection that already in 1835 Schumann planned the
composition of the "Musikalische Gedichte mit unterlegten Liedern" of Heinrich
Heine (*Tagebücher* [1971], 417). The question remains to be settled whether
he already knew Taubert's *Minnelieder* at that time, for the publication date of
the latter is not definite. According to Willi Kahl (*ZfMw*, 3:463), they appeared
in 1831. According to Elfriede Glusman, however, they were announced in the
Allgemeine musikalische Zeitung only in 1834.

Schumann. His aim was not the poetization of (instrumental) music but the "intimate amalgamation" and mutual interpenetration of music and poetry in the artwork of the future, that total or universal (*allgemeinsame*) drama.

Wagner's theory of the *gesamtkunstwerk*[25] rests on a series of axioms that are developed with astounding logical consistency. The syllogism formed by the premises says that the arts of dance, music and poetry ("the three purely human [*reinmenschliche*] art forms") are essentially inseparable and were originally united – in the lyric poetry and the drama of the Greeks [26]– that they are therefore "unfree" and "restricted" in isolation and can be "free" and "complete" only in their union in representative drama, the perfected artwork of the future (GS III, 68/69).

The idea of the reunion of the arts in a total work of art is, of course, one that had fascinated several artists and aestheticians before Wagner.[27] But only Wagner elaborated the idea into a comprehensive theory that is as original as it is radical.

One aspect of its originality is the criteria by means of which Wagner divides the arts into two "families." Wagner maintains that in the three

---

25 Richard Wagner, *Das Kunstwerk der Zukunft* (1849), GS, 3:42–177. Cf. Carl Dahlhaus, *Wagners Konzeption des musikalischen Dramas* (Arbeitsgemeinschaft "100 Jahre Bayreuther Festspiele," vol. 5) (Regensburg, 1971), and Stefan Kunze, "Richard Wagners Idee des 'Gesamtkunstwerks'," in *Beiträge zur Theorie der Künste im 19. Jahrhundert*, ed. Helmut Koopmann and J. Adolf Schmoll, vol. 2 (Frankfurt a.M., 1972), 196–229.

26 Cf. August Wilhelm Schlegel, *Briefe über Poesie, Silbenmaß und Sprache* (1795): "In its origins, poetry was inseparable from music and dance. In all its forms, from the simplest nature to the most sophisticated expansions of art, from the savage's leap of joy to Noverre's ballets, dance has never had to do without the accompaniment of music. Now, however, poetry and music are wholly independent of each other. Their works fashion themselves in isolation in the minds of different, often mutually misunderstood artists and have to be deliberately directed toward being made to appear one again by the sleights of recitation." Quoted from A. W. Schlegel, *Kritische Schriften und Briefe*, ed. Edgar Lohner, vol. 1 (Stuttgart, 1962), 145.

27 Paul Moos, *Richard Wagner als Ästhetiker. Versuch einer kritischen Darstellung* (Berlin/Leipzig, 1906), 124/125, referred to Herder, Goethe, Ast, Trahndorff und Schleiermacher. Peter Rumenhöller has drawn attention to ideas of Philipp Otto Runge. See Rummenhöller, "Romantik und Gesamtkunstwerk," in *Beiträge zur Geschichte der Musikanschauung im 19. Jahrhundert* (1965), 161–170.

"purely human art forms," dance, music and poetry, the human being becomes himself "object and matter of artistic treatment," while in the "pictorial arts," architecture, sculpture and painting, he represents Nature artistically (III, 123). Dance, music and poetry, in Wagner's view, are manifestations of "artistic man," who expresses himself in a threefold way: as bodily being, as feeling being and as thinking, rational being (III, 63–67). The "artistic matter" of dance is "the real, bodily being" (III, 71). Music is the "artistically conscious language" of the heart (III, 81). But poetry is "the creative process through which the work of art enters into life" (III, 103). Of all the arts, music "by its inmost nature" most needs the "marriage" with the other arts (III, 118).

Wagner's critics have time and again pointed out that his theory of the *gesamtkunstwerk* is replete with errors, exaggerations and faulty constructions.[28] No one will be able to deny that he made indeed numerous historical mistakes and that his speculations about the philosophy of history often served the purpose of proving the truth of his theses. Yet one cannot do justice to Wagner if one fails to realize that the radicalism of his views is nothing but a symptom of his consequential thinking. If one keeps in mind that his ideal was the reunion of all the arts in the drama, it appears only logical that he rejected all those genres that he thought did not correspond to this ideal. He had nothing but scorn for the pantomime (III, 80), the oratorio (III, 101) and the "closet drama" (III, 111–113). His disparaging judgments about these genres may seem tendentious and "unfair"; inconsistent they are not.

What has been said makes clear that because of his principles Wagner also had to be opposed to any further development of an independent instrumental music. For "pure" instrumental music is as "lonely" as the "closet drama." If Wagner's discussions of the development, nature and value of the symphony are not always entirely unequivocal, that is also owing to his intention of building a bridge between Beethoven's symphonies and his own artistic endeavors. From this intention springs his "violent" interpretation of Beethoven's Ninth Symphony, which in

---

28 See, for example, Moos, *Wagner as Ästhetiker*, 174–180, and Guido Adler, *Richard Wagner. Vorlesungen gehalten an der Universität zu Wien*, 2nd ed. (Munich, 1923), 167 ff.

Wagner's view is "the deliverance of music from its own intrinsic element to becoming a universal art." It, the last of Beethoven's symphonies, is "the human gospel of the art of the future. No progress from it is possible, for from it only the perfected artwork of the future can follow immediately, the universal [*allgemeinsame*] drama, to which Beethoven forged the artistic key" (III, 96).

Wagner was so caught up in his speculations in the philosophy of history and the theory of art that he could also not imagine the continued development of poetry as an independent ("lone") art. In his opinion, poetic art would in future be able to evolve further only in "intimate amalgamation" with music in the drama. In his essay *Zukunftsmusik* of September 1860, he wrote:

> In view of this irrefutable realization, poetry is likely henceforth to have only two ways of development open to it. Either a complete going over into the field of abstraction, pure combination of concepts and representation of the world by explaining the logical laws of thinking, and thus functioning as philosophy. Or *intimate amalgamation* with music, specifically the kind of music whose infinite potential has been revealed to us by Beethoven's symphony (VII, 111).

3. Liszt's Ideal of Program Music

The "intimate amalgamation" of music with poetry (literature) was likewise the declared aim of Franz Liszt's artistic endeavors. But whereas Wagner, led by the conviction that Beethoven's Ninth was the last symphony ever to be written, sought to realize this aim in the music drama, Liszt went the way of symphonic program music, in which he saw a means of progress in musical art. In a letter to Agnes Street-Klindworth of November 16, 1860, he described as the "great idea" of his Weimar period (1848–1860) the idea of "a renovation of music through the most intimate alliance with poetry" (*une grande idée: celle du renouvellement de la Musique par son alliance plus intime avec la Poésie*).[29] Liszt endeavored to expand the domain of symphonic music by incorporating poetic and philosophic ideas.

Liszt's big treatise on Berlioz is not only one of the longest but also probably the most important of the various apologetic writings about program music. Of the five chapters into which it is divided, two (the second and

---

29 *FLB*, 3:135.

third) contain detailed historic, aesthetic and philosophic discussions of the nature, legitimacy and necessity of program music. The discussions start out from some general reflections about the relation of music and poesy. Liszt is quite frank about the fact that he ranks music – "pure music," as he says – more highly than poetry. As to Robert Schumann and several of the Romantic writers, music is the "highest art" to him (IV, 30),[30] "heavenly art" (IV, 28), "echo from a remote ideal world" (Jean Paul[31]), "mysterious language of a distant spirit realm" (E. T. A. Hoffmann[32]), "spirit, soul that resounds immediately for itself" (Hegel[33]). Unlike Hegel,[34] Liszt cedes the highest place in the system of the arts to music, because he ranks feeling higher than thought and believes that feeling "incarnates" itself most purely in music (IV, 29). "Feeling itself lives and shines in music without pictorial dress, without a mediating action, without mediating thought" (IV, 30). By contrast, poetry (Liszt speaks of the arts of the *word*) can communicate feeling only with the aid of "the many and yet so confined forms of the understanding."

In view of this, it is only logical that Liszt never questions the legitimacy of pure instrumental music. On the contrary, he prays: "May heaven prevent that someone, in the zeal of pontificating about the use, justification and advantage of programs, should abjure the old faith by alleging that the heavenly art did not exist for its own sake, did not find sufficiency within itself, did not catch fire from its own divine spark and had value only as a representative of thought, as a reinforcement of the word!" (IV, 28/29).

---

30 For Wagner, too, music is "the highest, the most redeeming art" (GS, 5:191).

31 Jean Paul, *Die unsichtbare Loge, Vierter Sektor* (*Werke*, 1:60). Liszt (GS, 4:32) quotes the passage inexactly.

32 E. T. A. Hoffmann, "Der Dichter und der Komponist" (1813). *Die Serapionsbrüder* (1963), 83.

33 Hegel, *Vorlesungen über die Ästhetik III*, 197/198. On the interpretation of this "definition," see Adolf Nowak, *Hegels Musikästhetik* (Studien zur Musikgeschichte des 19. Jahrhunderts, vo.25), 150–153.

34 In Hegel's system of the arts, poetry ranks at the top. Music is the "second romantic art," followed by painting, sculpture and finally architecture, "the most incomplete art." See *Ästhetik III*, 131–133, 234/235. Cf. Monika Lichtenfeld "Gesamtkunstwerk und allgemeine Kunst. Das System der Künste bei Wagner und Hegel," in *Beiträge zur Geschichte der Musikanschauung im 19. Jahrhundert*, 171–177.

For all that, Liszt does not advocate "pure" instrumental music but rather program music. He obviates the possible objection that his plea for program music conflicts with his statements about music as the art of feeling by the argument that the program does not cancel feeing but rather gives precision to its contents (IV, 47). Besides, he intimates that the future of instrumental music lay only with an alliance with poetry. The highest artistic mission of the "poets among the composers," in his view, was to "enlarge" the limits of musical art (IV, 49).[35]

Of the arguments that Liszt advances on behalf of program music, three deserve to be emphasized. The first is a historical one: programs, he says, were "no more invented by Berlioz than by Beethoven," rather, program music can be traced back all the way to the 16th century (IV, 21–26). The second argument appeals to reception history: "for the last fifteen years" (that is since 1840), Liszt says, there have been more and more frequent attempts to supplement the symphonies, string quartets and sonatas of Beethoven with commentaries, and to explain "the impressions they make on us" in poetic and philosophic discourses. These attempts, he says, prove how great the desire is "to see the *leading thoughts* of great instrumental works defined precisely" (IV, 224/25). But the clinching argument is the third one: that vocal music, after all, has always had a "poetic basis" (IV, 32). Liszt now demands an analogous foundation for the new species of instrumental music. The program should provide what the text does for vocal music, "an added preface in readily understood language, by which the composer seeks to protect the listeners from the arbitrariness of a poetic interpretation of his work and to direct their attention from the start to the poetic idea, to a particular point of the whole" (IV, 21).

Program music and vocal music thus have the "poetic basis" in common. Both are opposed to "pure" instrumental music. We should note that this

---

35 It is worth mentioning that this idea was current at least 20 years before the publication of Liszt's treatise. Thus Ignaz Moscheles wrote in 1836, in a review of Schumann's F-sharp Minor sonata, about the "Beethoveners," who felt drawn "to the master's last works": "Art never stands still, these say, and therefore its youngest priests felt called upon to help it onward, to further widen the borders of its realm, and to still *pro*gress where Beethoven had already *trans*gressed." Quoted from Arnold Schering, "Aus den Jugendjahren der musikalischen Neuromantik," *JbP*, 24 (1917), 52.

"classificatory system" of the musical kinds was well-known long before the publication of List's treatise. Thus Carl Czerny, Liszt's teacher, laconically noted already in 1842, in an annotation (!) to his *Kunst des Vortrags* (The Art of Performance): "We distinguish pure music from that which, whether through title or text, is to depict a clearly expressed particular idea."[36]

We get more detailed information about Liszt's conception of program music from his discussion of individual musical and literary genres (IV, 51–57). The two theses Liszt proposes state that three genres, the oratorio, the cantata and the modern program symphony, "represent the epic in the musical area," and that "the musical like the poetic epic [are] a finished and fully developed form" (IV, 52). To clarify these at first rather paradoxical-sounding theses, Liszt categorically differentiates, evidently following Hegel,[37] between two kinds of epic poem, the "ancient" and the "modern epopee." About the ancient epopee of Homer he observed that in it "the grand deeds of a hero endowed with heroic human virtues" are foregrounded, "with a number of figures of the episodic narrative forming groups about him" (IV,53). In the modern epopee, on the other hand, the rationale and purpose of the poem was no longer "the depiction of the deeds of the hero but the delineation of affects that reign in his soul." Action and event here lose in importance, and the number of episodic figure is reduced. The wondrous is replaced by the fantastic. The action acquires a symbolic aura, a mythical substratum. As instances of this kind of epopee, which Liszt calls the "philosophic" one, he names Goethe's *Faust*, Byron's mysteries *Cain* and *Manfred* and Mickiewicz' *Dziady*.

What is instructive here is the comparison Liszt draws between the various literary and musical genres. He parallels oratorio and cantata with the ancient epic. "Oratorio and cantata," he notes, "have the tendency to describe in common with the epic." "Episode and apostrophe have almost the same position here as there, and the effect of the whole presents itself in both art forms as the solemn narration of a memorable

---

36 Carl Czerny, *Die Kunst des Vortrags der älteren und neueren Klavierkompositionen* (Vienna, 1842), 63.
37 According to Hegel (*Ästhetik III*, 395), three major stages can be distinguished in the developmental history of epic poetry: the oriental epic, the classical epic of the Greeks and Romans and the Romantic epic.

event, whose details serve solely the glorification of a single hero" (IV, 2). The program symphony, on the other hand, Liszt likens to the modern philosophic epopee. In both kinds what matters is the "narration of inward processes" (IV, 56). Liszt makes clear that he deemed only the symphonic program music capable of depicting "inward processes" and representing "characters" ("comparable to those drawn by the poet princes of our time" (IV, 57).

These reflections are at least partly shaped by considerations of the philosophy of history. In 1855, Liszt was convinced that the oratorio and the cantata had passed the heyday of their development. In both areas, he thought, it was difficult to still achieve success. Both genres had ceased "to awaken an interest like that evoked in the time when Handel animated them with the breath of the winged horse" (IV, 51), In the program symphony, on the other hand, he discerned, in 1855, the genre to which the future would belong. The program symphony seemed to him capable of giving expression to modern "ways of feeling" and contemporary "mentalities" (*Geistesstimmungen*) – in short, the "new manifestation of the human spirit" (IV, 55/56).

As paradoxical as it may seem, Liszt's treatise about Berlioz has so far never been scrutinized more closely. (Peter Raabe devoted all of a page and a half to it.[38]) There are reasons for this "neglect": the treatise includes a number of tiresome excursuses; the style is rarely concise; much in it seems superfluous; and some doubts have arisen as to Liszt's authorship. Our exposition, however, should have made clear that the essay is nonetheless enormously instructive. The views cited merit special attention not least because they enable us to realize that his often misunderstood program-symphonic work was not a matter of trivial illustration and tone painting but of representing "inward processes" – he repeatedly speaks of "affects" and "passions" – and conveying philosophic ideas through the medium of music. Goethe's *Faust* and Byron's mysteries, Dante's *Divina Commedia* and Shakespeare's dramas: masterpieces of this rank should, in his view, show modern program music the way.

---

38 Peter Raabe, *Liszts Schaffen*, 185/186.

At this point we need to raise the question as to the authenticity of the treatise. We have until now presumed that the views delineated were Liszt's own formulations. Yet we also know that Liszt's Weimar writings came about with the collaboration of the Princess Carolyne Sayn-Wittgenstein. Are the ideas formulated in the Berlioz treatise Liszt's own?

Peter Raabe, who was most likely the first to address this question in detail, opined that Liszt supplied the basic ideas, "especially for everything musical," and that the Princess, strung out what he wanted to say to such an extent "that one would best translate the expression '*developper*' she used for it with "flogging to death."[39] Émile Harasztis' judgment was more radical. According to it, only the sixteen pages of the treatise containing the analysis of the *Harold* Symphony can with certainty be ascribed to Liszt himself![40]

We think that the Berlioz treatise was placed in a bad light above all by Harasztis' derogatory remarks (he speaks of "obscure verbiage"). Several new observations make it appear certain that all the basic ideas of the treatise – not only "for everything musical" – derive from Liszt. To a large extent, however, the treatise is likely to have been formulated by the Princess, who "developed" Liszt's ideas. The following points are to be borne in mind:

1. The very first "draft" of the treatise occurs in a hitherto ignored letter to the Princess dated April 11, 1851 (FLB IV, 87). There Liszt explains, very tersely but to the point, the way in which Berlioz treats the Harold theme in the movements of the symphony.[41]
2. The elucidations of the technical principles of program music composition (GS IV, 68/69) are so precise that they cannot possibly have been formulated by a lay person. (The Princess Wittgenstein did not have an

---

39 Raabe, *Liszts Schaffen*, 175; *Wege zu Liszt* (Deutsche Musikbücherei, vol 13) (Regensburg, 1943), 46/47.
40 Emile Haraszti, "Franz Liszt, Écrivain et penseur. Histoire d'une mystification," *RMI*, 25 (1943), 17–28, and Numéro unique (Série spéciale) of the *Société française de musicologie 1944*, 12–24; Haraszti, *Franz Liszt* (Paris, 1967), 168/169.
41 See *Mahler and the Symphony*, 44 f.; 60 f.

eminent musical training at her disposal.[42]) Besides, these discussions in their sober factual diction also stand out from the bombastic rhetorical style of many parts of the treatise.

3. The treatise contains numerous references to the aesthetics of Hegel. Haraszti speaks inaccurately about one chapter and sneers that Hegel was the Princess' hobbyhorse. But it can be regarded as certain that Liszt, too, knew Hegel's aesthetics well. From a letter of his to the Countess d'Agoult it appears that he had made contact with Hegel's philosophy already in 1838.[43]

4. The important discussions of the epic character of the oratorio, the cantata and the program symphony undoubtedly constitute elaborations of Lisztean reflections. For the idea of an *épopée musicale* was one that had occupied Liszt long before his Weimar period. In an important letter of October 8, 1846, he wrote to the Countess d'Agoult that he had collected a large amount of [musical] fragments during his stay in Hungary, by means if which one could newly compose the musical epopee (*l'épopée musicale*) of this odd country, as whose rhapsodist he regarded himself.[44]

Summing up, we must emphasize that the views about the musical epopee set forth open new perspectives for a deeper understanding of Liszt's artistic intentions. They help us to realize that ever since the 1840s he regarded it as the area in which he wanted to work as an artist. Significantly, the principal works he created after 1848 belong to those genres he regarded as "epic": the program symphony, the symphonic poem and the oratorio. The *Faust* and *Dante* symphonies and most of the symphonic poems came about during the Weimar period. Then, in the 1860s, Liszt's great oratorios were completed: *The Legend of St. Elizabeth* (1862) and *Christus* (1866). A letter Liszt wrote on November 8, 1862, indicates that he regarded the

---

42 According to Julius Kapp, *Liszt. Eine Biographie*, 15th to 18th ed. (Berlin,/Leipzig, 1922), 116.

43 Letter to the Countess d'Agoult, December 1838.

44 *Correspondance de Liszt et de la comtesse d'Agoult*, ed. Daniel Ollivier (Paris, 1934), 2:368. It should be mentioned in this connection that already in 1838 Berlioz called the *Eroica* a "magnifique épopée musicale." See *À travers chants* (1971), 50.

symphonic program music and the oratorio indeed as the areas in which he wanted to achieve innovative, forward-looking creations. "After having solved the *symphonic* task I had set myself in large part as well as I could in Germany," he wrote to Franz Brendel, "I now want to fulfill the *oratorical* one (along with several related works)."[45]

It remains to be appended that Liszt was neither the only nor even the first one to parallel musical and literary genres. It is characteristic of the music as well as the thinking about music of the 19th century that such comparisons were very popular and frequent. To illustrate with some examples:

Hector Berlioz in 1830 described the *Symphonie fantastique* as "instrumental drama" (*drame instrumental*).

Gottfried Wilhelm Fink, the well-known editor of the *Allgemeine musikalische Zeitung*, in 1838 compared the "grand symphony" to a "dramatically conceived novella of feeling." "It [the symphony] is a dramatically designed story, developed in a psychological context and told in notes, about some emotional state of a mass assembly which, prompted by a main impulse, individually expresses its essential feeling in every kind of popular representation through every instrument drawn into the whole." There is no difference between the "novelistic poet" and the "tone poet," according to Fink, "except that the one creates with words, the other with notes"[46]

In 1840, Robert Schumann stressed the "novelistic character" of Schubert's "Great" symphony in C Major, whose "heavenly length" seemed to him "like a fat novel of four volumes, say, by Jean Paul."[47]

Some years later, Alexander Ulibischeff saw a correlation between the symphony and the ode, "in that one is the expression and the purest effluence of pure music, the other the loftiest effluence of lyrical or limitless poesy."[48]

---

45 *FLB*, 2:28.
46 Gottfried Wilhelm Fink, art. "Symphonie," in Gustav Schilling, *Encyclopädie der gesammten musikalischen Wissenschaften, oder Universal-Lexikon der Tonkunst*, vol. 6 (Stuttgart, 1838), 541–551; pp. 548/549.
47 Schumann, GS, 1:463/464. Some thoughts for this article are "preformulated" in a letter of Schumann's to Clara Wieck of December 11, 1839. See *Jugendbriefe*, 307/308.
48 Alexander Ulibischeff, *Mozart's Leben und Werke* (German adaptation of *Nouvelle biographie de Mozart* [1843]), 2nd ed. (Stuttgart, 1859) 4:212/213. And cf. Ambros, *Die Grenzen der Musik und Poesie*, x.

In 1862, finally, Eduard Kulke outlined a "theory" about the relation of symphony and symphonic poem. According to that, the symphony is related to the epic ("but with the addition of purely lyrical elements"), whereas the opera "is subject to the laws of the drama generally." The symphonic poem, however, stands, as it were, in the middle between opera and symphony and could also be called "symphonic drama" or "dramatic symphony."[49]

49 Eduard Kulke, "Symphonie und symphonische Dichtung. Eine Studie," *NZfM*, 56 (1862), 181–183.

XI. Schumann's Musical Poetics

"Why should there be no operas without text; that would be dramatic."
Schumann (1832)[1]

"The more specific a music is, the more individual pictures it spreads out
before the listener throughout the whole, the more it will captivate, and the
more everlasting it will be and new for all time." Schumann (1832)[2]

The thought that a renewal of instrumental music would be possible only
through the inclusion of poetic elements and ideas is among the leading
conceptions of the 19th century. Liszt was by no means the first composer to
advocate the "poetic solution of instrumental music." Before him, this claim
was entered already by Schumann and Berlioz. If one juxtaposes the views
of the three composers on this issue, one can, despite their basic agreement,
discern significant and instructive differences in their conceptions, which
deserve a closer analysis.

If, to begin with, we ask in what way Schumann's ideal of a "poetic music" manifests itself in his own compositions, we must remember that many
of his works bear characterizing titles and were demonstrably prompted
by personal experiences, mental images and literary impressions.[3] To cite
some examples:

1. Schumann revealed in a letter to Heinrich Dorn of September 5, 1839,
    that personal experiences occasioned the creation of several of his
    works: "Surely much of the struggle Clara cost me may be contained
    in my music and also perceived by you. The concerto, the sonata, the
    Davidsbündlertänze, the Kreisleriana and the Novelletten she occa-
    sioned almost single-handedly."[4]
2. The *Papillons* op. 2 (1830/31) grew from an impression of several pas-
    sages in the penultimate chapter (no. 63) of Jean Paul's *Flegeljahre*;
    in 1941, Wolfgang Boetticher showed that Schumann marked various

---

1   Diary entry, July 1832. *Tagebücher* (1971), 411.
2   Diary entry, July 1832. Ibid., 410.
3   On what follows, cf. also Edward A. Lippmann, "Theory and Practice in Schu-
    mann's Aesthetics," *JAMS*, 17 (1964), 310–345.
4   *Briefe. Neue Folge* (1886), 146/147.

paragraphs in his personal copy of that novel and furnished them with cardinal numbers that refer to the individual *Papillons* pieces.[5]

3. In adapting Paganini's G Minor *Caprice* (= Schumann op. 3, no. 6), Schumann, according to a note in his Diary (6–4–1832) had a fantastic image in mind: "Paganini in a magic circle – the murdered woman – dancing skeletons and drifting magnetic fog spirits."[6] Schumann thought that the conclusion of the piece "recalled" this image.

4. In letters to Clara, Schumann himself pointed to the "poetic " content of the *Phantasie* op. 17 (1836),[7] which is one of his most personal works; the three movements of the piece were originally to have been entitled "Ruin," "Victory Arch" and "Constellation" (*Sternbild*).

5. By his own admission, Schumann, in a presentiment of the death of his brother Eduard, had "visions of funeral processions, coffins, unhappy, despairing people" while composing the *Nachtstücke* (Night Pieces);[8] the work was originally to have been called *Leichenphantasie* (Funeral Fantasy), with the individual pieces to be named "Funeral Procession," "Odd Company" (*Kuriose Gesellschaft*), "Nocturnal Banquet" and "Choral Song [*Rundgesang*] with Solo Voices."

6. Schumann received the inspiration for his First Symphony op. 38 (1841) from a poem by Adolph Böttger; the four movements were originally meant to have titles, which were suppressed at publication.[9]

7. According to Schumann's own indications, the *Bilder aus Osten für Pianoforte* (Pictures from the East for Piano) op. 66 (1848) originated after his reading of Rückert's *Makamen des Hariri*; in a draft to the "Preface," Schumann writes that with the first five pieces, "specifics" from the narratives had "not exactly been before his eyes"; for the last

---

5 Boetticher, Schumann (1941), 331/332, 611–613. On the genesis of *Papillons,* see Wolfgang Boetticher, *Robert Schumanns Klavierwerke. Neue biographische und textkritische Untersuchungen*. Part I: *Opus 1–6* (Quellenkataloge zur Musikgeschichte, ed. Richard Schaal, vol. 9) (Wilhelmshaven, 1976), 49–77.
6 *Tagebücher*, 404.
7 *Jugendbriefe* (1910), 278, 302, 303.
8 Ibid., 301, 309.
9 See F. Gustav Jansen, *Die Davidsbündler* (1883), 245; Arnim Gebhardt, *Robert Schumann als Symphoniker* (Forschungsbeiträge zur Musikwissenschaft, vol . 20) (Regensburg, 1968), 25–27.

piece, however, he had had the image of Abu Seid "in extreme old age and as a penitent" in mind.[10]

8. About his Third Symphony op. 97, the so-called *Rhenish* (1850), Schumann remarked in a letter to Simrock that it "perhaps reflects a piece of life here and there";[11] the fourth movement originally bore the heading "In the Character of an Accompaniment to a Solemn Ceremony."[12]

An unbiased reader, looking at these facts, might think that Schumann's instrumental works exhibit at least some points of contact with program music. Yet according to a widely accepted view, Schumann ranks as an "absolute musician" and a virtual antipode to the composers of program music.[13] Many critics who revere him as a master of non-concretizable music, love to point to his statements according to which he had invented the titles to a number of his works after the fact.[14] However, this entire complex of questions requires a detailed, systematic scrutiny. For it can be

---

10 According to Boetticher, *Schumann* (1941), 330.

11 Quoted from A. Niggli, Erläuterungen der III. Symphonie, in *Robert Schumann's Symphonien u. A.* (Schlesingersche Musik-Bibliothek, Meisterführer no.13) (Berlin/Vienna, n.d.), 49.

12 Facsimile of p. 145 of the autograph in Werner Korte, *Schumann* (Potsdam, n.d.) fig. 17.

13 The notion, still widely current today, that Schumann was basically an "absolute musician" arose after 1850, as Boetticher (*Schumann*, 375–398) has shown. Theodor Uhlig, the friend of Wagner, maintained categorically in the *NZfM* in 1851 that "Schumann, as an absolute musician, is unable to understand music any other way." Before 1859, on the other hand, Schumann was deemed by many to be a composer who strove for the "characteristic" and for "definiteness of expression." "Already in the early works," Boetticher writes, "the question about a concrete content was regarded as crucial, and the interest was focused on secret biographical connections."

14 Reference is often made to a statement of Schumann's in the important letter to Simonin de Sire of March 15, 1839, which, however, is frequently torn from its context and misinterpreted. Precisely so as to exemplify the anchorage of his music in the "poetic," Schumann enumerates several works of his with titles (*Kinderscenen* op. 15, *Kreisleriana* op. 16, *Phantasie in drei Sätzen* op. 17, *Arabeske* op.18, *Blumenstück* op. 19, *Humoreske* op. 20) and adds by way of restriction: "The titles of *others* of my compositions always come to me only after I am already finished composing rhem" (*Briefe. Neue Folge* [1884], 134). As the context indicates, Schumann implied that the titles of at least some of the enumerated works came to him *before* or *during* the composition!

shown that at least in some instances Schumann's statements are contradictory. Thus Schumann, in publishing the third of his *Novelletten* op. 21 in a supplement to the *Neue Zeitschrift für Musik*, with verses from Shakespeare's *Macbeth* as motto, had emphasized in so many words that he had found "these words coming close to the sense of the music only later."[15] But from both diary entries and reports it emerges that Schumann had in fact conceived the piece from the start as "Macbeth Novellette."[16]

After what has been presented, it would be a vain endeavor to try to dispute Bötticher's thesis "that in his creative work Schumann let his imaginative life to a high degree be stimulated by literary impressions."[17]

Was Schumann really an opponent of program music, as is asserted so often? In his review of the *Symphonie fantastique*, he clearly implies that he did not like detailed programs. But it would be a mistake to conclude from this that he rejected every kind of non-autonomously conceived music. In the very same review, he warns against minimizing the importance of extra-musical elements in musical creation:

> As to the difficult question generally how far instrumental music may go in representing events and ideas, many are too timid in their views. It is certainly erroneous to think that composers set out paper and pen for the miserable purpose of expressing, describing or picturing this or that. But don't underestimate the role of chance influences and impression from the outside. Unconsciously, an idea often continues to have an impact alongside the musical imagination, the eye alongside the ear, and the former, this ever-active organ, then holds fast, among the notes and harmonies, certain outlines, which, with the progress of the music, can condense and develop to clear shapes (I, 84).

Schumann was the most committed pioneer of poetically inspired instrumental music. It would be wrong to stamp him an opponent of every kind of program music. His reserve vis-à-vis Berlioz' kind of the program music can be traced back to three reasons, which, it seems, have not been, or been insufficiently, taken notice of in past discussions.

---

15 Jansen, *Die Davidsbündler*, 74, 230.
16 On March 3, 1838, Schumann, according to Boetticher (*Schumann*, 318), noted in his diary that he had "made the Macbeth-Novellette."
17 Boetticher, *Schumann*, 313 ff. Cf. Karl H. Wörner, *Robert Schumann* (Zurich, 1949), 360.

The first reason was Schumann's conviction that detailed programs are deleterious because they force the listener's imagination from the start into fixed channels and leave it no room for unfolding freely. Schumann saw in this unavoidable "gagging" of the imagination an actual violation of the "rights" of the "tender-minded" German listener, who, in contrast to the French, did not want "to be led so rudely in his thoughts" (I, 83). He therefore thought that the main headings of the *Symphonie fantastique*'s five movements would have sufficed. (This latter remark, one should note, implies at least some concession.)

The second reason was Schumann's dislike specifically of the program of the *Symphonie fantastique*. Some allusions of his make clear that he particularly objected to Berlioz' synopsis of the Finale for aesthetic, moral and religious reasons, even felt them to be blasphemous.[18] Thus he wrote: "If one wanted to combat the entire direction of the zeitgeist that can tolerate a *Dies irae* as a burlesque, one would have to repeat what for years has been written and said against Byron, Heine, Victor Hugo, Grabbe and the like" (185).[19]

The third reason lay in Schumann's view that the artist had the right and the duty to keep occasion and process of his creative work from the public:

Man has a peculiar awe of the workplace of genius; he does not really want to know anything about the causes, tools and secrets of creation, just as Nature, too,

---

18 On Schumann's religiosity, see Boetticher, *Schumann*, 192–200.

19 Some (approving) remarks of Ludwig Börne and Heinrich Heine demonstrate that many in the 1830s took the program of the *Symphonie fantastique* to be an ironic denial of the existence of God. Thus Börne wrote in his *Letters from Paris* (No. 16, of December 8, 1830): "An odd symphony, a dramatic one of five acts, of course only instrumental music; but in order for it to be understood, [Berlioz] had a text explaining the action printed, as if for an opera. It is the most riotous irony, as no poet has yet expressed it in words, and all of it *godless*. The composer tells the story of his own youth in it." (Quoted from Schumann, GS, 2:380/381). And Heine wrote in the tenth of his *Letters on the French Stage* (*Sämtliche Schriften in zwölf Bänden*, 5:350): "It was in the Conservatoire de Musique, and a great symphony by him [Berlioz] was performed, a bizarre nightpiece, which only once in a while is lit up by a sentimentally white female's robe, which flutters aroun in it, or by a sulphuric lightning flash of irony. The best in it is a witches' sabbath, where the Devil reads mass and the Catholic church music is parodied with the bloodiest, most horrific farcicality."

exhibits a certain delicacy in covering its roots with soil. Let the artist therefore keep to himself with his labor-pains; we would discover ghastly things if with every work we could see all the way to the bottom of its origin (I, 83).[20]

If one thinks about this "principle," one can well imagine that the communication of so very a "personal" program for the *Symphonie fantastique* must have veritably seemed like exhibitionism to Schumann.

It is clear, then, that Schumann had several reservations about program music of the Berliozan sort. That does not mean, however, that he was a categorical opponent of every kind of program music. His article of 1843, "Sinfonien für Orchester" – in which he also discusses Ludwig Spohr's program symphony *Irdisches und Göttliches im Menschenleben* (Things Earthly and Divine in Human Life) – proves that he thought quite tolerantly about the controversial subject of program music. Though he admits to "having a prejudice against this kind of production," he qualifies it by stressing that what counts in this kind of music, too, is the result, and that the latter depends on whether the composer is a master (like Spohr) or a novice (II, 129). Already in 1835, Schumann had declared that the decisive criterion for the evaluation of a program-bound composition was "whether the music as such, without text and explanation, amounts to something" (I, 85). In 1843, as we have already noted, he formulated this principle with these words: "Before everything else, let me hear whether you have made beautiful music, then your program, too, shall be pleasing to me" (II, 129).

To sort out the principles of Schumann's musical "poetics," one also has to critically compare and assess his numerous statements about the point and appropriateness of titles. Confessedly, the initial result of such an assessment is discouraging. Many of the statements seem to contradict each other, so that doubts arise whether they will be at all reducible to a common denominator. Upon closer inspection, however, one will recognize

---

20 Schumann made a similar remark 15 years later in a conversation with Wilhelm Joseph von Wasielewski, explaining the deletion of the original title of the fourth movement of the *Rheinish Symphony* by saying: "One does not have to show people one's heart, a general impression of the work of art is better for them; at least they don't make wrong-headed comparisons then." (W. J. von Wasielewski, *Robert Schumann. Eine Biographie*, 3rd ed. [Bonn, 1880], 269.

that a good many of the contradictions are apparent ones only, and that Schumann's views on this question are steadier than they seem to be.

In many instances, Schumann emphasizes that he regards titles as not only admissible but downright required, as when it is a matter of preventing a "patent misconception of the character" of a piece, when pieces express "secret states of mind," where "a hint in words from the composer can led to a quicker understanding" (II, 24), and also when it seems necessary "to come to the aid of the listener's imagination by means of such intimations" (II, 104).

Schumann also was of the opinion that many of his contemporaries had wrong ideas about the function of titles and misused the latter, either because they erroneously believed that a musical work absolutely required a heading or an interesting title would guarantee the quality of the composition, or else by adding a title to already completed compositions that did not actually fit them. Schumann does not miss any opportunity in his reviews to make chiding remarks whenever he seemed to have come upon such notions. Thus in 1842, he wrote in a review of a work by Julius Schapler:

> It always remains a not very good sign for a piece of music if it *needs* a title; it then certainly did not well up from inner depths but was prompted only by some external intervention. Who would deny that our art can express a great any things, can even trace the course of an event in its own way; but those who want to determine the effect and worth of a piece produced in this way have an easy test available: they only need to strike out the titles (II, 112/113).

And in 1839, he observed about Etudes by Bernhard Eduard Philipp (I 435):

> What would be so strange if good friends sat together, the composer played for them and the latter suddenly, as if hit by a ray of light, exclaimed: "Couldn't one give a suitable heading to this or that piece, and wouldn't the opus gain indescribably thereby?" and the composer rejoices and titles the respective pieces with large letters. The present titles, too, are probably not derivable from any deeper reason, the music was there before the title and fulfills in a cursory way what the latter intimates (I, 435).

Schumann's statements about the purpose and appropriateness of titles are thus not contradictory, but rather indicate a differentiated thinking. Titles that in his view were justified by the music he regarded as allowable or even requisite. A few of his utterances, however, suggest that at times he had misgivings of a fundamental sort, fearing that titles hamper the listeners' imagination after all, and he sometimes let himself be guided by the thought that the educated music lover did not need any titles, since he could be trusted with guessing and understanding the composer's intention also without them! From this reflection springs the aphorism:

> Your saying, Florestan, that you love the Pastoral and the Heroic Symphony less because Beethoven himself so labeled them and thereby imposed barriers upon the imagination seems to me to be based on a just feeling. But if you ask me why, I would hardly know how to answer (I, 28).

And in the review of the *Symphonie fantastique*, we read explicitly:

> In a word, the tender-minded German, ill-disposed toward all personality, does not want to be led in his thinking so rudely;[21] even in the Pastoral Symphony, it offended him that Beethoven did not trust him to divine its character without his help (I, 83).[22]

Substantial insights into Schumann's mode of creation are conveyed finally also by his remarks about reviews of some of his works by Ludwig Rellstab. His reactions to Rellstab's discussions of the *Papillons* and the *Kinderszenen* are particularly instructive. On April 19, 1832, Schumann had sketched the "program" of the *Papillons* for Rellstab.

> Less for the editor of the *Iris* than for the poet and soulmate of Jean Paul, I take the liberty of adding some words to the *Papillons* about their origin, since the thread that is supposed to tie them together is hardly visible. You, dear sir, will remember the final scene in the *Flegeljahre* – dance of masks – Walt – Vult – masks – Wina – Vult's dancing – the exchange of masks – confessions – ire – revelations – hurrying off – concluding dream and then the departing brother.[23]

Rellstab's review of the *Papillons* is written as a coded response to Schumann's letter and debates the justification of program music. Rellstab criticizes, albeit in covert allusions, that Schumann had hidden so many subjective elements in his work that the composition would remain

---

21 This sentence contains a covert allusion to Rellstab's review of *Papillons*, which Schumann initially misunderstood. For detail, see below.

22 The objection that titles and programs restrict the imagination of the listener was a standard argument of the opponents of program music. See the remarks by Liszt in GS, 4:63/64.

23 *Jugendbriefe*, 167.

incomprehensible without a *key*, and that even with a key one could comprehend it "only externally." He therefore postulates:

> A work of art must be understandable, not via a foreign something, but independently, fully, by itself alone; its soul must live within it, not outside, otherwise it is no more than a corpse on a bier, whose soul dwells already above the stars.[24]

This statement signifies basically a rejection of any heteronomy aesthetics in music: Rellstab disowns not only esoteric program music but program music as such. (Yet it was he who coined the name *Mondscheinsonate*, "Moonlight Sonata," for Beethoven's op. 27/2!)

Schumann, however, after a first reading of the review, is likely not to have caught the "hardcore" of Rellstab's objections. For a diary entry of May 30, 1832, indicates that he thought at first, erroneously, that Rellstab was asking for more precise programmatic data.

> Then I read [the review]. The idea for a second issue of *Papillons* had been going round in my head all day anyway. Now I discovered something about "organic work of art" – about misunderstanding and "riddles of a thousand solutions." But that's the German for you: I gave him something to guess about Jean Paul and about the individual scenes, but he promptly demands to *hear* in black and white where Vult curses, how he curses – and where Jacobine is off to."[25]

During the next several days, Schumann did not enter anything about Rellstab in his diary. Yet we can assume that Rellstab's critique provided an impetus for renewed basic reflections about issues of musical creation. For it is notable in his diary entries that in the summer of 1832 he gave time and again thought to the potential of music to evoke images and, above all, about the possibility of an "opera without text,"[26] Several of these reflections entered into a letter he wrote to Rellstab on December 7, 1832. There he replied to the latter's strictures with counter-questions: "Only the 'beautiful corpse" grieved me. Is the song really one? And why shouldn't there be an opera without text? And what would ever be created whose

---

24 *Iris im Gebiete der Tonkunst*, no. 21 (May 25, 1832), 82. Schumann copied this and other reviews of Rellstab into the end of his second Leipzig "Lebensbuch," "for improvement" (!). See *Tagebücher*, 424 ff.

25 *Tagebücher*, 401.

26 Ibid., 410–413,

ground – conscious or unconscious to the authors – was not an objective [sic] one?"[27]

More vehement was Schumann's reaction in 1839 to Rellstab's review of the *Kinderscenen*, especially to his disparaging remarks about the titles of the pieces. He used the occasion of reviewing some piano etudes for a retort, reproaching Rellstab with inconsistency in judgment: in Henselt he approved of titles, "in others not, but without reasons" (I, 435; II, 429). To Heinrich Dorn, meanwhile, Schumann wrote point-blank on September 5, 1839, that Rellstab misconceived his mode of creation and totally misunderstood his intentions:

> But I have hardly encountered anything clumsier and more narrow-minded than what Rellstab has written about my *Kinderscenen*. He seems to think I set a screaming child before me and pick my notes accordingly. The opposite is the case. I do not deny that some children's heads were in my mind in composing; but the titles, of course, came about later and are really nothing but more refined cues for performance and interpretation. Rellstab, though, truly at times does not see far beyond the ABC and wants only chords.[28]

If we review the facts, observations and preliminary results presented, it appears that the principles of Schumann's musical "poetics" can be reduced to four points:

1. Schumann believed that music could and should express extra-musical material. In composing, he let himself be inspired by literary impressions, associated literary and visual with musical elements, was fascinated by the idea of an "opera without text,[29] and had had personal experiences of mental images appearing to him during composition and influencing the compositional process. But he was also of the opinion that the instrumental composer should not begin his work with the fixed intention of transmuting a prefabricated "program" into music.

---

27 *Jugendbriefe*, 195.

28 *Briefe. Neue Folge*, 147. On the relations between Schumann and Rellstab, see the remarks by Kreisig in GS, 2:450–4453.

29 As late as 1845, Schumann played with the idea of composing Goethe's *Hermann und Dorothea* as a "singspiel merely with piano"! See Boetticher, *Schumann*, 317n.8. It is incidentally worth noting that Wagner in *The Art Work of the Future*, lists, besides symphoniens, masses, oratorios and songs without words, also "operas without text" as a separate genre (GS, 3:101).

Such a procedure offended against his maxim that artistic creation was unconscious and unaccountable.[30]

2. Fundamental features of Schumann's instrumental composing are the striving for the characteristic and the "poetic," which to Schumann meant the "non-mechanical," the Romantic, the "special," the "rare " and "secret," the imaginative and fantastic, the new and original, the dreamlike. Particularly for understanding instrumental works whose subject was the "special," he regarded headings as requisite;[31] accordingly, he furnished numerous of his works with characterizing titles. But Schumann condemned the misuse many of his contemporaries made of titles and demanded that they should be appropriate to the "content" of the music and had "welled from the inner depths" (II, 112).[32]

3. Schumann let himself be guided by the conviction that even the characteristic and "poetic" music, which he championed, was to be judged and appraised primarily *as* music. Time and again he cautioned against the misconception that a title – as an indication of the extra-musical "content" of a composition – vouched in any way for the quality and beauty of the music, postulating that "The main thing is always whether

---

30 Jean Paul, *Vorschule der Ästhetik, III* §13: "The most powerful element in the poet, that which breathes the good and the evil soul into his works, is precisely the unconscious." Cf with this the following diary entries of Schumann: "The dark part of the imagination or its unconscious remains its poesy" (7/13/1831), and Florestan says that the great genius, too, had a model, from which it worked unconsciously" (8/8/1831). Quoted from Eismann, *Tagebücher*, 350, 359. Cf. also Schumann's essay "Charakteristik derTonarten" (1835): "The process by which the composer chooses this or that basic key for expressing his feelings is inexplicable like the working of genius itself, who simultaneously with the idea also presents the form, the vessel that contains the idea securely" (GS, 1:106).

31 It is noteworthy in this connection that as early as 1815, E. T. A. Hoffmann expressed the view in the first (and only) of his "Briefe über die Tonkunst in Berlin," that music should be concerned with the "expression of the individual" (*Schriften zur Musik*, 283).

32 Surprisingly, Liszt made similar demands. In his Berlioz article, he warned composers of the "misuse" that "was possible" with programs, and reminded his readers "that programs or titles can be justified only if they are a poetic necessity, an inseparable part of the whole and indispensable to its being understood" (GS, 4:27/28). The statement is formulated in such a way that one has to think its agreement with Schumann is not merely coincidental!

the music, without text and explanation, amounts to something in itself, and above all, whether spirit dwells in it" (I, 85). He advised composers who wished to test the value of externally inspired works to make a trial by striking the titles (II, 112/13).

4. Schumann, as we have shown, regarded titles as requisite but voiced objections to detailed programs. His verdict was evidently prompted by several considerations: the fear that detailed programs would leave the listener's imagination no latitude for free play; the notion that the artist had the right and the obligation to conceal occasion and process of his creations from the public; and the experience that content explanations are frequently misunderstood.

From what has been set forth, it appears that the difference between Schumann's "poetically" inspired instrumental work and program music is actually much smaller than commonly assumed. Many of Schumann's works are based on "inner" programs that Schumann, in accordance with his principles, suppressed or encrypted. The number of Schumann compositions that can be ranked as esoteric program music is apt to be much larger than has been suspected.

XII. Autobiographic Elements in Schumann's Music

That Schumann's early piano music is to a high degree autobiographical will, after what has been said, no longer come as a surprise. Many pieces are personal in character and owe their origin to personal experiences. The subject is frequently Schumann's relation to, and passionate love for, Clara Wieck. Many works have that love as their theme and express in music things experienced and longed for, fears, hopes, expectations, visions, dreams and fantasies.

We have already mentioned Schumann's letter to his former teacher Heinrich Dorn. On September 5, 1839, he wrote to him:

> Surely much of the struggle Clara cost me may be embodied in my music and also perceived by you. The concerto, the sonata, the Davidsbündlertänze, the Kreisleriana and the Novelletten she prompted almost single-handedly.[1]

The five works Schumann cites here originated essentially during the years 1836 to 1838 – a time of extraordinary mental distress. The "concerto" is the F-Minor Sonata op. 14, known to have been conceived as a concerto without orchestra. The "sonata" is he Sonata in G Minor op. 22, completed only in 1839. All five of these works, as well as the Fantasy op.17, composed already in 1836, were written for Clara. She is the addressee, although all are officially dedicated to other people.

Naturally, Schumann also comes to speak repeatedly of these works in his letters to Clara. He called the first movement of the *Fantasy* op. 17 "a deep lament about you."[2] The F-Minor Sonata he described as "one long cry of my heart for you."[3] Of the *Kreisleriana* he remarked that Clara would find herself in them. In nearly all of the works mentioned, Clara is

---

1 *Briefe. Neue Folge* (1886), 146 f.
2 Schumann to Clara, March 19, 1838, Clara and Robert Schumann, *Briefwechsel. Kritische Gesamtausgabe*, ed. Eva Weissweiler, 2 vols. (Basel/Franklfurt a.M., 1984, 1987), 1:126.
3 Schumann to Clara, February 12, 1838. *Briefwechsel*, 1:104.

present in the form of quotations from her compositions – quotations of profound symbolic significance.

The story of Schumann's passionate love for Clara, his relation to her father Friedrich Wieck, the vehement altercations with him – all this is too familiar to need rehearsing.[4] It may be less well-known that long separations from Clara imposed upon Schumann had enormous impacts on his psychic life as well as on his creative work. In October of 1837, Clara, accompanied by her father, embarked upon her very successful trip to Vienna, from which she returned only in May of 1838. Schumann's diaries reveal how much his thoughts circled about the distant beloved during this time, a time in which the *Novelletten* and the *Kreisleriana* came into being: she wholly dominated his thinking and feeling.[5] Characteristically, he was especially receptive during this time of separation and trial to great works of music and literature in which lovers have to overcome a critical situation. He evidently paralleled his own predicament with the situation of famous lovers, whose fate could move him to tears. Thus he identified with Beethoven's Florestan, with Goethe's Egmont, with Leander of the ancient Greek legend. Clara to him was Beethoven's Leonore. Goethe's Clärchen (!) and Suleika, and the Hero of the ancient legend. These circumstances are of considerable significance also for the interpretation of his early piano music.

Schumann's music is special also inasmuch as it closely mirrors his complex personality. This should not be taken only in the sense of the Romantic theory of art, according to which music is nothing other than the language of the heart and the soul.[6] What is meant, rather, is that his music resembles himself. Clara tellingly saw musical portraits of his nature in several of his compositions. Thus she observed about the G- Minor Sonata: "I love it as I love you. Your entire being is so clearly expressed in it."[7]

---

4 Nancy B. Reich, *Clara Schumann. Romantik als Schicksal. Eine Biographie* (Reinbek, 1993).
5 Robert Schumann, *Tagebücher*, ed. Gerd Niehaus, 3 vols (Leipzig, 1987), 2: 40 ff.
6 Schumann to Clara, April 13, 1838 (*Briefwechsel*, 1:138): "My music now strikes even me as so simply wondrously intertwined, in all its simplicity, all its intertwinings, so fully spoken from the heart, and it has that effect also on all for whom I play it, something I now like doing frequently."
7 Clara to Schumann, March 2, 1838. *Briefwechsel*, 1:108.

Schumann himself regarded the *Davidsbündlertänze* (David's League Dances) op. 6 as a kind of self-portrait. In this work he gave, seemingly for the first time, musical expression to the Romantic theme of the split personality. What is relevant here is not so much that the dances are "dedicated," as the title page of the autograph has it, to Walther von Goethe by "Florestan and Eusebius," but that Schumann precisely marked the respective contributions of the two fictive authors to the composition. Pieces by "Florestan" are signed Fl. in the first edition. Eusebius' contributions always have the monogram E. at the end. Joint contributions by both "authors" are marked Fl. and E.

Schumann himself felt his personality to be complex and self-contradictory. Highly sensitive, touchy, extremely irritable, endowed with an enormously active imagination, he was subject to extreme mood swings. As he once wrote to Heinrich Dorn, he saw in Florestan and Eusebius the two sides of his twofold nature.[8] He often complained of melancholy and depressive ill-humor, but he could also be cheerful and boisterous.[9] He could be "silly" on the one hand and "very serious" on the other, he once wrote to Clara.[10]

Among the many aspects his early piano music discloses, the communicative one is one of the most important. During the long period of separation from Clara, he felt the need to communicate, be in steady contact, with her. He had two means of doing so: writing letters and composing. His music was a kind of heart-to-heart talk for him– a way of being close to the distant beloved. He said so himself. Nobody could debar him, he asserts in a letter to Clara, from writing twice as much to her as she to him. "Most of all I want to do it with music – for that is, after all, the friendly messenger who best delivers what is written within." And in another letter we read: Oddly enough, however, when I write you as much as I do now, I can't compose: then you receive the music."[11] Undoubtedly, Schumann's enormous productivity in the years 1836 to 1849, is also rooted in this situation.

Another important aspect of his early piano music is the narrative one. From 1831 on, he lived for some time in Friedrich Wieck's house, He would entertain the twelve-year-old Clara with stories and stir her imagination. He challenged

8   *Briefe. Neue Folge*, 66.
9   *Briefwechsel*, 1:142.
10 Ibid., 146.
11 Schumann to Clara on Easter Monday 1838. *Briefwechsel*, 1:149 f.

her with riddles and charades and told her Arabian fairytales, doppelganger stories, penny dreadfuls and ghost stories.[12] Storytelling remained an essential form of communication in his dealings with Clara also in later years.[13]

There are clear indications that Schumann conceived several of his piano compositions as musical narratives. In a list of his works in the sketchbook Wiede II fol. 10 recto, he called some of his pieces "little stories."[14] As is well-known, he praised Franz Schubert's "Great" Symphony in C Major, which he had discovered in Vienna, for its "novelistic" character,[15] and found the literary genre of the novella to be especially appealing to him. In a letter to Clara he explained the coinage *Novelletten* to be an allusion to the British singer Clara (!) Novello. But the title of opus 21 is ambiguous and also means something like little novellas. Not only the *Novelletten* but also the *Kreisleriana* can be described as such.

Schumann's intention of telling stories musically becomes transparent also in the titles of some of his pieces. Thus the sixth of the *Phantasiestücke* op. 12 is entitled "Fable," and it is rather striking that the cantabile motto with which the piece begins and ends also forms the epilogue of the second *kreislerianum*. No less telling are the frequent recitative passages in the piano music. They all have in common the character of speaking, of narration. We might just recall the last of the *Kinderszenen* ("The Poet Speaks") and the fourth *kreislerianum*.

The *Phantasiestücke* op. 12, written in early July of 1837 – thus during the long separation from Clara[16] – have without exception quasi-poetical titles. At least two of these pieces, *In der Nacht* (At Night) and *Das Ende vom Lied* (literally The End of the Song, but also The End, or Upshot, of the Matter) appear to be related to Clara. Of all the pieces in this series, Schumann loved the night piece most. On April 21, 1838, he wrote about it to Clara:

I just had a letter from Krägen[17] – he tells me many lovely things about the Phantasiestücke and regularly enthuses in his way in them – the "Night" was

---

12 Schumann to Clara, January 11, 1832. *Briefwechsel*, 1:3.

13 See *Briefwechsel*, 2:558.

14 Facsimile in Wolfgang Boetticher, *Robert Schumanns Klavierwerke*, Part I, Plate 15.

15 Robert Schumann, GS, 1:464.

16 *Tagebücher*, 2:34.

17 Karl Philipp Krägen (1797–1879), composer and piano teacher, was a civil servant at the Dresden court and a friend of Schumann's.

"great and beautiful," he writes, and his favorite; mine nearly also. Later, after it was finished, I found the story of "Hero and Leander" in it. You know it surely. Leander swims every night across the sea to his beloved, who waits on the lighthouse, showing him the way with a burning torch. It is a beautiful old Romantic legend. When I play the "Night," I can't forget this image – first how he plunges into the sea – she calls – he answers – he happily through the waves to the shore – now the cantilena where they lie in each other's arms – then when he has to leave again but cannot part from her – until the night shrouds everything in darkness once more – Of course I imagine Hero exactly like you, and if you sat on a lighthouse, I would also still learn to swim. Tell me, won't you, if the image fits the music for you as well.[18]

The passage is instructive in several respects. For one thing, it helps us to realize that Schumann loved to comment poetically on his music. For another, it lets us conclude that he projected his own situation onto the story of Hero and Leander – the painful consciousness of being separated from his beloved and the vision of the longed-for union. His associations with sea and waves can also be explained from the billowing motion of the music at the beginning and the end of this passionate piece.

In der Nacht

Schumann gave hermeneutic explanations also for the last of the *Phantasiestücke*, "Ende vom Lied." They deserve all the more attention as

---

18 *Briefwechsel*, 1:154.

extra-musical associations here closely accompanied the compositional process. On March 4, 1838, Clara had conveyed her impressions of the pieces to him and had written about the last piece: "The End of the Song is the loveliest that any song has ever come to; in some places it reminds me vividly of Zumsteeg."[19] To this, Schumann replied on March 19: "I have to commend you all the more for recalling Zumsteeg together with the "End of the Song" – it is true, I was thinking at the time, well, in the end everything resolves itself into a merry wedding after all – but finally the pain for you came back in again, and so its sounds like wedding and funeral bells one with the other."[20]

The conclusion of the piece is in fact unusual and forms a notable contrast to the first three parts, which are quite positive in their nuances. Thus the song-like first part, to be recited "good-humoredly" and written in F Major, commences forcefully and rises all the way to *fortissimo*. The middle part in B-flat Major strikes up a very sprightly tone, and the third is a da capo of the first. But the following coda has surprises in store: it is located in the *piano*, *pianissimo* and *piu pianissimo* sphere and commences with bell-like sounds; it dies away in the low bass region.

A similar contrast also characterizes the seventh of the *Kreisleriana* op. 16 of May 1838. The two parts of which the piece is composed contrast with each other as brusquely as can be imagined. While the first part in C minor has a stormy character and is to be played very fast, the second, to be performed more slowly, sounds like a restrained coda; it begins in B-flat Major and closes with a fourth-six chord in E-flat Major, with chorale-like harmonies being particularly prominent. There can be no doubt that this uncommon conclusion conceals some poetic intention.

---

19 Ibid., 112. Johann Rudolf Zumsteeg (1760–1802), composer of operas, melodramas and ballads.
20 *Briefwechsel*, 1:121.

In contrast to the *Phantasiestücke* op. 12, neither the *Novelletten* nor the *Kreisleriana* have individual poetic titles. Even so, it unequivocally appears from Schumann's letters to Clara that both works are autobiographically conceived. Let us focus on the *Novelletten*. On February 6, 1838, Schumann wrote to Clara about them: "So I have also composed a ghastly amount for you in the last three weeks – facetious stuff, Egmont stories, family scenes with fathers, a wedding, in short, extremely amiable things – and the whole called *Novelletten*, because your name is Clara [like Clara Novello's] and Wiecketten doesn't sound good enough. But I always had the feeling that I had not yet hit the right thing in the music, had not yet found what I was looking for – And then on Saturday the postillion walked in, and he had it, and my eyes were opened: "that's what I had been searching for, your letter, your lovely, precious, heart-felt letter."[21]

---

21 Ibid., 90.

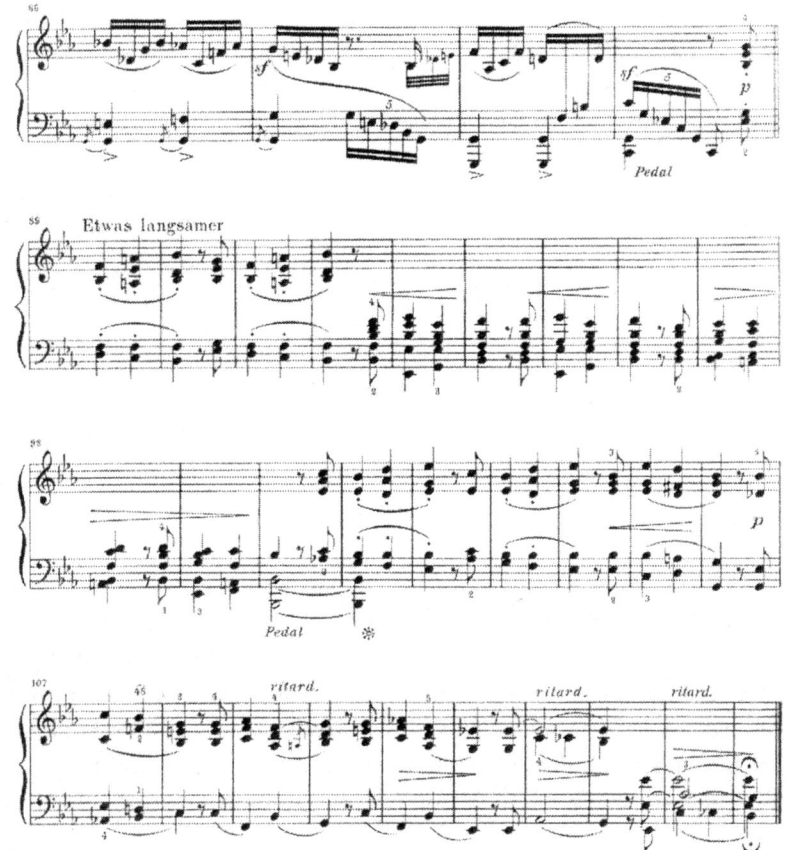

Explanations p. 182

Many of Schumann's allusions in this letter can be decoded. Thus his phrase "Egmontgeschichten" refers to his identification with the hero of Goethe's *Egmont* –a work he reread with great emotion after having heard Beethoven's music to the drama.[22] The formulation "family scenes with fathers" alludes to the altercations with Friedrich Wieck. But the "wedding" Schumann had in mind was his vision of a union with his beloved. If one

---

22 Cf. Hans Joachim Köhler, "Die Stichvorlagen zum Erstdruck von Opus 21 – Assoziationen zu Schumanns Novelletten," in *Schumann-Studien*, 3/4 (Cologne, 1994), 75–94; p. 83.

takes into account his entries in his diaries,[23] it is not difficult to figure out that the fifth *novellette* with the heading "Resounding and Festive," a piece having noticeable polonaise-like traits, evokes this nuptial scene.

A special matter is the second *novellette*. As is apparent from Schumann's index of his letters, he had originally thought of calling the two parts of the piece *Sarazene* and *Suleika*.[24] The copy he sent with a hand-written dedication to Franz Liszt on April 20, 1838, is headed *Sarazene*. Upon

---

23 *Tagebücher*, 2:50–53.
24 Ibid., n.189 and p. 477.

publication of the *Novelletten*, however, he suppressed both titles (as well as the title *Macbeth* for the intermezzo of the third number). Evidently he was not willing to divulge the cryptic meaning of the music. The secreted titles *Sarazene* and *Suleika* refer to Goethe's *Westöstliche Divan*, particularly to the book *Suleika*, from which Schumann copied two poems for Clara.[25] It needs little argument to infer that by the two names *Sarazene* and *Suleika* he meant himself and Clara. The contrast between the very fast bravura of the main part and the throughout tenderly melodious intermezzo is a stark one, yet the two parts felicitously join together to form a whole.

The final *novellette* is artfully composed of several pieces. Clara is present in it at several points in the form of the opening melody of her Nocturne in F Major – a piece for which Schumann had a special predilection.[26] Schumann quotes the theme in the middle of the second trio, marking it *Stimme aus der Ferne* (Voice from far away). Then he repeats it in embellished and differently harmonized form, and much later he works it in a third time. These quotations are intended to be evocative – as invocations of the distant beloved, who often appeared in Schumann's dreams and was repeatedly the object of hallucinations.

---

25 *Briefwechsel*, 1:152 f.
26 Ibid., 100.

My principal thesis asserted that a large portion of Robert Schumann's early piano music is autobiographical in nature. The examples adduced will have made clear how that was meant. Many pieces must be viewed against the background of Schumann's passionate relationship with Clara. Several compositions feel like monologues, while others have the character of lyrical communings with the beloved.

XIII. Berlioz' Conception of the "Instrumental Drama"

> "Le plan du drame instrumental, privé du secours de la parole,
> a besoin d'être exposé d'avance." Berlioz (1830)[1]

> "L'un veut faire de la symphonie un drame; l'autre prétend faire
> du drame un symphonie." Tierson on Wagner and Berlioz[2]

A close study of Berlioz' and Liszt's program music inevitably raises the question as to the specific difference between their poetico-musical ideas. What conceptions did Berlioz and Liszt have of program music, and how did they put them into practice?

Richard Wagner seems to have been the first to attempt an answer to these questions. In his essay "On Franz Liszt's Symphonic Poems" of 1857, he set forth the thesis that the "problem" of program music was how to treat the "poetic object" in such a way that the compositions would attain a musical form that was "grasped quickly" and "readily understandable"; and he did not hide the fact that he thought Liszt's "solution" to this problem more convincing than Berlioz'. Berlioz' "great mistake" in the love scene of his dramatic symphony *Roméo et Juliette* was that he clung to the motifs of the balcony scene and their disposition in Shakespeare, instead of sublimating "everything in them according to its concrete content of feeling" and thus presenting the scene "in very concrete ideal form" also musically. The result of this failure was, Wagner argued, that the listener lost the "musical thread." Liszt, on the other hand, succeeded in his symphonic poems in sublimating the poetic object in such a way that it could present itself to the listener's feelings "clearly, distinctly, densely and unmistakably"; the musical conception, Wagner felt, expressed itself with astonishing succinctness.

Wagner's arguments spring from his belief that drama and music constitute two entirely different realms in both nature and effect. Wagner took the

---

1 *Avertissement* to the program of the *Symphonie fantastique*, version of May 21, 1830. See n. 12, below.
2 Julien Tiersot, *Hector Berlioz et la société de son temps* (Paris, 1904), 303.

view "that in order to express the same idea, the dramatist has to resort to altogether different means than the musician." For the dramatist

> is much closer to common life and will be understood only if he presents his idea to us in an action that in its multifariously composed elements resembles an event in this life in such a way that every spectator thinks he is experiencing it for himself as well. The musician, by contrast, disregards the process of common life altogether, entirely omits its coincidences and particulars, and instead sublimates everything in them according to its concrete emotional content, which can be represented distinctly, of course, only in music.

Berlioz, in Wagner's view, would thus have had to deviate from his dramatic model in order to be able to create a musical work that was "comprehensible in and by itself."[3]

Wagner's writings, theories, theses and judgments had a colossal effect on musical journalism after his death. Even so one cannot but be struck by the vast extent to which his above remarks about Berlioz and Liszt have influenced subsequent views of the relation between the two "program musicians." Thus Liszt was regarded by many critics until 1950 – and perhaps is even today – as a more sterling musician than Berlioz. Hugo Riemann, for example observed in 1901 that Liszt's compositions revealed "a distinctly superior ability compared with Berlioz'," that "a victorious musical logic" pervaded "even those compositions of Liszt that are most obviously ruled by the old formal principles," and that Liszt never lost the thread, "as Berlioz so often did."[4] Fritz Volbach expressly took over Wagner's views in 1909.[5] Joseph Heinrichs thought in 1929 that he could reduce Berlioz' and Liszt's contrary art-theoretical conceptions to the duality of naturalism and idealism.[6] And Peter Raabe in 1931 saw the "fundamental difference" between Berlioz' and Liszt's manner in the fact "that Berlioz in composing was *continuously* influenced by the external impressions that had first prompted him to embark upon his task, whereas Liszt, though he also let

---

3   Richard Wagner, "Über Franz Liszts symphonische Dichtungen" (1857), GS, 5:182–198; pp. 193–195.
4   Hugo Riemann, *Geschichte der Musik seit Beethoven (1800–1900)* (Berlin/ Stuttgart, 1901), 365/366.
5   Fritz Volbach, *Die deutsche Musik im neunzehnten Jahrhundert* (Kempten/ Munich, 1909), 135–137.
6   Joseph Heinrichs, *Über den Sinn der Lisztschen Programmusik* (1929), 21–23.

himself be put into the creative mood by images and poems, would rather depart abruptly from his model than tolerate letting his musical feeling be forced in any way."[7]

An examination of the question to what extent the views cited here help to explain the supposed "fundamental difference" between Berlioz and Liszt must be reserved for a separate study. Another, and arguably more important, aspect of the matter deserves our attention here. I am referring to the fact that the literary genres Berlioz and Liszt had in mind for their programmatic conceptions were entirely different ones. Berlioz's point of departure was the drama, whereas Liszt's was the epic along with the lyric! It is imperative to subject these different conceptions to a careful scrutiny.

Roméo et Juliette, Berlioz' *symphonie avec choeurs* of 1839, is the first dramatic symphony of "world literature."[8] For the first time in the history of the symphony an attempt was made in this work to express a drama – or, more exactly, the emotional content of several scenes in a drama – symphonically. Berlioz must have been aware from the beginning that for his attempt to succeed a program, that is, a text explaining the scenic events, would not be suffice and therefore decided to include choruses and soloists whose task would be by means of sung and recited words to prepare the "mind" of the listener for the symphonically "interpreted" scenes from Shakespeare's tragedy. In a preface to the piano score of 1859, Berlioz wanted it to be clearly understood that although voices were frequently used, his work was neither a concert opera nor a cantata, but a symphony with choruses.

> If singing is present almost from the beginning [he explained], it is in order to prepare the listener for the dramatic scenes, whose feelings and passions are to be expressed by the orchestra; and also in order to introduce the choral masses, whose unheralded entrance might have damaged the unity of the work, more gradually within the musical development.[9]

---

7 Peter Raabe, *Liszts Schaffen*, 89.

8 On the genesis of *Roméo et Juliette*, see Jacques Barzun, *Berlioz and the Romantic Century*, 2 vols., 3rd ed. (New York/London, 1969; 1st ed. 1950), 1:309–319, and my remarks in *Mahler and the Symphony*, 14.

9 The text of the preface is reprinted in the Berlioz edition, 73 f. The piano score of *Roméo et Juliette* appeared in 1859 in Paris and, with French and German text, at Rieter-Biedermann in Winterthur.

Only the very last scene of the symphony, he added, the scene of reconciliation between the two families, appertained to opera or oratorio.

Essential for a deeper understanding of the work's peculiar nature is also Berlioz's comment that the dialogues and "duets" between Romeo and Juliet in the garden and graveyard scenes would not be sung but were entrusted to the orchestra, and this for three reasons. For one thing, his work was not an opera but a symphony. For another, duets had been composed for voice a thousand times already, "and by the greatest masters"; it therefore seemed both advisable and enticing to try a different mode of expression for a change. And thirdly, the sublimity of love in Shakespeare's tragedy had suggested a musical treatment that gave free play to the composer's imagination, something "the fixed meaning of sung words would not have permitted"; it had therefore seemed advisable to have recourse to the language of instrumental music, "a richer, more diverse, less determined language, and one incomparably more effective, especially in such a case, by its very indeterminacy."

It should not be necessary to emphasize that these elucidations of Berlioz' are of eminent significance. They not only give us insight into his intentions, but also help us to realize that Wagner's critique of *Roméo et Juliette* is at least partially unjust. Berlioz had certainly recognized the problem inherent in a "translation" of a dramatic story into symphonic music, and he dispensed with the "word" – that is to say, the faithful adoption of the scenic motifs of the drama – in the garden scene precisely because he believed that he could express the emotional content of the scene better by purely symphonic means.

It is now generally agreed that Berlioz' *Roméo et Juliette*, the first "dramatic symphony" of world literature, represents a milestone in the history of 19th-century symphonic music. Opinions are less unified about the work's relation to Berlioz' preceding symphonies, the *Symphonie fantastique* and the *Harold Symphony*. While the leading Berlioz biographer Jacques Barzun regards the first two symphonies as stepping-stones to the dramatic symphony,[10] Paul-Marie Masson thought in 1923 that the term *symphonie dramatique* also fit the earlier works, and that it was in fact a more exact

---

10 Barzun, *Berlioz*, 1:156/157, 247, 320 ff.

one than the common designation *symphonie à programme*. A *symphonie dramatique*, according to Masson, consists – in contrast to the overture – of several movements, which have titles and all refer to one and the same subject. One could therefore speak of a genuine sequence of episodes or scenes. Such a symphony did not just set the mood for a drama or for meditations about a drama, but took the place of the drama itself, thanks to the suggestive power of the orchestral language and to the detailed literary commentary attached.[11]

In thinking about the question whether and to what extent the *Symphonie fantastique* and the *Harold Symphony* belong to the genre of the dramatic symphony, one may find that Masson's observations do justice to at least one aspect of the matter, inasmuch as Berlioz himself regarded the *Symphonie fantastique* as an "instrumental drama" (*drame instrumental*). He called it that already in the first official program version, which appeared on May 21, 1830, in the Parisian paper *Le Figaro* (as an announcement of the planned but then cancelled premiere).

The text of its preamble reads:

> Le Compositeur a eu pour but de développer, dans ce qu'elles ont de musical, différentes situations de la vie d'un artiste. Le plan du drame instrumental, privé du secours de la parole, a besoin d'être exposé d'avance. Le programme suivant doit donc être considéré comme le texte parlé d'un Opéra, servant à amener des morceaux de musique, dont il motive le caractère et l'expression.[12]

---

11 Paul-Marie Masson, *Berlioz* (Les Maîtres de la musique (Paris 1923, 1930), 125 ff.

12 The very first version of the *Symphonie fantastique*'s program is contained in Berlioz' famous letter to his friend Humbert Ferrand of April 16, 1830. See Hector Berlioz, *Correspondance générale*, ed. Pierre Citron (Paris, 1972), 1:318–320. A second version was published in *Le Figaro* on May 21, 1830. The printed program versions diverge in detail. See Julien Tiersot *Berlioz*, 331, and Tiersot's series of articles "Berlioziana" in *Le Ménestrel*, January 3, 1904 to December 1, 1906, especially the articles in the edition of June 26, July 3 and 10, 1904. A first compilation of the various program versions can be found in Theodor Müller-Reuter, *Lexikon der deutschen Konzertliteratur* (Leipzig, 1909), 200–210. See also Edward T. Cone, *Hector Berlioz: Fantastic Symphony. An authoritative Score – Historical Background – Analysis – Views and Comments* (London, 1971), 18–35, and Wolfgang Dömling, "Die Symphonie fantastique und Berlioz' Auffassung von Programmusik," *Mf*, 28 (1975), 260–283. On the genesis and conception of the *Symphonie fantastique,* see also Julien Tiersot's

The *Symphonie fantastique* accordingly pertains to the dramatic genre. Berlioz explains it as a sui-generis drama, a "drama without text" or perhaps (to apply Schumann's terminology) an "opera without text." Since the "instrumental drama" lacked the support of a verbal text, Berlioz says, it was necessary to explain the layout of the drama in advance. The program fulfilled a similar function as the "spoken text of an opera, which introduces the musical sections and justifies their character and expression." Berlioz is evidently referring to the recitative – as also emerges from a long note he added as an additional explanation to one edition of the program. There he writes: "If the lines of this program were suited to being recited or sung between the movements of the symphony like the choruses of antique tragedy, their meaning would undoubtedly not have been so misunderstood."[13]

Ludwig Börne's judgment about the *Symphonie fantastique* indicates, incidentally, that at least some of the visitors to the famous premiere on December 5, 1830, understood Berlioz' intentions correctly. In his *Letters* from Paris (no. 16, dated December 12, 1830), he wrote: "A curious symphony, a dramatic one, in five acts, of course only instrumental music; but in order that one would understand it, [Berlioz] had a text explaining the action printed, as for an opera."[14] Note that Börne here calls the work expressly "a dramatic symphony in five acts!"

Berlioz' conception of the *Symphony fantastique* thus takes its bearings from musical drama,[15] i.e., the opera. Yet as original as the idea of an "instrumental drama" may seem, it was not unexampled. Ludwig Spohr's violin concerto *in modo di scena cantante* op. 47 (composed in 1816) had already appeared in 1820. In 1826 and 1827, Beethoven's last five string

---

important essay "The Berlioz of the Fantastic Symphony," *MQ*, 19 (1933), 303–317.

13 "*Si les quelques lignes de ce programme eussent été de nature à pouvoir être récitées ou chantées entre chacun des morceaux de la symphonie, comme les choeurs des tragédies antiques, sans doute on ne fût pas mépris de la sorte sur le sens qu'elles contiennent.*" Quoted from Masson, *Berlioz* (1930), 145n.1

14 Quoted from Kreisig, "Anmerkungen zu Schumann,"*GS*, 2:381.

15 Note that in his memoirs, too, Berlioz speaks of both the *Symphonie fantastique* and the supplementary "monodrame" *Lelio ou Le retour à la vie* as of a "musical drama": "*Le sujet du drame musical n'est autre, on le sait, que l'histoire de mon amour pour miss Smithson, de mes angoisses, de mes rêves douloureux ...*" See *Memoires de Hector Berlioz* (Paris, 1870), 184.

quartets came out, which Berlioz admired,[16] and which exhibit a plethora of vocal and programmatic traits – one may think of the *cavatina*, of the *Heilige Dankgesang eines Genesenen* and the recitative passages in nearly all of the quartets.[17] In the summer of 1832, Schumann, as we have shown, was fascinated by the idea of an "opera without text,"[18] and in the same year, Mendelssohn's *Songs without Words* appeared. As we can see, the thought of a renewal of instrumental music through assimilation to vocal music occupied a number of composers in the first third of the 19th century.

If we now ask wherein the "dramatic" element in the *Symphonie fantastique* consists, we need first to consider the subject of the work. A closer look at the famous program reveals impressions from the reading of several literary works. Berlioz himself referred to Chateaubriand's *René* and Goethe's *Faust* in his letter to Ferrand and in his memoirs. No less important will have been the impressions he received from De Quincey's *Confessions of an English Opium Eater* (Musset's French translation of the work had appeared in 1828) and from Victor Hugo's ballad no. XIV, "La Ronde du Sabbat" (1826).[19] Berlioz' "achievement" lies in having "converted" several "motifs" from these works into an original and personal program, which is designed in the manner of a scenario, and which, with all its fantastic, "depth-psychological" and dreamlike qualities, nevertheless exhibits a consistently progressive, single-minded "action." In dramaturgical terms, one could compare the first three numbers to a drama's exposition; the fourth movement would be the peripety and the fifth the catastrophe.

But of the symphony's music, too, it can be said that that it is dramatic and operatic. It is *dramatic* inasmuch as the last two movements constitute a heightening over the first three. It is *operatic* in that the five uncommonly distinctive movements, each having an unmistakable character, contrast

---

16 See Barzun, *Berlioz*, 1:99.

17 On Beethoven's "instrumental scenes," see my *Beethoven's Eroica*, appendix.

18 The assumption that Schumann might have heard of Berlioz' *drame instrumental* already in the summer of 1832 is not very likely. Liszt's piano score of the *Symphonie fantastique*, on which Schumann based his famous review, did not appear until 1834.

19 See J.-G. Prod'homme, "Berlioz, Musset and Thomas de Quincey, *MQ*, 32 (1946), 98–106; Barzun, *Berlioz*, 1:162–169; Nicholas Temperley, "The Symphonie fantastique and Its Program," *MQ*, 57 (1971), 593–608.

with each other to a degree that is nearly unparalleled in the symphonic tradition before Berlioz.[20] Even more significant is the fact that Berlioz also employs "musico-scenic" means, thereby evoking associations with actual scenes in the listener. Thus the *idée fixe*, the thought of the beloved, is "present" in all the movements, recurring repeatedly as a reminiscence motif. The *valse* of the second movement can be thought of as music for a ball scene even in a "fantastic" opera. The dialog of the two woodwinds at the start of the third movement, the *Scène aux champs*, suggests the presence of two imaginary shepherds. The "execution scene, in which the fourth movement (*Marche au supplice*) culminates, is "illustrated" musically with extreme realism. The last movement, finally, could be likened to a "fantastic" opera finale in which a great many personages appear on stage!

A number of critics have tried to explain Berlioz' striking predilection for theatrical effects in terms of a compensatory need. Since Berlioz, the born but hapless opera composer, was denied success in the musical theater, they argue, he transplanted the drama into the concert hall. Whether or not this explanatory attempt can do justice to one or more aspects of the matter, certain it is that Berlioz had a special gift for the "scenic" (several of his symphonic movements, in fact, bear the nomenclature *Scène*[21]) and was probably the first to introduce an abundance of stage-musical means and artistic tricks into the symphonic realm.[22] It is to such tricks that the ability of his music to evoke "spatial" sensations in the listener is due.[23]

Our investigation should have proved that there is in fact a close connection between Berlioz' *drame instrumental* and his *symphonie dramatique*. Except for the use of vocal parts in the latter, the difference between them is smaller than it would seem. Both have dramatic subjects, both are based on a "scenario." The scenario of the *Symphonie fantastique* is Berlioz'

---

20 Consider only the succession of keys: C Minor/ C Major, A minor/ A Major, F Major, G Minor/G Major, E Minor/C Major!

21 Cf. Rudolf Bockholdt, "Die Idée fixe der Phantastischen Symphonie," *AfMw*, 30 (1973), 190–207; p. 206.

22 See my *Mahler and the Symphony*, 44 f., 57 f., 86 f., 104 f., 124 f., 167, 237 f., 245, plates I-III, XXXIII, XXXV, XLIII.

23 On "spatiality" in Berlioz' music, see Edward C. Bass, "Musical Time and Space in Berlioz," *MR*, 30 (1969), 211–224., and remarks by R. Bockholdt in *AfMw*, 30 (1973), 204–207.

invention; the scenario for *Roméo et Juliette* he "arranged" after Shakespeare's drama.

We cannot conclude this discussion without noting that Berlioz' ideas of the *drame instrumental* and the *symphonie dramatique* had a strong impact on several composers during the second half of the 19th century (after the publication of Berlioz' symphonic works[24]). Especially in Russia they fell on fertile soil. Milij Balakirev, the theoretician of the Group of Five, picked up Berlioz' idea of the *instrumental drama* and passed it on to Tchaikovsky, who can be accounted one of the greatest composers of "instrumental dramas."[25]

---

24 The score of the *Symphonie fantastique* appeared in 1845/1846; the score of *Roméo et Juliette* came out only in 1857.
25 See Nikolai van der Pals, *Peter Tschaikowsky* (Potsdam, 1940), 35–37, 64/65; Constantin Floros, *Peter Tschaikowsky* (rowohls monographien), Reinbek bei Hamburg 2006, 117–121.

XIV. Liszt's Conception of the "Musical Epopee"

> "Pendant mon séjour en Hongrie, j'ai recueilli quantité de fragments à l'aide desquels on recomposerait assez bien *l'épopée musicale* de cet étrange pays, dont je me constitue le Rhapsode." Liszt (1846)[1]

As already intimated, Liszt's Berlioz treatise was conceived as a promotion of program music, not as a polemic against absolute music. Liszt's aim in publishing this treatise was to foster an understanding for program music's right to exist: to attack absolute music was not his intention. All the same, he made no secret of his belief that program music was the only timely and "progressive" species of instrumental music of the day.

We gain new perspectives for determining the specific differences between Berlioz' and Liszt's program music from the observation that they sought to realize the jointly desired "poetic solution to instrumental music" along different ways: whereas Berlioz had the "instrumental drama" in mind from the start, Liszt's conception of program music had been kindled by the idea of a "musical epopee" and an "instrumental lyricism."

In the Berlioz essay, Liszt, as we have shown, had explained in detail why he regarded the modern program symphony as a pendant to the "philosophical epopee" of Goethe, Byron and Mickiewicz. Instrumental music, in his view, was primarily the art of feelings; the nature of the "philosophic epopee" he perceived as the "narration of inner processes," by which he meant "mental states" (*Seelenzustände*), "affects," "passions." This kinship, he thought, justified the attempt to downright "fuse" instrumental music and "philosophic epopee," pure feeling and "inner processes" dressed in words. These reflections issued in the formulation:

> The sung word has ever fostered and fashioned a *connection* between music and literary or quasi-literary works. Our current endeavor, however, aims at an *amalgamation* of both, which promises to become a more intimate one than has hitherto been attained. More and more, the masterpieces of music incorporate the masterpieces of literature (IV, 58).

---

1 Liszt to the Countess d'Agoult on October 8, 1846. *Correspondance*, 2:368.

The crucial question is how this "amalgamation" of instrumental music and literature is to be effected. Liszt's statements indicate that he viewed the process as one of transformation: the composer lets himself be inspired by a literary work, a poem, a legend, a myth, endeavors to grasp the key concept (the "poetic idea") of the text and submits to its guidance in the act of composition. As an "alien content," the "poetic idea" determines the musical "content" and the form of the composition. The purpose of the program is to direct the attention of the listener in advance "to the poetic idea of the whole, to a particular point of it" (IV, 21). In a like sense, we read elsewhere that with the help of the program the composer indicates "the direction of his ideas and the point of view, from which he conceives his subject" (IV, 56/57).[2]

On the basis of these principles, it is possible, in theory as well as in practice, to bestow the "character" of any literary genre by "transubstantiation" upon instrumental music. As Liszt put it:

> The program has the ability to transmit the kinds of character to instrumental music that are virtually identical with the various poetic forms. It can give it the bearing of the ode, the dithyramb, the elegy, in short, of every type of lyrical poetry. And even after the instrumental music has long since expressed the unique moods of these diverse genres, it can gain new, undreamt-of advantages through a statement of the matter, from the approach of certain ideas, the elective affinity of certain figures, from the separation or connection, lining up or merging of certain poetic images and inferences (IV, 52).

We can see from these quotations that besides the "musical epopee" Liszt was thinking also of a novel "instrumental lyricism."[3]

---

2 Liszt similarly motivated the demand for programmatic explanations of compositions already in a letter to George Sand of January 1837. It was not useless, he wrote, "for a composer to indicate the spiritual outline of his work in a few lines and, without lapsing into petty explications and anxiously observed details, to express the *idea* that has served as the basis of his composition" (GS, 2:130).

3 The term *Instrumentallyrik* occurs, as far as we can tell, not in Liszt's writings but (for the first time?) in an essay by Hans von Bülow, published in 1856, on Wagner's *Faust* Overture. See Hans von Bülow, *Ausgewaählte Schriften 1850–1892* (Leipzig, 1911), section one, 203–231; p. 206. Bülow tries to explain that Wagner's work should not be called either a dramatic overture or a character portrait. It was rather an "atmospheric picture" (*Stimmungsbild*), which be-

Epic and lyric poetry were thus firmly built into the Lisztean concept of program music. Only drama had no place in it. If one inquires into the reasons for this conspicuous exclusion, one may detect that, from theoretical considerations as well as personal inclination, Liszt had principal misgivings about the stage, the scenic and the dramatic! For one thing, he was convinced that "in its own unique language," instrumental music could reproduce inner processes and characters but could not represent any action, which is, of course, the key element of drama (IV, 56). For another, he held that the "limited space" of the stage hindered the viewer from giving full scope to his imagination. In his review of Adolph Bernhard Marx's book, he speaks expressly of the "insufficient reality of the stage," dismisses stage props as "instruments too clumsy for the true reproduction of certain sublime scenes," and frankly confesses his preference for the very *Literaturdrama*, i. e., closet drama (GS V, 212–215), against which Wagner had fulminated a few years earlier in *Das Kunstwerk der Zukunft*.[4] Highly instructive as to Liszt's pronounced antipathy to the stage is also what his disciple Felix Weingartner has to tell. In his *Erinnerungen an Liszt*, he asserts that a sense for the dramatic was "not strongly developed" in Liszt and continues:

> When he visited an opera, he rarely looked at the stage; for the most part he read along in a full score or a piano score. He was indifferent to the scenic action. That also explains why he only very reluctantly permitted the theatrical performance of his *Heilige Elisabeth*, even though a poetic stage representation is advantageous to the effect of that work.[5]

If from the standpoint we have reached we look back at the artistic aims of Wagner and Berlioz, we can see that partly contrary positions clearly stand out. Whereas Berlioz had come forward as the composer of momentous dramatic symphonies and stage works, and Wagner's endeavors were devoted exclusively to the music drama as total work of art, Liszt foremost regarded the musical epic has his artistic domain, musical epic meaning to

---

longed to the "purely instrumental lyricism." On Bülow's essay, see Friedrich Rösch, *Musik-ästhetische Streitfragen* (Leipzig, 1897), 92–106.
4   Wagner, GS, 3:111–113.
5   Felix Weingartner, *Akkorde. Gesammelte Aufsätze* (Leipzig, 1912), 42–57; pp. 50/51.

him the oratorio[6] and the symphonic program music. In the 'fifties, he concentrated his creative efforts on the latter;[7] in the 'sixties, he turned to the "oratorical task." While Wagner condemned the closet drama and had a strong antipathy against the oratorio,[8] Liszt had a distaste for the stage, greatly prized *Literaturdramen*, and composed such major oratorios as *Die Legende von der heiligen Elisabeth* and *Christus*.

At this point we need to raise the crucial question how Liszt's theoretical thoughts about program music are related to his own creative works. Do his ideas about the "musical epopee" and "instrumental lyricism" offer a "key" to a better understanding of his symphonic works? We think the answer must be an unqualified yes. The following should be borne in mind:

Liszt composed no instrumental dramas and no dramatic symphonies in Berlioz's sense. There are no works of his that could set alongside the *Symphonie fantastique* or *Roméo et Juliette*. The poems and subjects that served as "models" for most of Liszt's symphonic poems belong generally to the epic or lyric genre. To be specific:

Liszt had a predilection for poems saturated with philosophical reflections. Outstanding examples are Victor Hugo's *Ce qu'on entend sur la montagne*, Lamartine's meditation *Les Préludes* and Schiller's *Die Ideale*. The subject of Hugo's poem, on which the Mountain Symphony is based, is the dualism of Nature and Humanity and concludes with the philosophic aporia why God contaminated the harmonic song of Nature with the clamor of the human race. The matter of the symphonic poem

---

6 In the review of Marx's book (GS, 5:214), he says expressly: "The character of the oratorio is distinctively epic: consequently, lyrical and dramatic elements can appear in it only as episodes."

7 Liszt's symphonic work, it is worth remarking, essentially "takes over" from Berlioz' symphonic oeuvre. Berlioz' last major symphonic work, the *Symphonie funèbre et triomphale*, dates from the year 1840. The *Marche funèbre pour la dernière scène d'Hamlet* was composed in 1848. Liszt's earliest symphonic works came about in the 1840s: the "Mountain Symphony" and the symphonic poem *Tasso*. See Peter Raabe, *Die Entstehungsgeschichte der ersten Orchesterwerke Liszts* (diss.) (Jena, 1916, Leipzig, 1916).

8 Typical are his disparaging remarks in *Das Kunstwerk der Zukunft*, where he speaks of "oratorios – those sexles operatic embryos"(GS, 3:101) and, another time, of the "unnatural monstrosity of the oratorio" (GS, 3:119).

Les Préludes is the reflection that in the final analysis it is death that determines the tenor of life, which is conceived as a series of preludes. The "poetic" theme of the symphonic poem *Die Ideale* is the relation of art and life, artist and ideal.

It is, moreover, profoundly indicative that several of Liszt's programs formulate ideas that clearly gesture toward the area of the "philosophic epopee." Thus Liszt wants the symphonic poem *Heroïde funèbre* to be understood as a kind of elegy about "pain," whose funeral banner "waves over all times and places." He identified the central idea of the symphonic poem *Tasso* (after Goethe and Byron) as the antithesis of suffering and triumph conceived as the fate of the artist. In the programmatic preface to this work, he writes that it is truly said of poets that although their life is often burdened with a curse, the blessing on their graves never fails. *Lamento e Trionfo*, a favorite idea of Liszt's, signifies therefore the belief in the posthumous victory of great individuals and ideas, the faith in the posthumous rehabilitation of the unappreciated and oppressed, and finally also the conviction that lofty conceptions will have an effect even after the death of their authors. Liszt similarly summarized the basic idea of his *Prometheus* in terms of an antithesis, that between *Malheur et Gloire*, misfortune and glory. In his preface to the work he writes he had tried to infuse his music with the feelings and sensations that, with the changing phases of the Prometheus myth, constitute its (or his) essential character, namely boldness, suffering, perseverance and deliverance.

Other symphonic poems that are epic in their subject are *Mazeppa* (after Victor Hugo), *Die Hunnenschlacht* (after the monumental painting of the same title by Wilhelm von Kaulbach) and *Hungaria*. The composition of that work was probably inspired by a poem by Mihaly Vörösmarty, which has the character of a national epic.

The symphonic poem *Hamlet* after Shakespeare is a case *sui generis*. Its subject is unquestionably "dramatic." But Liszt called the work expressly a prelude to Shakespeare's play. It is thus a "dramatic" overture.

Finally there are Liszt's two greatest symphonic works: the *Faust* and the *Dante* symphony. They, too, cannot be classified as "dramatic symphonies." For one thing, Dante's *Divina Commedia* is an epic, not a drama

(Hegel called it "the true art epic of the Christian Catholic Middle Ages"[9]). For another, Liszt regarded Goethe's *Faust* not as a stage work but as the archetype of the "philosophic epopee." Thirdly, as we shall presently see, he wanted the three movements of the symphony to be understood as "three character portraits": Faust, Gretchen and Mepistopheles.

---

9   Hegel, *Ästhetik III*, 349/350, 406/407. Cf. also Georg Lukács, *Die Theorie des Romans. Ein geschichtsphilosophischer Versuch über die Formen der großen Epik*, 2nd ed. (Berlin, 1974), 50/51, 59/60.

XV. Liszt's *Faust* Symphony: A Semantic Analysis

> "Dry analysis alone does not suffice here. It is, to be sure, the approved method for determining the musical construction and for identifying the parts, – but it can never give us the spiritual bond, and it is that, after all, which, with Liszt as with every musician working poetically, forms the innermost core of his works." Richard Pohl in 1862 about the *Faust* Symphony[1]

> "More important is that absolutely new imaginative conception that is manifested in the major works (in the *Piano Sonata* and the two outer movements of the *Faust Symphony*, to name two examples), and in virtue of which these works are among the outstanding musical creations of the nineteenth century." Béla Bartók in 1936 about Liszt[2]

1. Aspects of the Investigation

The *Faust* Symphony of 1854 was, and is, regarded as one of Franz Liszt's most distinguished works. Many have seen, and see, in it the crowning achievement of his entire oeuvre.[3] Liszt himself counted the symphony among his best works. In a letter to Louis Köhler of May 24, 1856, he called his nine previous symphonic poems – *Mountain Symphony, Tasso, Les Préludes, Orpheus, Prometheus, Mazeppa, Festklänge, Héroïde funèbre* and *Hungaria* – prolegomena to the *Faust* and the *Dante* Symphony.[4]

Recognized even by his opponents as one of Liszt's major works, the *Faust* Symphony was destined to become a prime bone of contention during the time of the vehement disputes between the New Germans and the Conservatives. The New Germans raised it above everything that had

---

1 Richard Pohl, *Franz Liszt. Studien und Erinnerungen* (Gesammelte Schriften über Musik und Musiker, vol 2) (Leipzig, 1883), 250.

2 Béla Bartók in *Liszt problémák* (Liszt Problems) (Budapest, 1936), 53–57. Quoted from Paula Rehberg/Gerhard Nestler, *Franz Liszt. Die Geschichte seines Lebens, Schaffens und Wirkens* (Zurich/Stuttgart, 1961), 576/577.

3 Thus Julius Kapp (*Liszt. Eine Biographie*, 15th-18th ed. [Berlin, 1922],160, 172/173), Sacheverell Sitwell (*Franz Liszt* [Zurich, 1958], 189) and many others.

4 *FLB*, 1:223.

been done in the area of symphonic music since Beethoven. Thus the musicologist Richard Pohl observed in 1862 that there was "nothing worthier and more qualified to stand at the side" of Beethoven's last and greatest works than the *Faust* Symphony: it constituted the "summit of Liszt's hitherto artistic work" and was "without doubt the greatest symphonic work of our time."[5] By contrast, the Conservatives saw in the work an important piece of evidence for the failure of a supposedly wrong-headed and disastrous aesthetic. For Eduard Hanslick, the bitterest opponent of the New German School and all program music, the Mephisto movement of the symphony – a movement of "naked ugliness" and "indescribable tastelessness" – showed most palpably "by what arid rational operations Liszt produces 'music'." And the first movement was in Hanslick's view a "ghastly patchwork" and "downright comical," a "bungled Berlioz regarding himself as Goethe."[6]

Of greater weight, to be sure, are the judgments of Anton Bruckner, Richard Strauss and Béla Bartók. According to a previously overlooked report by August Stradal, the *Faust* Symphony was the only symphonic work of Liszt's that Bruckner knew intimately and greatly esteemed. Bruckner admired "the themes, the colossal structure, the instrumentation, the harmonic daring."[7] Richard Strauss, in turn, wrote on November 19, 1890, to his friend Ludwig Thuille that during a Weimar performance of the symphony he had once again become concretely aware "that Liszt is the only symphonist who *had* to come after Beethoven and who represents a gigantic advance over him." Similarly to Bruckner, Strauss admired Liszt's "flourishing invention," the "precision in poetic-musical expressiveness," the "sureness in instrumentation."[8]

5   Richard Pohl, *Liszt*, 320.
6   Eduard Hanslick, *Aus dem Tagebuche eines Musikers (Der "Modernen Oper" VI. Teil). Kritiken und Schilderungen* (Berlin, 1892), 238–241.
7   August Stradal, „Erinnerungen aus Bruckners letzter Zeit," Zeitschrift für Musik, 99 (1932), 973. For details about Bruckner's relation to Liszt, see my *Brahms and Bruckner as Artistic Antipodes*, ch. XIX.
8   *Richard Strauss und Ludwig Thuille. Briefe der Freundschaft 1877–1907*, ed. Alfons Ott (Munich, 1969), 114/115, 197/198.

These verdicts are hardly exaggerated. The more closely one studies the *Faust* Symphony, the clearer it becomes that it is indeed one of the most significant, boldest and most original symphonic works of the 19th century. In its time it was a work of the foremost avant-garde. Viewed from a historical perspective, it astonishes by the many "modern" traits it exhibits. These include above all the structure of the "Faust" themes, the audacity of the harmonic blueprint, the rhythmic-metric innovations and Liszt's amazing art of thematic metamorphosis.

The central question the *Faust* Symphony raises is the question as to the semantics of the music. Liszt did not attach a program, nor did he speak of his intentions. It sufficed him to label the three movements "Faust," "Gretchen" and "Mephistopheles" and to give the work the title *Eine Faust-Symphony in drei Charakterbildern* [character portraits] *(nach Goethe)*.

Why this terseness? There are several possible reasons. It is conceivable, to begin with, that Liszt dispensed with detailed explanations, and even poetic mottos, because he felt he had drawn the three characters in a very personal and rather free manner.[9] Or one could surmise that he decided to do without a detailed program because he wanted to give the listeners' imagination free play, or, more probably, because considering the popularity of Goethe's drama – Pohl wrote in 1862: "The educated German clings to his Faust as to a gospel"[10] – he credited the listeners with being able to "gather" his intentions and his interpretation of the material from his music.[11] That, to be sure, would be a rather utopian expectation, as the intentions of the author in the case of so complex a work as the *Faust*

---

9   Richard Wagner gave listeners to his *Faust* Overture (composed in 1839/1840, revised in 1850) some aid in understanding the work by prefixing verses 1566–1571 from Part I of Goethe's tragedy to the score as a motto: The god who through my bosom flits Can deeply stir my inmost soul; Yet, though he high above my powers sits, Can exercise no outward rule;And thus existence is mere deadly weight,Death wished for, life to me a thing to hate. (tr. E.B.-K)

10   Pohl, *Liszt,* 272.

11   Liszt thus did not add any (detailed) programs to the *Dante* Symphony (1856) or the symphonic poem *Hamlet* (1858), either – two compositions based on well-known masterpieces of world literature.

Symphony can be ascertained only after a detailed study of the score and only with the aid of a systematic semantic analysis.

Of the many studies of, and commentaries on, the *Faust* Symphony, there are maximally only four or five that are really relevant. Let us review them in chronological order.

On September 18, 1857, Franz Brendel reported in the *Neue Zeitschrift für Musik* about the work's premiere. (It had taken place on September 5 in Weimar on the occasion of the unveiling of the memorial statues of Goethe and Schiller.) He wrote very appreciatively about the "Faust" and "Gretchen" movements, as well as about the "Chorus mysticus" added to the composition in 1857, but had reservations about the "Mephisto" movement. Brendel was probably the first to realize that in the "Mephisto" the themes of the "Faust" movement are travestied and distorted.[12]

Also in 1857, Leopold Alexaner Zellner, a Viennese Liszt devotee, published the first technical analysis of the symphony.[13]

In 1862, a series of articles by Richard Pohl appeared in the *Neue Zeitschrift für Musik*, to date probably the most extensive as well as weightiest treatise on the *Faust* Symphony. Pohl was the first to make an attempt to gloss the themes and particular passages of the symphony with verses from Goethe's *Faust*.[14] In doing so, he was fully aware of the hypothetical character of his co-ordinations, saying: "since Liszt himself did not comment on the matter, an absolute determination will be hard to make."[15] Pohl's treatise formed the basis of the subsequent hermeneutic

---

12 Franz Brendel, „F. Liszt's neueste Werke und die gegenwärtige Parteistellung. I. Das Concert in Weimar am 5. September," *NZfM*, 47 (1857), 121–124.

13 Leopold Alexander Zellner, in *Blätter für Musik*, nos. 78–79 (Vienna, 1857).

14 Richard Pohl, "Liszt's Faust-Symphonie," *NZfM* (1862). Reprinted in Pohl, *Liszt* (1833), 247–320. (We consistently quote from this edition.) The study consists of six chapters: I. Rückblick und Umblick; II. Die Faust-Poesie und die Faust-Musiken; III. Liszt's Auffassung der musikalischen Faust-Idee; IV. Erster Satz: Faust; V. Zweiter Satz: Gretchen; VI. Mephisto uind Schlußchor. Liszt commented briefly about Pohl's articles in a letter to Franz Brendel of August 29, 1862 (*FLB*, 2:23).

15 P: 283.

commentaries by Lina Ramann,[16] Arthur Hahn,[17] Otto Klauwell,[18] Hermann Kretzschmar,[19] Georg Göhler,[20] Max Chop,[21] Hans Engel[22] and Rudolf Kloiber.[23]

Some new ideas were presented in 1900 by Rudolf Louis in his Liszt monograph. He believed that Liszt had from the outset dispensed with "hanging on the poet's coattails," preferring to obtain the "extract," or essence, of Goethe's poem. There was "no trace" to be found in the symphony of individual facts and events of the dramatic action. Liszt had wanted solely to interpret the three chief characters of the tragedy, Faust, Gretchen and Mephisto, as representatives of the earth, heaven and hell.[24]

A substantial addition to the research on the *Faust* Symphony, finally, was made by László Somfai in a study published in 1962. Somfai largely disregarded the hermeneutic problem of the work, concentrating instead on elucidating the symphony's genesis, from the first sketches to the publication of the score by Schuberth in 1861.[25] He was able to show that after writing

16 Lina Ramann, *Franz Liszt als Künstler und Mensch*, vol. 2, pt. 2 (Leipzig, 1894), 169–198.
17 Arthur Hahn, *Franz Liszt. Symphonishce Dichtungen* (Schlesinger'sche Musik-Bibliothek, Meisterführer no. 8) 162–179-
18 Otto Klauwell, *Geschichte der Programmusik*, 162–172.
19 Hermann Kretzschmar, in Alfred Heuß, ed., *Erläuterungen zu Franz Liszts Sinfonien und sinfonischen Dichtungen*. Bound ed. of the „Kleine Konzertführer" (Breitkopf & Härtels Musikbücher) (Leipzig, 1912), 23–35.
20 Georg Göhler in his introduction to Eulenburg's miniature score ed. of the *Faust* Symphony (No. 77, E.E. 3647) (Leipzig, n.d.).
21 Max Chop, *Franz Liszts symphonische Werke I* (Reclams Universal-Bibliothek no. 6519; Erläuterungen zu den Meisterwerkender Tonkunst, vol. 34) (Leipzig, 1924), 13–40.
22 Hans Engel, *Franz Liszt* (Potsdam, 1936), 105–107.
23 Rudolf Kloiber, *Handbuch der symphonishcen Dichtung* (Wiesbaden, 1966), 52–57.
24 Rudolf Louis, *Franz Liszt* (Vorkämpfer des Jahrhunderts. Eine Sammlung von Biographien) (Berlin, 1900), 65–67.
25 Láslό Somfai, "Die musikalischen Gestaltwandlungen der Faust-Symphonie von Liszt," *Studia Musicologica Academiae Scientiarume Hungaricae*, 2 (1962), 87–137.

down the first version of the score in 1854, Liszt still made an unusually large number of changes in various details.[26]

Two questions, above all, crystallize out from the foregoing:

1. Are there indeed no allusions to scenes and events of the dramatic action to be found in the *Faust* Symphony?
2. Are precise and verifiable statements about the semantics of the music and Liszt's conception of the Faust story possible?

It seems to me that we can already answer the second question in the affirmative. One thing has to be kept in mind, however: precise statements are possible only if we succeed in deducing extra-musical motifs from the music itself. The challenge is to correlate tectonic and semantic aspects with each other, to combine technical with semantic analysis.

2. Liszt's Observations about Goethe's *Faust*

In 1931, the noted Liszt critic Peter Raabe proposed a somewhat willful thesis about the *Faust* Symphony, one that has to be discussed, especially also because it gained considerable attention in the more recent research (Somfai). According to Raabe, Liszt probably never departed more from his model than he did in the *Faust* Symphony. The admirers of the work, who emphasize how faithfully Goethe's *Faust* is mirrored in Liszt's, were mistaken. The work reflects Liszt's personal experiences, knowledge and convictions. The first movement, Raabe says, is a "personal confession"; the "Gretchen" movement discloses Liszt's conception of the "eternal in woman"; the last movement Liszt was able to write because he had learned "that there is a power that falsifies and shreds everything great and nobly

---

26 The autograph score of 1854 is now in the possession of the national library Széchényi in Budapest. A vital prerequisite for Somfai's study was provided by the restaurateur Deszö Sasvári, who in 1960 opened the stuck-together leaves of the manuscript and thereby made possible an insight into the altered portions. The earliest drafts of the *Faust* Symphony are found in a sketchbook from the middle of the 1840s, which is preserved in the Liszt Museum in Weimar (*Ms. N 4*). The score was published in Leipzig by the J. Schuberth Verlag in 1861 and 1866. The printing of 1861 (publisher's no. 2646) served as source for the edition of the symphony in the *Gesamtausgabe* (I, 8 and 9).

thought." The outer movements of the symphony are therefore but "images of the Faustian element in Liszt's soul."[27]

Raabe bases this bold thesis on three things: first, a letter of Liszt's to Frau Therese von Helldorff, from which Raabe gathers that Liszt "basically did not have much sympathy with Faust as Goethe has depicted him as a character"; second, on a statement of Liszt's to the Princess Wittgenstein, where he says: "Every subject that is connected with Goethe is dangerous for me to treat"; and third, on the consideration that Liszt did not unreservedly revere Goethe himself, either.

Considering the momentousness of Raabe's thesis, it is clearly necessary to test his arguments more closely. A careful scrutiny reveals that Raabe has partly misinterpreted the quoted passages and drawn conclusions from them that are quite inadmissible. Let us pursue the matter.

Frau von Hellsdorff had written to Liszt about her partiality for Byron's *Manfred*, and he replied from Rome on September 22, 1869 that he shared her predilection.

> In my youth [he wrote], I admired Manfred passionately, and I visited him far more often than I did Faust, who, to put it delicately, seemed to me, despite his fabulous reputation as a poetic work, basically 'bourgeois' as a character. That made him more multifarious, more complete, richer, more communicative, whereas Manfred condenses himself, becomes torpid, conjures up oblivion so as not to bleed with remorse, and, failing to recognize the inexpressible mystery of redemption, plunges from the height of his foolhardiness into infinity. The personality of Faust fritters away his energies, loses himself in small things; he hardly acts, lets himself go, vacillates, experiments, lets himself be led astray, reflects, bargains, and is interested solely in his little happiness. Manfred is completely different, incomparably prouder and firmer. By an absolute act of will, he rejects in immeasurable disdain everything that is nature and life – with the exception of a single being. Certainly it would hardly occur to him to put up with the bad company of Mephisto, and if he had loved Gretchen, he might have killed her, but he would never, like Faust, have abandoned her in sheer cowardice.[28]

This passage shows that in 1869 Liszt felt indeed greater sympathy for Manfred than for Faust. The reservations he had about Faust were largely ethical ones, as when he charges Faust with cowardice in abandoning Gretchen. But we have to consider that Liszt made these allegations in

---

27 Peter Raabe, *Liszts Schaffen*, 81–83.
28 The original French text of the passage is quoted by Raabe, *Liszts Schaffen*, 82.

1869, fifteen years after the completion, and nearly 25 after the first sketches, of the symphony. Liszt sometimes changed his mind about literary matters,[29] and how he thought about Faust at the time of conceiving the symphony is something we don't know. And something else has to be taken into account: Liszt's remarks suggest that Goethe's highly differentiated, psychological characterization of Faust must in fact have fascinated him. For he concedes that Faust as a character is more diverse, more complete, richer and more communicative than Manfred. (One is bound to think of the great wealth and notable differentiation of the Faust themes in Liszt's symphony.)

Let us now look at the second statement. Raabe quotes the sentence: "Every subject that is connected with Goethe is dangerous for me" from a letter of March, 1854; notes that the sentence was written only a few months before Liszt started to work on the *Faust* Symphony; and gives the impression that it refers to Goethe's *Faust*. If one reads the entire letter to the Princess Wittgenstein,[30] one realizes that Raabe has taken the sentence out of context and misinterpreted it. The sentence refers not to *Faust* but to an article about Beethoven's music for Goethe's *Egmont*, an article that Liszt had coauthored with the Princess.[31] Liszt is writing to the Princess from Gotha that the article must not appear prior to his return to Weimar, as he had several major and many minor comments to make about it. Why did Liszt express this request? Several facts suggest that the Princess, whose thinking about Goethe (as about all things German) was highly critical,[32] to all appearances found so much to object to in *Egmont* that Liszt felt compelled to put on the brakes. Thus he wrote to

---

29 An example is Liszt's assessment of Hamlet. See my *Mahler and the Symphony*, 211–213.

30 *FLB*, 4:182/183. The original French wording of the sentence in question is: "Tout sujet qui touche à Goethe est dangereux à traiter pour moi."

31 Franz Liszt, "Über Beethoven's Musik zu 'Egmont'" (1854), GS, 3:29–36.

32 Richard Wagner writes in his Autobiography: "Specifically, you could not speak well about Goethe with *him* [Liszt], especially in the presence of the Princess Caroline. About Egmont, whom he thought he had to hold in low regard because he let himself be 'duped' by Alba, even we almost got into unpleasantness, since Liszt seemed in a mood for it." See Wagner, *Sämtliche Schriften und Dichtungen*, 15:125.

her: "Besides, there are many excellent things in the article about Egmont that we will be able to use; but it is requisite that we go over it once more together." In the published version of the article, Liszt and the Princess emphasize the poetic qualities of Goethe's drama, praise the drawing of several of the characters in it (the Regent, Macchiavelli, Alba, William of Orange), but criticize the character of Egmont, whom they regard as an "immature youth."

Liszt was certainly no uncritical admirer of Goethe. But it would be altogether wrong to think that there was "a wide chasm" between him and Goethe, as Raabe maintains. Numerous utterances, overlooked by Raabe, document that Liszt admired *Faust* and counted it among the loftiest works of world literature. Thus Hector Berlioz tells in his memoirs that on the day he first met Liszt in Paris – it was the day before the premiere of the *Symphonie fantastique* on December 5, 1830 – he had spoken with him about Goethe's *Faust*.[33] Liszt confessed not to have read it as yet; "soon afterwards he enthused as much about him as I did."[34] In his essay about "Berlioz and his Harold Symphony," of 1855, Liszt cites Goethe's *Faust* (along with Byron's *Cain* and *Manfred* and Mickiewicz' *Dziady*) as the archetype of the modern "philosophic epopee" that he had in mind as model for the modern program symphony.[35] In a letter to the Princess of June 12, 1876, Liszt describes *Faust* as a "sublime dramatic epopee" – "despite all the confused stuff that is in it and from which one can never disentangle oneself, say what you will." And he adds "The Commentaries on the Apocalypse seem almost clearer to me than those on 'Faust'!"[36]

---

33 Hector Berlioz, *Literarische Werke. Erste Gesamtausgabe*, 10 vols. (Leipzig, 1903–1921) 1:138.
34 This comment refers, of course, to Part One of *Faust*. The second part of Goethe's tragedy did not appear until 1832.
35 Franz Liszt, "Berlioz und seine 'Harold'-Symphonie" (1855), GS, 4:53.
36 *FLB*, 7:143/144. The original French text runs as follows: "Si j'étais Intendant d'un théâtre quelconque, ce serait un devoir de propager la mise en scène de la sublime épopée dramatique de Goethe – malgré tout embruillamini qu'il y a là-dedans, et dont on ne sortira jamais, quoi qu'on dise. Les commentaires de l'Apocalypse me semblent encore plus clairs que ceux de Faust!" From another letter of Liszt to the Princess, dated May 13, 1876 (*FLB*, 7:157), it appears that his remark about the confusion in *Faust* refers to the second part of the work. It also appears from the correspondence with the Princess that Liszt was well

In his last years, finally, he told his pupil August Stradal: "I should not have written a *Faust Symphony*, but only the *Dante Symphony*. People don't trust my clerical views for that reason. And yet Dante's *Divina Commedia* and Goethe's *Faust* lead by different paths in the end to the same heavenly heights.[37]

From what has been said it appears that Raabe's thesis about Liszt's distant relationship to Goethe and to *Faust* and about the supposed freedom with which he shaped his *Faust* Symphony cannot be upheld. There is no basis for Raabe's assumption that Liszt had never departed more widely from his model than he did in the *Faust* Symphony.[38] We must not forget that on the title page of his work Liszt expressly states that it was a Faust Symphony *after Goethe*.[39] Raabe also misconceives a fundamental principle of Liszt's symphonic program music, that is, the intention of amalgamating literary and musical elements.[40] "The masterpieces of music," Liszt wrote in 1855 in his essay about the *Harold* Symphony, "more and more incorporate the masterpieces of literature."

---

versed in the secondary literature about Goethe's *Faust*. Thus in one letter he mentions a work by the Tübingen aesthetician Friedrich Theodor Vischer (*FLB*, 7:284). In 1851, Liszt read Goethe studies by Hermann Hettner (1821–1882) and Adolf Stahr. See his letter to Adolf Stahr of May 26, 1851 (*FLB*, 8:87). The Princess Wittgenstein, incidentally, also authored a commentary on Goethe's *Faust*. See La Mara, *Liszt und die Frauen*, 2nd ed. (Leipzig, 1919), 89.

37 August Stradal, *Erinnerungen an Franz Liszt*, quoted from Rehberg/Nestler, *Liszt*, 442.

38 Raabe seems to have revised his opinion later. In his book *Wege zu Liszt*, published in 1943 in Regensburg (Deutsche Musikbücherei, 13:93/96), he connects the *Faust* Symphony more closely to Goethe's tragedy.

39 Equally groundless is Somfai's thesis, directly following Raabe, that Liszt wanted partout to "cast something else into notes" than merely Goethe's *Faust*. Our investigation will show that Somfai's view that Liszt had fused "at least two other outstanding literary experiences – or more exactly, universalized human types, characters", namely Manfred and Prometheus (!) with his Faust, cannot be supported by any evidence.

40 For Liszt's conception of program music, see, ch. X, 3, above.

3. Themes and Structure of the "Faust" Movement

Another fundamental principle of Liszt's program music was the demand that the subject of a composition (the "poetic idea") must determine the form. By applying this principle, Liszt sought to free his music from the schematism of "classical" form and to open up its unlimited possibilities of formal shaping.

Viewing the *Faust* Symphony from a distance, one might think at first that Liszt's novel ideas about the relation of "content" and "form" did not apply to it.[41] For the sequence of movements faintly reflects the model of Beethoven's Ninth Symphony: three instrumental movements – a first one ("Faust"), a slow second one ("Gretchen") and a scherzo-like third ("Mephisto") – followed by a Finale that includes a male chorus and a tenor solo (the *Chorus mysticus*). How original Liszt's conception is one recognizes only if one takes a closer view of the symphony's themes. What proves to be novel is not only that each of the three instrumental movements is based on a different number of particular themes – the "Faust" movement, not counting the episodic parts, is based on five themes, the "Gretchen" movement on two, the "Mephisto" movement on several emblematic figures that characterize Mephisto – but above all that the "Faust" themes recur in the "Gretchen" and the "Mephisto" movement. They play a major role in the middle part of the "Gretchen" movement, and they also provide the foundation of the "Mephisto" movement, as Liszt lets them pass there in review in varied and distorted form – the "Mephisto" movement thereby proves to be a kind of defamiliarized negative of the "Faust" movement.

This mode of formation obeys not purely musical principles but rather a "poetic," that is to say programmatic, "necessity." By picking up the "Faust" themes in the middle part of the "Gretchen" movement, Liszt intimates that Faust has entered Gretchen's life. By inverting the "Faust" themes in the "Mephisto" movement into the negative, he signals that he is adopting Goethe's conception of Mephisto as the "spirit of negation,"

---

41 On Liszt's observations about the relation of content and form, see my *Mahler and the Symphony*, 37–40.

who cannot create anything of his own, but can only "deny" and "destroy" (*Faust I*, 1338–1344).

In the letter to Frau von Helldorff cited above, Liszt writes in 1869 that Faust as a character is *"plus varié, plus complet, plus riche, plus communicatif"* than Manfred. If one looks at the head movement of the *Faust* Symphony with this remark in mind, the impression obtrudes itself that List had similar thoughts about Faust already in 1854. For the "Faust" movement exhibits a structure of astonishing complexity and differentiation. It is not only rich in contrasting themes but governed by enormous agogic, expressive, harmonic, and metric variations – in sharp contrast to the "Gretchen" movement. The tempo alone, if I have counted correctly, changes seventeen times. The expression is subject to constant fluctuation. The mode changes perpetually: sections in major, in minor and in major/minor alternate with wholly ambiguous ones. (The harmony exhibits a remarkable wealth of mediantic relations of thirds.) No less remarkable is the frequent change in time: 4/4 and 3/4 meters alternate constantly, often within one and the same theme. The earliest score even included a 7/8 measure. On December 14, 1854, shortly after completing the first version of the score, Liszt, writing to his American pupil William Mason, mentioned the *"mesures horribles"* of 7/8, 74/ and 5/4 that alternate with 4/4 and 3/4 time.[42] Liszt was clearly aware of the outrageous innovations of the *Faust* Symphony!

The five strongly contrasting themes of the "Faust" movement are structured differently and, with great art, rendered sharply distinctive: each has its own physiognomy. Let us look at them more closely.

---

42 *FLB*, 1:186. On William Mason (1829–1908), see Alfred Goodman, *Die amerikanischen Schüler Franz Liszts* (Veröffentlichungen der Musikforschung, vol. 1) (Wilhelmshaven, 1972), 19–39.

Theme I

The structure of theme I (*Lento assai*) is dictated by augmented triads and sighing formations. The theme is composed of three motif groups (a+b+c) that merge seamlessly into each other. Motif group Ia is the famous "dodecaphonic" theme:[43] a sequence of four broken augmented triads in

---

43 The designation "dodecaphonic" for Theme I was coined by J. Milstein in his book *F. Liszt* (Klassiki muzykalnoj kultury), 2 vols., 2ⁿᵈ ed. (Moscow, 1971; 1ˢᵗ ed. 1956), 1: 408. On the "dodecaphonic" aspect of the theme, see also Serge

symmetric rhythms. Motif group Ib, a sighing phrase of the oboes, clarinets and bassoons marked *dolente*, is harmonized by augmented triads. Motif group Ic, developed from a three-note sighing motif of the violins (m. 5), reveals itself upon a closer look as a sequence of sighing formations on the degrees of the augmented triad.

The theme has become very famous because it cannot be grasped in terms of the functional theory of harmony (function theory). It eludes any classification by the traditional modes, is wholly ambiguous, although it is anchored tonally and mediantically: the notes a^b and e prove to be tonal "centers."[44]

After a very long pause (m. 11), the theme is played a second time (mm. 12–22), appearing in transposition to the minor upper sixth and the major upper third. The basic form of the theme and its transposition relate to each other like a first and second phrase: the first phrase begins in a^b and ends in e; the second phrase begins in e and ends in a^b.[45]

Since the theme is not firmly grounded in a specific key, it evokes the impression of groping and searching: it is somehow roaming.[46] Intoned for the most part in unison, it has traits of a monologue.

Gut, *Franz Liszt. Les éléments du langage musical* (Éditions Klincksieck, 1975), 111–115.

44 Liszt transposed the motif group Ia to the minor upper sixth, but the groups Ib and Ic to the major upper third, so as to be able to close on the a^b (instead of the c), the beginning of the theme.

45 Hugo Riemann (*Geschichte der Musik seit Beethoven*, 421) and Hans Engel, (*Liszt* [1936], 106/107), made unsuccessful attempts to explain the tonality of Theme I as C minor.

46 Arnold Schönberg, *Harmonielehre* (Leipzig/Vienna, 1911), 2217, 266–295), includes the augmented triad among the *vagierende* (roving) chords.

Theme II

Theme II (*Allegro agitato ed appassionato*) forms a radical contrast to Theme I. It is written in a clear key (C Minor, the main key of the movement), is fully harmonized and passionate and pressing in character. (It was notated originally in 7/8 time.) Yet there is also a link to Theme I: the three-note sighing motif from the *dolente* group (Ic) forms an element also of Theme II. Another important motif of Theme II is borrowed from Richard Wagner's *Faust* Overture of 1839/1840. As not previously noted, the measures 83–87 of Liszt's theme paraphrase mm. 367–375 of Wagner's overture:[47]

---

47 Liszt knew Wagner's overture, having conducted it on May 11, 1853, in Weimar. For details, see below.

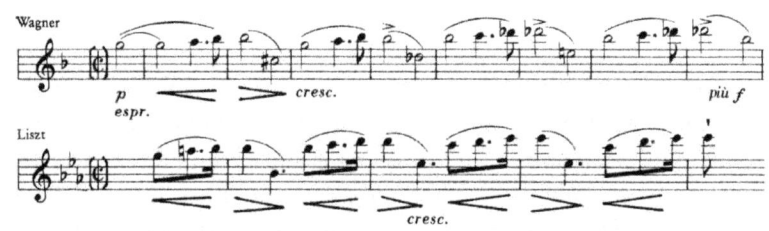

Theme III

Theme III (*espressivo ed appassionato molto*), in turn, has again a physiognomy all its own. It has a dramatic (recitative) character and is structured dialogically: a four- and five-bar melodic sighing phrase is recited in diverse variants in alternately high and low position by the oboes and clarinets, on the one hand, and the bassoons, cellos and double basses, on the other. The second violins and the violas accompany with tremolo. This theme undergoes a great deal of modulation.

Theme IV

The germ of Theme IV (*Affettuoso poco Andante*) is the *dolente* group of Theme I. The repeated head motif of the *affettuoso* theme is nothing other than an amazing metamorphosis of Ib + Ic. However, the characteristic interval of the *dolente* motif, the descending major seventh, is now transformed into a minor seventh. That and a different harmonization give the theme, notable also for its permanent alternation between 3/4 and 4/4/ time, an entirely different character. The marking *affettuoso* fits the expressive content well. Theme IV is in D Major (E Major) but frequently diverges to minor, and frequently includes soft minor sounds in its harmonization, so that it would not be unfair to say that it belongs more to the major/minor mode.

Like Theme III, Theme IV is orchestrated in a dialogic manner: the melodic motifs are presented alternately by individual winds (*cantando*) and, at the beginning, by the solo viola (*dolce, con grazia*).

Theme V

Theme V (*Grandioso, poco meno mosso*), finally, is designed dualistically. "First" and "second" phrase of the theme contrast strongly with each other. The "first phrase" (in 4/4 time) has a solemn, ceremonial character, the "second" (in 3/4 time) a lively, buoyant one. (The contrast becomes even more pronounced in the recapitulation [mm. 503–519], where the "first phrase" is to be recited *rall.* and the "second" one *accel.*) Theme V is written diatonically and is in D Major (E Major); the especially "pure" pentatonic structure of the head motif is particularly striking.

How are these themes integrated into the plan of the movement? Unquestionably, the "Faust" movement (like the "Mephisto" one) reveals the basic outline of the sonata form. One can readily argue for a division into exposition (mm. 1–296), development (mm. 297–358), recapitulation (mm. 359–581) and coda mm. 582–654). Upon closer inspection, however, one discovers that the movement has at bottom a two-part design. The following structural schema will illustrate the design of the movement, the sequence of its themes and tempos and its harmonic blueprint.

PART ONE
Exposition

Mm. 1–22 *Lento assai*	Theme I (in the character of a slow introduction); tonal center: a^b
Mm. 23–65 *Allegro impetuoso*	Of the two parts of this section, the first (mm. 23–44), based on the tritone and the diminished seventh chord, is a *hapax legomenon*:[48] it does not recur in the recapitulation. The second part (mm. 45–65) opens with the now fully harmonized "dodecaphonic" theme (Ia) . The part concludes with the several times repeated third-fourth chord.
Mm. 66–70 *Lento assai*	Theme Ib recited solo by the bassoon. This section was originally preceded by another exposition of the "dodeca-phonic" theme, beginning on *c*.
Mm. 71–110 *Allegro agitato* *Ed appassionato*	Theme II in C minor; a modulating passage closes on B_7
Mm. 111–146 with *espress. ed appass.* *molto*	Theme III (functioning as a transitional passage),[49] beginning E 6/4 and leading to D_6
Mm. 147–166 *Meno mosso* *miserioso e molto* *tranquillo*	This section (which does not recur in the recapitulation) is unique: *characterized by* long-held harmonies of the winds and rising and falling figurations of muted violins and violas, accompanied by clarinets and pizzicato violins and violas playing broken triads in the rhythm of the head motif. The section begins on D_6 and closes on C^6_5
Mm. 166–178 *plintivo*	Development of the three-note sighing motif (m. 5) from Theme I. Episodic character: the section does not recur in the recapitulation.
Mm. 179–202 *Affettuoso* *Poco Andante*	Theme IV (secondary subject) in E Major

---

48 Occurring only once in a given piece.
49 Pohl (280), erroneously calls Theme III a *Seitenthema* (secondary theme).

Mm. 202–224 *Allegro con fuoco*	Transition to Theme V; mm. 213–224. Exposition of a new motif (*marcato*)
Mm.225–250 *Grandioso, poco meno mosso*	Theme V (final theme) in E Major
Mm. 250–296 *Un poco accelerando il tempo*	Mm. 250–271: antagonism between the *dolente* motif (Ib) and the *marcato* motif; mm. 272–280: Theme V in E Major; mm. 281–296: a *stringendo* part based on a progression of fourths.

Development

Mm. 297–318 Tempo I *Allegro agitato assai*	To begin with (mm. 297–304), a development of the head motif (Ia). intoned in *stretto* by tenor trombones and trumpets; the strings play *strepitoso* the head motif of Theme II. This section issues in a precipitous part (mm. 305–310), whose "melody," a descending line in the woodwinds, emphasizes the degrees of the augmented triad.
Mm. 319–334	Theme II in C$^\#$ Minor.
Mm. 335–358	Development of the *rinforzando* motif of Theme II; the harmonic foundation of the passage mm. 349–354 is the diminished seventh chord on *b*.

PART TWO
Recapitulation

Mm. 359–381 *Lento assai, wie zu Anfang*	Theme I (as in exposition); tonal center: a^b
Mm. 382–399 *Andante mesto. Nicht schleppend*	Development of the *dolente* motif (Ib), beginning in A minor; an accompanying figure in the rhythm of the head motif (Ia). In between (mm.388–391), a reminiscence of Theme III.
Mm. 400–420	Development of the "dodecaphonic" theme (Ia); from m. 407 the augmented triads change to perfect ones.
Mm. 421–449 *Allegro agitato ed appassionato molto*	Theme II in C minor (as in the exposition)
Mm. 450–490 *Affettuoso, poco Andante*	Theme IV, first in E Major, then (mm. 472–490) in C Major

Mm. 491–502	Appearance of the *marcato* motif (now *tranquillo*)
Mm. 503–518 *Maestoso*	Theme V in C Major
Mm. 519–547 *Poco a poco sino al fff*	– partly mm. 250–271 (antagonism between Ib and the *animando marcato* motif)
Mm. 548–581 *Allegro con fuoco*	Theme V in C Major (– mm. 272–296)

Coda

Mm. 582–598	– mm. 297–310 of the development
Mm. 599–610 *Andante maestoso assai*	Theme V (first phrase) in G♭ Major intoned by the trombones and answered echo-like by the woodwinds
Mm. 611–654 *Più mosso, molto agitato*	The motifs of mm. 611–618 are developed from the head motif of Theme V and are complemented by the three-note sighing motif (m. 5). Mm. 619–635: Theme Ia in the brass. Mm. 636–645 (*impetuoso*): Theme Ib in a significant rhythmic meta-morphosis. The movement closes mm. 646–654 with the *dolente* motif in unison (cellos sand double basses).

If one looks at the movement with preconceptions derived from classic sonata movements such as those of Beethoven, one will have to admit that the proportions are not well-balanced. The development, with its 62 bars, is one fifth, even one sixth, the length of the exposition (in a recording by the new York Philharmonic Orchestra under Leonard Bernstein, the exposition lasted twelve minutes, the development only two). One could argue that this imbalance is to some extent compensated by the fact that both the exposition and the recapitulation are interspersed with development-like passages. Even so, an impression of disproportion remains. That shows, however, that one cannot well measure Liszt's advanced works with the yardstick of traditional art. One can grasp the special character of the "Faust" movement's formal design only once one realizes that the movement is at bottom bipartite: exposition and development constitute the first part (358 bars), recapitulation and coda the second (296 bars).[50] (In the

---

50 Richard Pohl (*Liszt*, 291/292) first recognized the bipartite design of the "Faust" movement. See also Gernot Gruber, "Zum Formproblem in Liszts Orchester-werken – exemplifiziert am ersen Satz der Faust-Symphonie," in *Liszt Studien 1*.

recording cited, the two parts last exactly 14 minutes each.) Typically, the exposition merges into the development, as the recapitulation does into the coda, and it is also symptomatic that the coda starts with the same section as the development. (Bars 582–598 of the coda correspond to bars 297–310 of the development.) It remains to note that in the first version of the *Faust* Symphony, the recapitulation of the "Faust" movement was longer. It included the sequencing section of the *espressivo* theme (Theme III) as well as the episodes *misterioso* and *plintivo* that were deleted in the final version[51] – we would add: not to the detriment of the movement, whose two parts, as we noted, now have, if not the same number of bars, yet the same length in playing time.

4. Harmonic Symbolism: The Augmented Triad as Emblem of Faust

In recent years, the notion has more and more established itself that Liszt is among the boldest harmonists of the 19th century. Many see in him an even more audacious innovator than Richard Wagner. A study of the harmonies in the *Faust* Symphony can show that this opinion is not without foundation.

The harmony of the "Faust" movement is, as we have shown, strongly differentiated in terms of modes: portions in major, minor and major-minor alternate with wholly ambiguous ones. Among the latter, we can include the sequences of augmented triads that determine the structure of Theme I.

Ernest Newman surmised in 1946 that Liszt might have received the impulse toward the augmented triads from the theories of his Berlin friend Carl Friedrich Weitzmann,[52] who in 1853 (one year before the writing-down of the *Faust* Symphony) published a book about the augmented

---

Kongress-Bericht Eisenstadt 1975, ed. Wolfgang Suppan (Graz, 1977), 81–95. Somfai, *Studia musicologica*, 2 (1962), 111, sees the movement as a four-part sonata form, erroneously locating the beginning of the development at m. 250. Equally erroneous are Kloiber's data, according to which the development is supposed to comprise mm. 319–420

51 Somfai in *Studia musicologica* 2 (1962), 111.
52 Ernest Newman, "A Forgotten Chapter of History," *SundayTimes*, September 1946.

triad.[53] Humphrey Searle, however, rightly remarked that Theme I with the characteristic triads is notated already in a sketchbook dating from the mid-1840s,[54] and the excerpts from the sketchbook published by Somfai confirm this objection.

Quite apart from that, however, Weitzmann calls the augmented triad (as well as the diminished one) a "dissonant triad." He maintains the dissonant part of the triad, the augmented fifth, was to "sharp" that it required both preparation and resolution.[55] Liszt, on the other hand, emancipates the chord completely from these rules, using it in a completely free manner. The augmented triads appear, as Hermann Erpf noted, at the beginning of the *Faust* Symphony altogether without any functional linking[56] – the first instance in the history of music![57]

Yet these "symmetric major-thirds," as Erpf calls them, are not "atonal." The note *a-flat* proves to be the tonal center of the first theme, its "opposite pole" being the note *e*. Together they form a kind of axis.

Now it is highly significant that in the first version of the symphony, between the *Allegro impetuoso* and the *Allegro agitato* (where now the *Lento assai* fragment appears [mm. 66–70]), another complete exposition of the first theme had been placed, one significantly beginning with the note *c*. Theme I was thus originally to have been recited three times, beginning the first time with *a-flat*, the second time with *e*, the third time with *c*. Liszt, we can see, initially planned to base the beginning of the symphony systematically on mediantic relations – more exactly, major-thirds relations. The major thirds not only determine the structure of the augmented triad

---

53 Carl Friedrich Weitzmann, *Der übermäßige Dreiklang* (Berlin, 1853). Weitzmann calls the augmented triad the „mysterious chord" (9).

54 Humphrey Searle, The *Music of Liszt*, 2nd ed. (New York, 1966; 1st ed. 1954), 68.

55 Weitzmann, *Der übermäßige Dreiklang, passim*. See Also Weitzmann, *Harmoniesystem* (Leipzig, n.d. [1860]), 30–33.

56 Hermann Erpf, *Studien zur Harmonie- und Klangtechnik der neueren Musik* (Leipzig, 1927), 169.

57 In 1859, Adolph Bernhard Marx wrote about the augmented triad in his *Allgemeine Musiklehre*: " If we raise the fifth of the major triad, the augmented triad shrills at us; a sequence of such chords, however, has not been dared as yet (at least until now), – and we would also not know how to motivate it. " Quoted from Weitzmann, *Der übermäßige Dreiklang*, 4.

but were also supposed to determine the relation between the three statements of the theme.

If we now analyze the harmonic construction of the entire movement, we will realize to our amazement that it, too, is designed according to major-thirds relations; the movement is systematically erected on the "centers" *a-flat*, *c* and *e*. The principal key of the movement is C Minor. C Minor is the key of Theme II. The tonal "center" of Theme I is the note *a-flat*. The secondary theme and the final one (Themes IV and V) are in E Major in the exposition and partly in E Major, partly in C Major in the recapitulation. The following diagram will illustrate the blueprint of the movement:

Theme II Themes IV and V (recapitulation) c/C

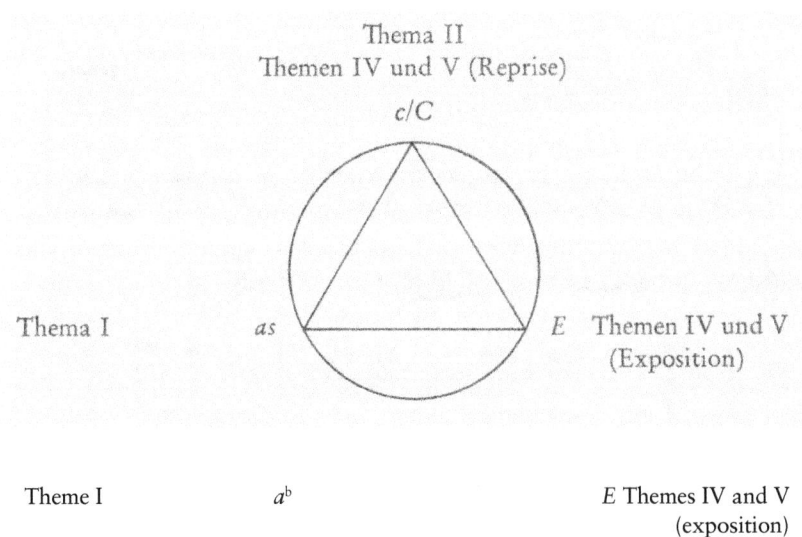

Thema II
Themen IV und V (Reprise)
c/C

Thema I   *as*   E   Themen IV und V
(Exposition)

Theme I a^b E Themes IV and V
(exposition)

We now can begin to grasp the "modernity" of the *Faust* Symphony to its full extent. The head movement of the *Faust* Symphony is to all appearances the first movement in musical history that is constructed on the basis of relations resulting from the division of the octave into three equal parts. To be sure, mediantic relations in sonata movements are current already before Liszt. Beethoven in particular chose the key of the upper major third as the key of the secondary subject, famous examples being the G-Major Sonata op. 31:1 of 1801–1802 and the Waldstein Sonata op. 53 of 1803–1804.

The late Schubert had a striking predilection for the "three-keys plan."[58] Thus the exposition in the first movement of the String Quintet op. 163 (1828) is based on the keys C Major, E Major and G Major. But no one before Liszt had dared to contrast a tonal center with the major upper and the major lower third as "counter-centers"!

How forward-looking Liszt's procedure was one realizes only once one includes Béla Bartók, a Liszt admirer,[59] in one's consideration. Ernö Lendvai has drawn attention to the fact that the division of the octave into three equal parts forms an important "axial system" in Bartók.[60] Thus the first movement of the Concerto for Orchestra (1943) is divided by the five appearances of the main theme as follows: F (exposition), D^b (1st half of the development), A (2nd half of the development), F (recapitulation, coda). A similar order governs the head movement of the Sonata for Two Pianos and Percussion (1937): C (exposition), E (1st half of the development), $G^\#$ (2nd half of the development) C (recapitulation).

To return to the "Faust" movement: The major-thirds relations discussed determine not only the harmonic construction of the movement but also the structure of individual passages. Thus the precipitous chromatic line into which the development of the head motif issues in mm 305–310 and mm. 590–598 is structured in chains of major thirds.

---

58 See Felix Salzer, „Die Sonatenform in Schubert" (typed diss.) (Vienna, 1926); excerpts in *Studien zur Musikwissenschaft* 15 (1928), 86–126.

59 Béla Bartók writes in his autobiography: „The renewed study of Liszt – especially of his less popular creations, such as the Années de pélerinage, Harmonies poétiques et religieuses, in the Faust Symphony, in the Dance of Death etc. – led me, past some less attractive externalities, to the heart of the matter: it disclosed the true significance of that artist to me; for the continued development of music, I discovered in him much greater genius than in Wagner and Strauss." See Bence Szabolcsi, *Béla Bartók, Weg und Werk, Schriften und Briefe* (Leipzig, 1957), 145.

60 Ernö Lendvai, *Einführung in die Formen- und Harmonienwelt Bartóks*, ibid., 97/98.

In mm. 519–534, the *dolente* motif is sequenced in a kind of development in major thirds, and the chordal progression *c-Ab-E-c* forms a highly characteristic "cadence" in mm. 619–622:

What is the semantics of the augmented triad and the major-thirds relations in the "Faust" movement? That question will have to be discussed in the next chapter section: But this much can be said here already: if we consider the exposed position the augmented triads have in the movement, and the relevance of the mediantic relations for its harmonic construction, it is plausible that Liszt applied the augmented triad deliberately as an emblem of Faust.

5. The Semantics of the "Faust" and "Gretchen" Movements

Richard Pohl's discussion of the *Faust* Symphony is of relevance for the history of Liszt research to the extent that it represents the first attempt to say anything more specific about the semantics of the music. Pohl's "procedure" consisted in annotating the themes and specific passages of the symphony with verses from Goethe's tragedy. Since there were no explanations of Liszt's to support this procedure, he had to be fully aware of the hypothetical character of the correlations.

Pohl assumed that the five themes of the "Faust" movement would reflect the "the main aspects of the Faustian character" and thus interpreted the themes as follows. Theme I expressed the "basic trait of the Faustian character, his entire being," namely *doubt*, sorrow, ill humor and discontent; contempt for the world, for science, as well as for his own endeavors; a hopeless inner bleakness." Theme II was the theme of "the passionate *quest* for a higher knowledge, and for mightier deeds; of restless striving without any inner satisfaction; of the struggle for freedom." Theme III was the theme of "ardent *yearning* for an unknown happiness; the cry for deliverance from the inner torments." Theme IV was the theme "of *love*, as general love of God and Man." Theme V, finally, was the theme "of *pride*, of the powerful consciousness of highest knowledge."[61]

Pohl had no objective grounds for his "designations": his procedure was purely subjective. Yet his correlations set a precedent: the later commentators all derived their support from him (even when proposing variant interpretations).

It will hardly be necessary to say that we cannot continue in Pohl's way. Our question today must be: in what way can sound, well-grounded insights into the semantics of the symphony be gained? If, to start with, we try to

---

61 Pohl, *Liszt*, 276–284.

concretize the semantics of the "Faust" themes, the following reflections may help us on our way.

As paradoxical as it may sound, we can win important initial clues for a semantic determination of the "Faust" themes from the "Gretchen" movement, drawing certain conclusions retroactively from the way in which Liszt treats the "Faust" themes there. It is therefore requisite to include the "Gretchen" movement in our considerations already here.

That movement exhibits a tripartite ABA' construction with fairly evenly balanced proportions. Two similar or even identical outer parts enclose a contrasting, thematically independent middle one. (A: mm. 1–110; B: mm. 111–207; A': mm. 208–291; coda: mm. 292–304.) Liszt furnishes the outer parts mostly from the "Gretchen" themes – those marked (except for the introductory idea) *semplice* and *amoroso* – while the middle part features the "Faust" themes. We can tell not only from Liszt's expression marks *dolce amoroso* (mm. 83 and 92) and *soave con amore* (mm. 187/188) but above all from the shape of the music itself that Gretchen's character portrait is centered on her love for Faust. The middle part of the movement – like the Adagio of Berlioz' *Romeo et Juliette* – is conceived literally as a love duet": in mm. 111–162, the motifs are recited in dialogue form, that is to say, alternatingly by instruments in the middle and upper ranges.[62]

Now it is significant that not all of the "Faust" themes appear in the middle part of the "Gretchen" movement. Liszt opens that part with the *dolente* motif of Theme I, which is repeatedly intoned on different degrees and marked with the terms *patetico* (mm. 111, 120) and *dolente* (m. 130).[63] There follow Theme III (mm.138–162) *espress. con intimo sentimento*, Theme IV (mm. 163–187) and Theme II (mm. 188–207) *soave con amore*. Theme V does not appear in the middle part; Liszt saves it for the coda

---

62 *The Andante amoroso* (mm. 354–388) in the head movement of Liszt's *Dante* Symphony of 1856, too, is shaped as a symphonic love duet. On the tectonics and semantics of the *Dante* Symphony, see my *Mahler and the Symphony*, 193–196.

63 In its character, this section of the "Gretchen" movement (mm. 111–135) resembles the *Andante mesto* (mm. 381–399) of the "Faust" movement.

(mm. 292–304), which cites the head motif of the theme several times like a reminiscence.

But what is particularly conspicuous is that the "dodecaphonic" theme (Ia) is not found anywhere in the "Gretchen" movement. I seems permissible to conclude that this theme must characterize a region that is alien to Gretchen. That can only be the region of scientific speculation: Faust, after all, does not confront Gretchen as a scholar. The "dodecaphonic" theme, notable for its quasi-mathematical structure, refers thus to Faust's learnedness, his penchant for reflection and speculation, his thirst for knowledge, the pensive side of his personality. We recall that Liszt wrote to Frau von Helldorff in 1869 about Faust that he wavers, experiments and reflects. The choice of unusual (experimental) means in Theme Ia, such as the functionless sequence of augmented triads, fits well with this.[64]

By contrast, Themes III and IV clearly have reference to Gretchen. For Liszt assigned them a central position in the "Gretchen" movement. Both themes, moreover, are instrumented in dialogue form in the "Faust" movement – Theme III also in the "Gretchen" movement. In the "Faust" movement, Liszt has the core motif of Theme III be played alternately in an upper and a lower range:[65] clarinets and oboes alternate with bassoons and low strings. The oboe, however, is used chiefly as Gretchen's instrument in the *Faust* symphony. If we also keep in mind that Theme IV is marked *affettuoso*, it its patent that Themes III and IV refer to Faust's relationship with Gretchen, in other words, to the amatory side of Faust.

The following givens (like everything else, not hitherto considered) also seem to support this interpretation. On May 11, 1852, Liszt had performed Richard Wagner's *Faust* Overture of 1829/1840 from manuscript in Weimar. Upon returning the score to Wagner on October 7, 1852, he wrote to

---

64 Not as a further argument but as a mere parallel, it deserves to be noted in this connection that in *Also Sprach Zarathustra* (1896), Strauss – 42 years after Liszt and certainly under the impact of the *Faust* Symphony – characterized science by means of a twelve-tone theme!

65 We should note that Theme III is structured dialogically already in the Weimar Sketchbook. See the musical example in Somfai in the *Studia musicologica* (1962), 116.

him that the work was very much to his liking – except for the secondary subject in F Major (mm. 118 ff.; Liszt speaks of the "middle section"), which he regarded as "insufficient." It lacked "gracefulness," and it did not have the "right relation or contrast" to what precedes and what follows. He therefore advised Wagner: "If instead of this [motif] you were to insert a soft, tender, gretchen-like modulated, melodic section, I think I can assure you that your work will gain a great deal."[66]

Wagner replied on November 9, 1852, that Liszt had "sensed" the crucial point of the matter with the right instinct, conceded that what was lacking in his overture was indeed "Woman"[67] and added:

> Perhaps, however, you would quickly understand my tone poem if I were to call it "Faust in solitude"! – I wanted to write an entire Faust symphony at the time: the first part (the completed one) was just that, the "solitary Faust" – in his yearning, despairing and cursing: Woman" exists in his mind only as a vague figment of his yearning, not in its divine reality: and it is this inadequate image of his longing that he smashes in his despair. Only the second movement was then to present Gretchen – woman: I already had the theme for her – but it was just a theme – : the whole was discontinued – I wrote my "flying Dutchman." – There you have the whole explanation![68]

Liszt's letter shows that to his imagination a (one-movement) Faust Overture without a "soft, tender, Gretchen-like modulated, melodic" secondary subject was unthinkable. Is it not reasonable to presume that he was guided by this idea also in composing his own *Faust* Symphony? His formulation "soft, tender, gretchen-like modulated, melodic section," in

---

66 *Briefwechsel zwischen Wagner und Liszt* (Leipzig, 1887), 1:193/194.

67 Ibid., 200.

68 The quoted passage in Wagner's letter is important, because it enables us to surmise that Liszt may have modeled the plan of shaping the *Faust* Symphony in the form of three character portraits (with the "Gretchen" movement in second place) on Wagner's precedent. Wagner also reports about the Faust Overture in his autobiography (*Sämtliche Schriften*, 13:237–238). The theme of the "Gretchen" movement mentioned by Wagner is, incidentally, noted down on a sketch leaf (preserved in the Richard Wagner Archive in Bayreuth) that primarily contains drafts for the *Flying Dutchman*. The theme was published by Egon Voss in his book *Richard Wagner und die Instrumentalmusik. Wagners symphonischer Ehrgeiz* (Taschenbuch der Musikwissenschaft 12) (Wilhelmshaven, 1977), 184.

any case, fits the *affettuoso* theme so well that one could think it was meant for it.

That leaves Themes II and V. What semantics did Liszt attach to them? Some clues can be gathered from the expression marks of the themes. In the "Faust" movement, Theme II always appears with the labels *agitato* and *appassionato*. An intensification of this expressive content is signaled by the epithets with which Liszt provides the theme's characteristic head motif elsewhere in the movement: we find the note *furioso* in mm. 117 and 124, *ardito* (bold) in mm. 202/203, *strepitoso* (uproarious) in m. 297 (at S), and finally *violente* in m. 312 . Theme II, we can say, therefore characterizes Faust's highly strung, passionate and immoderate nature, his vehemence and tendency to extremes. In ll. 187–207 of the "Gretchen" movement, however, the theme appears in a wholly changed form: it has been turned into the major mode and is now to be played *soave con amore* (!) Liszt thereby intimates in a manner both unmistakable and poetic that love has radically transformed Faust.

Let us now look at Theme V. In the exposition, it appears with the mark *grandioso* (at O), in the recapitulation with the labels *Maestoso* (m. 503, at Gg) and *Allegro con fuoco* (m 548, at Jj), and in the coda with the direction *Andante maestoso assai* (m. 599, at Nn). In m. 503, the trumpet voice, to which the melody of the theme is entrusted there, has the note *nobile*. Most of these descriptions closely fit the particularly solemn character of the theme's first phrase, which is purely diatonic and plagal in harmonization. An important clue for a semantic determination results from the observation that the *grandioso* theme is the only one of the "Faust" themes that is recalled in the *Chorus mysticus* (at K), which permits the conclusion that the *grandioso/maestoso* theme characterizes the grand and eternal in Faust. We will come back to that.

Summing up, we can say that the symphonic character portrait Liszt has drawn of Faust is indeed "multifarious, complete and rich," as Liszt had said in the letter to Frau von Helldorff. Liszt's music with its vehement contrasts and enormous expressive fluctuations conveys the complexity and contradictoriness of the Faustian nature. The five sharply individualized themes mark diverse facets of Faust's personality and of his all-embracing intellectuality, diverse aspects of the polarity of the "two souls" in the one breast.[69] The dodecaphonic theme (Ia) refers to Faust's learning, his penchant for reflection and speculation, his thirst for highest knowledge and the brooding, pondering trait of his character. Theme II characterizes his ardor and lack of moderation, his vehement, high-strung nature, his tendency toward opposites. Themes III and IV depict him as lover. Theme V, finally, characterizes the great and eternal in him. We see that these findings differs substantially from Pohl's correlations.

If few were to look for a motto for the "Faust" movement, the most fitting would seem to be the famous lines in which the scene of the Easter Walk culminates (*Faust I*, 1112–1117):

> Two souls, alas! within my bosom dwell,
> The one forever parting from the other;
> The one, in gross and earthy lover's lust
> Holds to the world with grappling organs clinging;
> The other fiercely rises from the dust,
> To spheres of lofty forebears winging. (tr. EB-K)

The literary critic Gerhard Storz has commented on this scene as follows:

> Abruptly the mood changes, as so often during the nocturnal monologue: Faust's recollection, awakened by the peasants and by Wagner, darkens in self-torment.... Once more in quick reversal, the curve of Faust's sense of being rises again.... [I]nto the sunset above the quiet landscape, Faust imagines a superhuman flight beyond all limits. At this point the alteration of up and down, depression and euphoria recurs particularly rapidly, particularly closely and vehemently. Precisely because of that, Faust for the first time becomes conscious himself of this change ... [T]he restless two-cycle rhythm of up and down, tension and release corresponds to and springs from the polarity of the two souls in the one breast.... Here it is *the world*, there it is *the high ancestral spheres*... "Upward", "above" – that direction means nothing other than Faust's claim to total freedom and superhumanity... And then the other, lower pole asserts itself, "the world."[70]

We find that Storz' commentary agrees perfectly with our technical and semantic analysis of Liszt's music.

---

69 Hans Joachim Moser, *Goethe und die Musik* (Leipzig, 1949), 119, rightly notes that the themes of the "Faust" movement (he speaks of four themes) give "a stronger intimation of the comprehensive spirituality of Faust than any theater music hitherto dedicated to the subject."

70 Gerhard Storz, *Goethe-Vigilien* (Stuttgart, 1953), 175 ff.

The following observation casts some additional light on Liszt's conception of Faust. Our analysis of the thematic material and its treatment in the "Faust" movement has shown that Liszt accorded a special relevance to the motif group marked *dolente* (sorrowful) in the first theme. For this motif group proves to be in fact a kind of leitmotif for the entire movement. It not only recurs repeatedly in the course of the movement but beyond that is used as an integrating element in several themes and theme complexes. Thus the three-note sighing motif Ic is artfully integrated into the *appassionato* theme (Theme II); the *plintivo* episode (mm. 166–177) is developed from it; and it is from the *dolente* group that Liszt gained the *affettuoso* theme (Theme IV) (this metamorphosis is, as already noted, truly astonishing). In a portion that follows the *grandioso* theme (mm. 250–271 and 519–533), Liszt antagonistically confronts the *dolente* with the *marcato* motif. In the recapitulation, the *dolente* motif is treated development-like (*Andante mesto*, mm. 382–399). And it is the *dolente* motif, finally, that in mm. 646–651 determines the somber ending of the movement. The preferential use of the *dolente* motif is without doubt programmatically motivated: Faust, in Liszt's conception, is a sufferer.

We cannot conclude this discussion without questioning the semantics of two unique episodes in the "Faust" movement – the *Allegro impetuoso* and the *misterioso*. Both episodes are in part composed of motivic elements that have nothing in common with the "Faust" themes. What is the significance of these elements?

Looking, to begin with, at the *Allegro impetuoso*, we can discern two parts. The second (mm. 45–65) opens with the "dodecaphonic" theme (Ia), which now appears in full harmonization. The first part (mm. 23–44), however, is based on independent material, namely on tritonic motif formations and on the diminished seventh chord (b-d-f-a^b).

Now, as is yet to be explained, both the tritone (*diabolus in musica*) and the diminished seventh chord are insignia of Mephisto in the *Faust* symphony. Mephistophelian elements therefore play a role already in the *Allegro impetuoso* of the "Faust" movement. That means that in Liszt's view Faust is unthinkable without Mephisto![71]

Mephistophelian elements, moreover, become visible and audible in two additional places in the "Faust" movement: in the development and in the coda. Thus the dramatically turbulent development issues, in mm. 349–353, into the repeatedly intoned diminished seventh chord on *b*. The passage in the coda (*impetuoso*, mm. 636–645), to be sure, has nothing to do with the diminished seventh chord. But the *dolente* motif appears here (mm. 636–639), in a conspicuously distorted variant that is typical of the "Mephisto" movement (see, e.g., the passage at B). The conclusion of the "Faust" movement thus points toward the "Mephisto" movement.

Faust-Satz T. 636—638

Mephisto-Satz T. 22—25

---

71 We have to note already here that mm. 23–44 of the "Faust" movement largely correspond to the sections mm. 1–10 and 36–47 of the "Mephisto" movement.

Seemingly altogether out of place in the "Faust" movement is the *misterioso* episode (mm. 147–166). Its character differs noticeably from that of the other portions. Dynamics, harmony, instrumentation, motifs – everything appears exceptional. The dynamics never leaves the *piano* and *pianissimo* sphere; the harmony is determined by perfect triads and seventh chords; violins and violas are divided into two groups each, of which one plays *arco* the other *pizzicato*; the woodwinds and muted horns intone long-held harmonies; muted violins and violas execute constantly ascending and descending figurations. (The broken triads in the clarinets and the violins and violas playing *pizzicato* in the rhythm of the head motif were added later.)

The passage, which has something impressionistic, atmospheric-ethereal, can refer only to the sign of the Macrocosm, which Faust perceives in the Book of Nostradamus (*Faust I*, 447–453):[72]

> How everything together weaves,
> One in the other works and lives!
> How heavenly powers rise and sink
> And chains of golden buckets link,
> Come with fragrant blessings winging
> From heaven to earth, their censers swinging,
> With harmonies the cosmos ringing! (tr. EB-K)

If one accepts this correlation,[73] one will simultaneously realize that the three instrumental movements of the *Faust* Symphony are not only designed as character portraits but also make reference to specific scenes of Goethe's tragedy. Our subsequent analyses will adduce further evidence for this thesis.

---

72 This was surmised in passing by Pohl (*Liszt*, 288), who, however, writes: "The mysterious whispering of the violins makes us think of the play of elves in a clear night under a full moon."

73 There is a striking similarity to the *misterioso* episode in the impressionistic-seeming F-sharp Major passage in Arnold Schönberg's sextet *Verklärte Nacht* (Transfigured Night, after Richard Dehmel) op. 4 (1899). The page illustrates the verse: "Oh look, how clear the universe shimmers."

241

6. Tectonics and Character of the "Gretchen" Movement

It does not take a detailed analysis of the "Gretchen" movement to perceive that it stands in sharpest contrast to the surrounding movements: a mere listening to the symphony will yield that perception. To make concrete statements about the character portrait Liszt has symphonically limned of Gretchen, however, one will have to scrutinize the music of the movement and to confront it with that of the "Faust" movement.

We have until now concerned ourselves only with the development-like middle part of the "Gretchen" movement, noting that it is composed of "Faust" themes and is conceived as a symphonic love duet. We now have to add the outer parts of the movement in our inquiry. Let us, to begin with, try to gain an overview of the tectonics of the movement. The following diagram will illustrate the structure of the composition, the sequence of its themes and its key relationships.

First Part
(consisting of "Gretchen" themes)

Mm. 1–15 *Andante soave*	Introduction (flute and clarinet quartet)
Mm. 15–51	Gretchen Theme I (*dolce semplice*); main key: A♭ Major; modulation to E♭ Major, b♭ minor, f minor and A Major
Mm. 52–57	Episode "He loves me – loves me not" (*Faust I*, 3181–3184) in A Major
Mm. 58–82	"Gretchen" Theme I (in A♭ Major)
Mm. 83–98	"Gretchen" Theme II (*dolce amoroso*) in A♭ Major
Mm. 99–110	Transition to c minor

Development-like Middle Part
Designed as symphonic love duet
(consisting of "Faust" themes)

Bewegteres Tempo	
Mm. 111–137	development, in duet form, of the *dolente* theme from "Faust" Theme I in C Minor, F# Minor, and G Minor (expression marks: *patetico*, *appass.*, *dolente*)
Mm. 138–162	development in duet form of "Faust" Theme III (mediantic modulation)

242

Mm. 163–187	"Faust" Theme IV (beginning in B Major)
Mm. 188–201	"Faust" Theme II (*soave con amore*) beginning in F♯ Major and after a modulatory passage concluding on the fourth-sixth chord of C Major. (The autograph score of 1854 shows this theme to be a later insertion)
Mm. 201–207	Transition (~ mm. 45–51)
	Varied Repetition of the First Part
Mm. 208–245 *Andante soave.* *Tempo I*	"Gretchen" Theme I (~ mm. 15–51)
Mm. 246–251	Transition (~ mm. 71–77)
Mm. 252–262	Reminiscence of "Faust" Theme IV (cf. mm. 171–187)
Mm. 263–280	"Gretchen" Theme II (*dolce amoroso*) (~ mm. 83–98)
Mm. 280–291	These bars were inserted only in 1880.[74]
	Coda
Mm. 281–304 *Un poco più lento*	Reminiscence of "Faust" Theme V

The first part of the movement conveys the impression of great simplicity, unity, firmness and economy. Two themes sufficed Liszt for portraying Gretchen: the *semplice* and the *amoroso* theme. (For the "Faust" movement he needed five). They are certainly sharply individualized, yet do not really contrast with each other. Both are in the same key (A♭ Major)[75] and have the same time signature (3/4 time), and both have a classicistic aura, especially by comparison with the boldness of the "Faust" Themes.[76]

---

74 See Liszt's letter to Friedrich Stade, December 11, 1880 (*FLB*, 2:302–304).

75 The "Gretchen" theme was originally sketched in A Major and in 3/2 time. Liszt had planned from the start to entrust the *semplice* them to the oboe. See the musical examples in *Studia musicologica*, 2 (1962), 122/123.

76 If one wants to explain why the "Gretchen" movement became the favorite part of the *Faust* Symphony already during Liszt's lifetime, one must not fail to refer to the simplicity, catchiness and also the classicistic traits of the movement. Significantly, it was the only part of the symphony that found any favor with Hanslick. "Although Liszt's Gretchen," he wrote, "conducts herself in a more refined manner in the Andante, has moments of grace and tenderness, her

Semplice Theme

naivety is that of certain of Makart's pictures of children, in which adolescent girls languish with screwed-up eyes and teeth gleaming covetously from under a raised upper lip." By contrast, Hans Joachim Moser (*Goethe und die Musik*, 119) cavilled that the "Gretchen" movement had something "that tastes more of Gounod than of Goethe: this Gretchen is more of a perfumed sentimental ingénue than a free-city petty bourgeoise." Both judgments seem to me to miss the essence of the movement.

With respect to harmony, too, the part is by and large extraordinarily tight in construction. A♭ Major is Gretchen's key, the ¾ time is her time signature, the oboe is her instrument. Exceptional features are found only in the passages mm. 45–51 and 52–57, that is, the star flower episode ("He loves me – he loves me not")[77] and the measures that lead up to it. They are the only ones that are in the remote key of A Major and in 4/4 time, and the only ones that are out of keeping also in an agogic respect: mm. 45–50 are to be performed *rallentando*, mm. 54/55, on the other hand, *poco crescendo ed accelerando*. With this exceptional configuration, Liszt intimates that, moved by her love for Faust, Gretchen "comes out of her shell."

A genuine contrast to the first part is provided by the middle section. It is development-like and given a livelier tempo, it strongly modulates, and it is also instrumented more richly. To the woodwinds and strings that create the timbre of the first part, trumpets, trombones, timpani, cymbals and harp are added in the second.

The recapitulation exhibits several deviations from the exposition. For obvious programmatic reasons, the flute and clarinet quartet of the beginning and the "He loves me ..." episode are absent. (Both were included in the autograph score of 1854; they were deleted later.) The *semplice* Theme appears in a figural variation (mm. 208–230). In addition, the *amoroso*

---

77 Pohl (*Liszt*, 298) was the first to recognize that mm. 52–57 illustrate the star-flower episode. Peter Raabe's unsuccessful attempt (*Liszts Schaffen*, 98) to cast doubt on this identification can be explained only on the basis of Raabe's prejudicial opposition to any programmatic interpretation of Liszt's works. See my *Mahler and the Symphony*, 47–50, 70 f. and 211–213.

Theme is preceded by a section that quotes the fourth "Faust" theme as a reminiscence (mm. 252–262): Gretchen is no longer the same after he encounter with Faust.

Altogether, the character portrait of Gretchen in the outer parts of the movement is drawn with great tenderness and softness. In its simplicity, unity and firmness, it forms a quiet opposite pole to the complex, conflicted and restless image of Faust.

Liszt was convinced already in 1848 that everything complicated and artificial was alien to Gretchen's nature. That emerges from a letter of March 30, 1848, to Bedřich Smetana. Smetana, then still a young, unknown composer, had sent Liszt his *Morceaux caractéristiques* op. 1 with the question whether he could dedicate them to him. Liszt thanked him, accepted the dedication and permitted himself a critical remark about the title of the first piece, which was contrapuntally composed and entitled "Gretchen in the Woods." "The canon form," he wrote to Smetana, "seems too scientific to me for 'Gretchen'. The simple title 'In the Woods' would be preferable in my opinion."[78]

7. The Thematic Stock of the "Mephisto" Movement and Liszt's Technique of Distortion

> "'Doesn't Mephistopheles,' [Eckermann] said, "also have demonic traits?"
> 'No,' Goethe said, 'Mephistophles is much too negative a being; the demonic, however, manifests itself in a quite positive energy'" Goethe to Eckermann, March 6, 1831

Franz Brendel observed already in 1857 that Mephisto in the third movement of the *Faust* Symphony "travesties, inverts, ridicules and grotesquely distorts" the themes of the "Faust" movement.[79] The angle nearest at hand from which one should view the "Mephisto" movement is indeed Liszt's technique of distortion. Wherein consists this technique? What programmatic idea does it serve? To what extent does it permit inferences about Liszt's conception of Mephisto? These are the questions that obtrude themselves upon a closer look at the movement.

---

78 *FLB*, 8:58.
79 *NZfM*, 47 (1857), 122.

Let us begin by examining the thematic stock. The fact that Liszt for the most part based the movement on Faust themes led critics to conclude that Mephisto was intended to be drawn as a "characterless" figure. The originator of this notion appears to have been Richard Pohl. In 1862, he stated:

> One cannot call Mephisto a *character* – he is only a *principle*, but for that very reason as systematic and logical as no character will ever be. He knows nothing of the stormy casting about between conflicting sensations and passions, the wavering between good and evil; and as little of the immersion of the self in and merging with another self. He knows no self-deception and no self-forgetting, no love and no longing. For that very reason, however, he also always knows exactly what he wants and does not want and – what he stakes! He risks into immensity, and although he loses in the end he risks with a boldness that, a genuine demonic trait, concisely characterizes his entire nature.
>
> Since Mephisto is no real character, he also has no characteristic motifs, not even a mood motif; his being consists in absolute *negation*.[80]

In 1894, this thought was elaborated by Lina Ramann as follows:

> While Liszt outlines the inner portrait of both Faust and Gretchen by means of fixed characteristic motifs, he grants Mephisto no character themes at all. Evil is after all the Proteus that assumes any form and therefore possesses none of his own. His character is to have no character. Consequently, Liszt has him pick up the Faust themes one after the other in scorn and derision, triflingly distort them to absolute grotesques, play catch-ball with them, tear and pluck them to pieces. He does not touch the two Gretchen themes, however – over them he has no power.[81]

Exactly thirty years later, in 1924, Max Chop voiced the same opinion:

> Besides his devil's phiz, Mephisto has nothing to show for that he can call his own. He always fastens himself to the created only in order to destroy it. His is the Protean nature, which to achieve its purpose can assume any shape and attribute so as to deceive, and therefore remains without any real individuality. A "character" without character. Therefore he also lacks, in this musical setting, the personal note to crystallize about a motif or theme.[82]

Only in 1931, Peter Raabe observed that Liszt incorporated into the "Mephisto" movement also a theme from an older composition, the concert movement for piano and strings posthumously edited under the title

---

80 Pohl, *Liszt*, 307.
81 Lina Ramann, *Liszt*, II/2, 186.
82 Max Chop, *Franz Liszts symphonische Werke*. 1:31.

Malédiction (Raabe-Liszt-Index No. 452).[83] Humphrey Searle added precision to Raabe's observation by noting that the borrowed theme is the only new theme in the movement.[84]

With the "Faust" themes and the theme borrowed from *Malédiction*, however, the thematic substance of the "Mephisto" movement is not yet exhausted. It has not previously been observed that Liszt did give Mephisto a personal leitmotif after all and that besides the already identified theme he borrowed some additional elements from the concert piece.

The "Mephisto" movement is actually based on the tone symbol of Lucifer as Mephisto's leitmotif; four themes from the "Faust" movement; the *Malédiction* theme; and a curse rhythm as leit-rhythm. We will discuss these elements in what follows. But first we should point out that the "Mephisto" movement is constructed in sonata form and divides into an introduction (mm. 1–53), an exposition (mm. 54–329), a development (mm. 330–431), a recapitulation (mm. 432–616) and a coda (617–674). The symphony concludes with the *Chorus mysticus* added in 1857.

Liszt opens and closes the introduction to the movement with the Lucifer symbol, a tritonic motif (*diabolus in musica!*), which each time is sounded three times. The motif, which later appears in significant augmentation also in the coda, serves quasi as identity badge for Mephisto, who is "of Lucifer's kind" (*Faust II*, l. 11770); his harmonic emblem is a diminished seventh chord. Liszt took both, the symbol and its emblem, from the Finale of the *Symphonie fantastique* of his friend Berlioz.[85]

---

83 Raabe, *Liszts Schaffen*, 53.

84 Humphrey Searle, *The Music of Liszt*, 47 f., 79.

85 A comprehensive investigation of the symbolism in Liszt's works shows that Liszt uses the tritone as symbol of disaster in the widest sense, that is: as symbol of Lucifer, Mephisto and hell generally (in the *Dante* Sonata and the *Dante* Symphony, in the *Faust* Symphony, in the first and the second *Mephisto Waltz*), as symbol of the Tartarus (in the *Requiem* for male chorus), as symbol of curses (*Malédiction* for piano and strings), of boldness and suffering (*Prometheus*), of sorrow and death (*Hungaria*), of mourning and lament (*Gran Festival Mass*), as symbol of the ghostly, ghastly, monstrous (as in the melodramas *Lenore* and *Der traurige Mönch* [The Sad Monk]), as symbol of rage (first *Mephisto Waltz*, *Legend of St. Elizabeth*), of doubt (second *Mephisto Waltz*), of the grave (*From the Cradle to the Grave*), of the evil omen (*Unstern* [Disastrous Star])]. See Floros, *Mahler and the Symphony*, 177–190.

Berlioz, Symphonie fantastique *(1830), "Songe d'une nuit du Sabbat"*

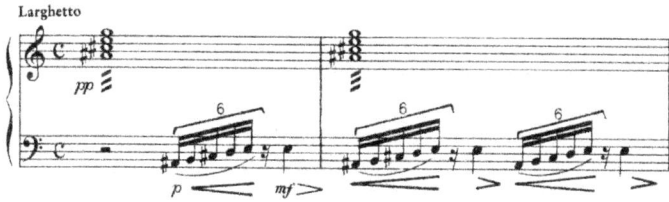

Liszt, "Mephisto" Movement (1854)

Of the five main themes of the "Faust" movement, four recur in the "Mephisto" movement, albeit always in changed form: the first theme, the *appassionato* theme, the *affettuaos* theme and the *grandioso* theme. The only "Faust" theme the movement dispenses with is the *espressivo* one.

How are the themes treated? The first thing one notices is that Liszt by and large does not touch their diastematic shape. The recasting takes the form of altered tempi, altered rhythms, changed articulation and changes in ornament. (In that Liszt follows Berlioz' procedure in the Finale of the *Symphomie fantastique*). The stately tempi are without exception changed into lively ones; the longer note values are shortened throughout; *legato* is mostly modified into *staccato*; a number of notes acquire brief appoggiaturas or are ornamented by auxiliary notes.

Theme II (metamorphosis)

Nearly all of the "Faust" themes are "dismembered," "decomposed" into their elements by characteristic rests or sharper caesuras. At times, Liszt splits off a motif from one of the themes, varies it rhythmically and in articulation and "develops" it, a particularly instructive example being the treatment of the chromatic motif from the *appassionato* theme in the "Mephisto" introduction, mm. 11–20

In this way, the character of the "Faust" themes is radically transformed – Liszt exhausts nearly every possibility of metamorphosis – and the themes are accordingly often furnished with new expression marks. With particular frequency the terms *marcato* and *scherzando* can be registered in the "Mephisto" movement. The expressive "Faust" themes and motifs repeatedly obtain a grotesque or "jocular" character. The *dolente* motif (mm. 4–5) appears in the "Mephisto" introduction (mm. 22 ff.) in nearly unrecognizable transformation, marked *marcato e scherzando*.

250

The *grandioso* theme is now to be played *giocoso*!

Liszt headed the movement *Allegro vivace, ironico* – a label that can be related to Faust's calling Mephisto "Du Spottgeburt von Dreck und Feuer," "you mocking [i.e., monstrous, abortive] birth of dirt and fire" (l. 3536). The term *ironico* points from the start to one tendency of the movement, that of persiflage.

8. The Concert Piece *Malédiction* as a Source of the "Mephisto" Movement

"Mephisto" and "Curse" Motifs in the *Faust* Symphony

The *Orgueil* theme with the Curse rhythm in the Concert Movement *Malédiction*, GA I, 13, p. 1854

The borrowed Malédiction theme in the "Mephisto" Movement, GA I,
8–9, p. 124

Our discussions will have shown that a closer study of the themes in the
"Mephisto" movement and of Liszt's technique of distortion can yield interesting insights for the semantic analysis of the composition. Even more
significant conclusions, however, will result from a close scrutiny of the
Malédiction theme and, beyond that, of the *Malédiction* concert movement,
from which Liszt borrowed the theme.

Our analysis starts from the observation that the *Malédiction* theme appears in several shapes in the "Mephisto" movement. It appears in more or
less "complete" form – that is, as a rounded-off phrase – in mm. 188–195
and 204–211, where it frames the theme of the famous fugue in three-
fourths time.

In that form, the theme measures eight bars and is composed of two
(similar) diatonic, but rhythmically pithy motifs and a chromatic extension.
A comparison with the other variants of the theme shows, however, that the
chromatic extension does not occur elsewhere and that the characteristic

trait of the theme is the pithy rhythm of the head motif. It consists of a half-note or whole not as "upbeat," two accentuated short eighths and a quarter note, followed by a quarter rest, with the eighth notes being repeated echo-like. The rest is a constitutive part of the rhythm.

Curse rhythm in the winds, "Mephisto" sextuplets in the violins

In this form (and some variants, often reduced to the two eighths and the rest), the rhythm recurs – even separated from the *Malédiction* theme – so insistently and often that one has to assume that it has a tone-symbolic significance and fulfills the function of a leitrhythm.[86] The observation

---

86 About leitrhythms in 19th-century music, see Floros, *Mahler and the Symphony*, 207–218.

that this characteristic rhythm is first intoned by the winds at the end of the introduction (mm. 47–52), as a motif complementary to the "Mephisto" motif (the diminished seventh chord, the harmonic emblem of Mephisto, here being "resolved" into a dissonance, the altered third-fourth chord) suggests that it must be connected with the latter.

Liszt borrowed the *Malédiction* theme, as already noted, from the concert movement in E Minor/E Major published posthumously in the *Gesamtausgabe* (I, 13) under the title *Malédiction für Klaviersolo und Streicher* (Piano Solo and Strings). Bernhard Stavenhagen, the work's editor, pointed out in 1915, in the critical commentary on the edition, that the word *Malédiction* was not necessarily the actual title of the piece. In the copy revised by Liszt that served as source for the edition, it stood above the first tempo marking (*quasi moderato*) written in pencil by Liszt – a noteworthy entry, which seemed so weighty to Stavenhagen that he did not hesitate to use it as the title for the concert piece.

Stavenhagen's decision provoked some sharp critical remarks from Peter Raabe. He favored the view that the word *Malédiction"* was not the title of the work "but a specification Liszt meant only to mark the first theme," and noted that in the above-mentioned copy Liszt labeled other themes and motifs with "catch-words" as well, namely *Orgueil, Pleurs-angoisses, songes?* (or *vagues?*) and *raillerie*. According to Raabe, the catch-terms "Curse, Pride, Tears, Anxieties, Dreams, Mockery" are meant as "instructions for the performer" (!) and document that Liszt "already early on created the kind of music that wants to render certain feelings, but without any 'course of action'."[87]

A detailed analysis of the concert piece, however, leads to the conclusion that Raabe's critique of Stavenhagen is groundless and that the work rightly bears the title *Malédiction*. Stavenhagen accidentally hit on the truth!

Let us consider first that Liszt's "catch-words" in the copy can by no means have been meant only as "instructions" for the performer (Raabe's regrettable tendency, as we have noted, was to lower the importance of the programmatic component in Liszt's music!), but constitute a kind of program. The situations they intimate readily combine into a "logical"

---

87 Raabe, *Liszts Schaffen*, 54 f.

sequence. Besides, the printed score, too, swarms with expression marks that clearly have a programmatic meaning.[88]

Even more revealing is the fact that the motivic and rhythmic elements of which the first complex, the one marked *Malédiction*, is constituted plays an almost domineering role in the course of the movement. The pithy two-eighth rhythm marked *con furore* recurs countless times and, besides, also forms the characteristic component of the head motif of the second theme (*Orgueil*). From yet another short motif of the *Malédiction* complex (mm. 7–8) Liszt also obtained the final section marked *raillerie* (mm. 118 ff.). (The concert movement is constructed in sonata form: exposition, mm. 1-`162, development, mm. 163–228, recapitulation, mm. 229–342.)

There can be no doubt that this concert movement is based on an unspoken program around the idea of a curse, and likewise that in *Malédiction* we may see the counterpart to *Bénédiction du Dieu dans la solitude*, a piano piece of 1847 from the *Harmonies poétiques et religieuses* (GA II,7). *Malédiction* and *Bénédiction*, cursing and blessing, damnation and salvation: one can see that the opposition of Evil and Good must have fascinated Liszt long before the composition of the *Faust* Symphony in 1854.

The most surprising result of our investigation, however, is this: Liszt borrowed from the concert movement *Malédiction* not only the one "theme" of the "Mephisto" movement but a series of additional elements: to begin with, the leitrhythm described above (in its reduced form of two eighth notes it is identical with the *con furore* rhythm of the *Malédiction* piece); secondly a short motif from the *Malédiction* complex (mm. 7–10) that is sequenced on rising degrees in the sense of an intensification (*steigerung*) (mm. 37–45 of *Malédiction* resemble mm. 355–360 of the "Mephisto" movement); and finally the three-note head motif of the

---

88 Some examples: *con furore*, mm. 1, 7, 228; *appassionato con forza*, m. 51; *molto appassionato ed espressivo*, mm. 70 f.; *teneramente amoroso*, m. 76; *teneramente*, m. 106; *con passione*, mm. 113, 296; *agitato*, m. 138; *impetuoso*, m. 140; *energico nobilmente*, mm. 164 f.; *Recitativo. Patetico, tremolando con energico, disperato*, m. 198; *Andante lacrimoso*, m. 199; *strepitoso*, mm. 219, 304; *avec enthousiasme*, m- 243; *pomposo*, m. 292.

Malédiction complex, which appears with a symbolic significance in the *Allegro impetuoso* of the "Faust" movement.[89]

Liszt's concert movement *Malédiction* thus proves to have been an important "source" for the composition of the *Faust* Symphony and especially the "Mephisto" movement.

9. The Curse as Key Idea of the "Mephisto" Movement

After what has been said, it should require no lengthy argument that Liszt imported the elements of the *Malédiction* concert movement just identified into the *Faust* Symphony precisely because of their semantics. There can be no doubt that all of them represent diverse forms of one and the same idea also in the symphony, that is, the idea of a curse. To both the *Malédiction* theme, in all of its manifestations, and the leitrhythm of the "Mephisto" movement Liszt attached the semantics of the curse.

Having once grasped these connections, one will be amazed to discover that Liszt has modified three of the "Faust" themes in the "Mephisto" movement with Mephisto's curse rhythm. The model on which this rhythm is structured ("upbeat" – two or three notes on the accentuated part of the measure – then a rest) gleams through the "Faust" themes and gives the movement a high degree of uniformity. Mephisto's curse rhythm puts his stamp, as it were, on the "Faust" themes. (Only the "dodecaphonic" theme is not touched by it.)

The curse, in Liszt's view, is thus *the* characteristic of Mephisto and also forms the idiom in which he "speaks." Mephisto, the "spirit of denial," cannot create anything of his own, but can only "negate" and "destroy" (*Faust I*, 1338–1344). He decomposes the "Faust" themes and, cursing, ridicules everything that constitutes its "content": the thirst for knowledge, Faust's passion and lack of moderation, love and his *nobiltá*.

In Goethe' tragedy, the curse idea occurs twice in crass form: the first time in the Study scene (ll. 1583–1606), where Faust, in despair over his earlier faintheartedness about committing suicide, curses everything earthly and Christian and thereby definitively succumbs to Mephisto's power

---

89 Cf. the passage headed *Recitativo patetico* in *Malédiction* (m. 198) with *Faust* Symphony, 1st movement, mm. 28–31, 36–39.

(shortly afterwards, he concludes the pact with him); the second time in the Burial scene (ll. 11735 and 11815), where Mephisto is about to realize that he has lost the struggle with the angels over Faust's soul: "And as is proper now, I curse you one and all."

We cannot rule out the possibility that Liszt had Faust's curse in mind in conceiving the "Mephisto" movement. It may be regarded as certain that the movement refers also to the lines from the Burial scene. In the coda of the movement Liszt has described the "downfall" of Mephisto and his *satans* with almost pictorial vividness. In mm. 645–654, the coda reaches its climax in the threefold *fortissimo* appearance of the Lucifer motif. The motif appears here simultaneously in ascending and descending direction and is coupled with the curse motif, which in mm. 651–654 resounds in the trumpet and later in the timpani. That is followed in mm. 655–670 by Mephisto's (Lucifer's) downfall: the music "glides" in countermovement from above and from below towards the middle – initially in the rhythm of the curse motif! Harmonically, the passage is built on the chordal progression E^b – G^b – A – C, the degrees of the diminished seventh chord, which recurs altogether five times.

Then harp arpeggios mark the reversal. Horn and cello anticipate the (Gretchen) theme of the tenor solo *Das Ewig-Weibliche zieht uns hinan*, "The Eternal-Feminine draws us on high," from the *Chorus mysticus*. With that, the scene of the action changes. The burial scene is followed in Goethe's tragedy by the Mountain Gorges scene. We shall see that this is also the case in Liszt's symphony.

10. Liszt's Setting of the *Chorus mysticus*

Our analysis of the "Faust," "Gretchen" sand "Mephisto" movements has shown that Liszt – contrary to the views of Louis, Kretzschmar and Raabe – has not merely composed three *character portraits* of Faust, Gretchen and Mephisto, but beyond that has associated his music with certain scenes of Goethe's tragedy. At certain points of the score, the connection with Goethe's drama is particularly obvious. Thus Mephistophelian elements, as we have seen, play an important role already in the "Faust" movement. (In Liszt's conception, the figure of Faust is unthinkable without the Mephistophelian component.) The *misterioso* episode of the "Faust" movement, referring to the nocturnal study scene, illustrates the *harmonia mundi*, emblematized by the sign of the Macrocosms, which Faust contemplates in the Book of Nostradamus. The *accelerando* passage in the "Gretchen" movement illustrates the starflower episode ("He loves me – he loves me not"). The middle part of the movement is conceived as a symphonic love duet – one can't help thinking of the Garden scene (*Faust I*, 3184–3194). The coda, finally, refers to the Burial scene and vividly evokes the downfall of Mephisto and his satanic crew. The picture thus gained is confirmed by a semantic analysis of the choral conclusion to the symphony added in 1857.[90] Liszt marked the part that is based on the verses of Goethe's concluding *Chorus mysticus* (*Faust II*, 12104–12111) *Allegro mistico*.

---

90 In the printed score, Liszt himself offers the option of dispensing with the final chorus and letting the symphony close purely instrumentally, and he composed 10 concluding measures specifically for this case. In concert practice, the conclusion with the chorus has long since become prevalent. During Liszt's lifetime, however, the question whether the symphony should end with or without the chorus was one on which opinions were divided. (See Liszt's letter to Franz Brendel of August 29, 1862; *FLB*, 2:26.) While Brendel (*NZfM*, 47 [1857], 123) and Pohl (*Liszt*, 317) championed the vocal version, Wagner preferred the instrumental one. In his autobiography, he writes (*Sämtliche Schriften*, 15:120/121): "If anything convinced me of the masterful power of poetic conception of this musician [Liszt], it was the original conclusion of the Faust-Symphony, which was given tenderly and gossamery, with a last, all-overcoming reminiscence of Gretchen, without any violent drawing of attention." Wagner makes it quite clear that it was the Princess Wittgenstein who in 1857 prevailed upon Liszt to set the *Chorus Mysticus* to music. Somfai, too, incidentally, wrote in favor of the purely instrumental conclusion (*Studia musicologica*, 2, [1962], 95). Yet

Two new observations in the score now help us to realize that the music of the orchestra, which provides the "frame" for the tenor solo and the male chorus, is not only conceived as an incidental "background" of the *Chorus mysticus*, as one would be inclined to assume, but that it refers to specific passages in the famous Mountain Gorges scene.

Typical is, to begin with, Liszt's original prescription *schwebend*, "hovering," four bars after H. It would be a mistake to dismiss this as a mere expression mark. We should remember that according to Goethe's "stage directions" the Pater Ecstaticus, the angels "in the higher atmosphere" and the Mater Gloriosa are said to "hover." Liszt's marking should therefore be understood as a corresponding musical "stage direction." In the text, too, there is repeated talk of the "hovering" of the Mater Gloriosa. Thus we read at the very beginning of the hymn by the Doctor Marianus (ll. b11989–11996):

> The view is free at last,
> The spirit recovering,
> There women are moving past
> Upwardly hovering.
> The Glorious One within,
> Star-crowned mid the maidens,
> The heaven's majestic queen,
> I divine by the radiance.

And the chorus of the penitent women chants (ll. 12032–12036):

> To the heights you rise [*schwebst*],
> Eternity's place,
> O hear our cries,
> Thou peerless in praise,
> Thou full of grace! (tr. E.B.-K.)

Very remarkable is also a "reminiscence" of the *grandioso* theme from the "Faust" movement at K, a few bars before the conclusion of the work. Liszt here cites, as the *only* figure from the manifold world of the "Faust" themes, three times in the low instruments, the pentatonic head motif of the *grandioso* theme, which in the first movement is once also marked *nobile*.

Brendel seems to me to be right in thinking that "only through this final chorus does the work round off to a complete whole and without it could, in my view, not at all succeed as such."

This portentous "reminiscence motif" at this point in the symphony can refer only to the choir of angels hovering "in the higher atmosphere," who carry "Faust's immortal part" and say of him (ll. 11934 f.):

Saved is the *noble* member of
The spirit world from evil.

These observations permit the conclusion that Liszt wanted to characterize Faust's nobility with the *nobile* theme, that is, the nobility of his "immortal soul." Strangely enough, the semantics of this theme was not divined by any of the commentators. They all took the *grandioso/nobile* theme to be a "hero theme"!

XVI. Richard Strauss and Program Music

> "C'est à peu près le seul musicien original de la jeune Alle-
> magne; il tient à la fois de Liszt par sa remarquable virtuosité
> dans l'art de jouer de l' orchestra, et de notre Berlioz par son
> souci d'étayer sa musique sur de la literature." Debussy about
> Richard Strauss.[1]

From a musicological point of view, Richard Strauss presents the image
of a composer who during the first half of his life was a revolutionary
and thereafter a conservative. The "young" Strauss, the composer of the
tone poems, of *Guntram*, *Salome* and *Electra*, was notorious as an avant-
gardist. Johannes Brahms counted him among the innovators in music.[2]
His symphonic works represented a non plus ultra of modernity and their
boldness strongly impressed Béla Bartók[3] and Arnold Schönberg.[4] The
"mature" Strauss, on the other hand, the composer of *Der Rosenkavalie*,
Ariadne auf Naxos and *Arabella*, was frequently branded a reactionary.[5]
He did not follow the development into atonality. What distinguishes several of his operas since *Rosenkavalier* is a creative synthesis of Wagnerian
and Mozartian principles. Characteristically, the late Strauss regarded his

---

1 Claude Debussy in an article about Strauss, published on March 30, 1903, in
   Gil Blas. See Debussy, *Monsieur Croche et autres écrits* (1971), 134.
2 Richard Specht (*Johannes Brahms. Leben und Werk eines deutschen Meis-
   ters* [Hellerau, 1928], 382) records about the late Brahms: "He was very
   pessimistic in his views about the future of music, refused to speak about
   the innovators who had rallied around Richard Strauss, and prophesied the
   demise of the art ..."
3 Béla Bartók writes in his autobiography: "From this stagnation, I was torn as
   if by lightning by the first performance of *Also Sprach Zarathustra* in Budapest
   (1902); the work, received by most musicians there with utter dismay, filled me
   with the greatest enthusiasm: at last I glimpsed a new direction, a new way. I
   plunged into a study of Strauss' scores and started to compose once more." See
   Bence Szabolcsi, ed., *Béla Bartók. Weg und Werk. Schriften und Briefe*, 144.
4 Schönberg's earliest contributions to program music, the string sextet *Verklärte Nacht* op. 4 (1899) and the symphonic poem *Pelleas and Melisande*
   op. 5 (1902/1903), would certainly be unthinkable without Strauss.
5 See Hermann W. v. Waltershausen, *Richard Strauss. Ein Versuch* (Munich,
   1921), 124/125.

operatic oeuvre "as perhaps a final afterglow of the evolution of world theater into the realm of music."[6]

Regardless of this Janus-headedness, so typical of Strauss, nearly his entire opus is still alive today. In German-speaking countries, his operas are a stock-in-trade of the opera houses, and one cannot imagine the repertoire of the major symphony orchestras without his symphonic music. Several of his tone poems can be called downright popular. Even so, one cannot maintain that it is easy to find the right access to his music. To be sure, one can appreciate Strauss' tone poems as "pure" music. One can, in listening, concentrate on the purely musicals aspects of his symphonies and admire the brilliance of the instrumentation, the colorful sound, the mastery of compositional technique, the verve of the melodies and the cunning harmonies. But it remains questionable whether that takes one to the essence of the music. For Strauss' symphonic music is program music; it is inspired by extra-musical subjects. As program music, it places special demands on the listener: it wants to direct his imagination into specific channels, it presupposes a certain "knowledge," and it raises questions as to the correlation between subject and music.

The symphonist Strauss, as we know, took his cue from Berlioz and from Liszt, whom he especially revered, and whom he championed time and again.[7] It is no wonder, therefore, that the "aesthetician" Strauss, too, was entirely under the spell of Liszt's aesthetics, at least in his "early" years. The more one attends to Strauss' art-theoretical creed, which he formulated in letters to Hans von Bülow and the Slovakian composer Johann Leopold Bella, the clearer it becomes that he appropriated Liszt's principles almost in their entirety. Thus he voiced highly emotional commitments to program music, which he derived from Beethoven, and in which he saw the possibility of "an independent further development of our instrumental

---

6   Quoted from Otto Erhardt, *Richard Strauss. Leben · Wirken · Schaffen* (Olten/ Freiburg, 1953), 331.
7   Strauss wrote to Ludwig Thuille on November 19, 1890: "From Liszt's work entering the life of musical sound I became very vividly aware again that Liszt is the only symphonist who had to come after Beethoven and who represents a gigantic step forward from him." See Richard Strauss and Ludwig Thuille, *Briefe der Freundschaft, 1877–1907*, ed. Alfons Ott, 114, 197.

music."[8] Like Liszt, he believed in the dominance of content (the poetic idea) over form and that new contents could produce new forms. He took music to be the art of expression *per se*, and he categorically rejected the autonomous aesthetics of Eduard Hanslick. But whereas Liszt did not attack absolute music in his treatise on Berlioz (his sole concern was to awaken sympathy for program music), Strauss made no bones about his view of absolute music as an anachronism and as a "lesser" art. On March 313, 1890, he wrote to Bella:

> Program music – music as such!
> Absolute music – its fabrication by means of a certain routine and artisanal technique possible for any halfway musical person.
> The first – true art!
> The second – skilled craft!
> Now today's music has, of course, oddly enough taken its point of departure from No. II and has been guided to its true destiny only by Wagner and Liszt.[9]

Characteristic of Strauss' art-theoretical position is also his Beethoven interpretation: like Liszt, Tchaikovsky and Mahler, Strauss was fully convinced that Beethoven's instrumental work was inspired by "inner" programs, which Beethoven mostly concealed.[10]

What, then, is Strauss' position in the history of program music? Nearly all those who took up this question thought that his symphonic oeuvre greatly exceeded Berlioz and Liszt. Their reasons for this view, however, diverge widely. Strauss' adherents declared his tone poems to be the *telos*, the culmination of program music. They interpreted Berlioz' and Liszt's symphonic works as stages preliminary to the Straussian symphonies. Strauss seemed to them the founder of a novel realistic style of symphonic music.[11] Strauss' critics, on the other hand, reproached him with having

---

8   Strauss to Hans von Bülow, August 24, 1888. See „Hans von Bülow/Richard Strauss Briefwechsel," ed. Willi Schuh and Franz Trenner, in *Richard-Strauss Jahrbuch 1954* (Bonn, 1953). 7–88; p. 69.

9   Quoted from Willi Schuh, *Richard Strauss. Jugend und frühe Meisterjahre. Lebenschronik 1864–1898* (Zurich, 1976), 154.

10 Cf. my *Mahler and the Symphony*, 15–18.

11 Gustav Brecher wrote about *Don Quixote* and *Ein Heldenleben* in 1900: "For the first time a recklessly realistic style is used boldly and grandly here, such as until then had hardly been guessed at, but one that embodies the natural and ultimate consequence of *music as expression*." See Gustav Brecher, *Richard*

degraded music to the level of a mere illustrative art. Ever since Debussy, who compared Strauss' tone poems to "picture books" and "cinema,"[12] one often encounters the notion that Strauss' symphonies exhibited an affinity with film music.[13]

Can Strauss' music really be called a model case of merely illustrating program music? The question cannot be answered adequately without differentiating. There are tone poems of Strauss' that are close to the Lisztean concept of program music, and others that diverge from it. To the first category belong the tone poems *Macbeth, Don Juan, Death and Transfiguration* and *Thus Spake Zarathustra.* In all four of these, what matters to Strauss – as it does to Liszt – is the "narration of inner processes."

About the tone poem *Macbeth* (1887–1890), Strauss wrote to his uncle Carl Hörburger on January 11, 1888, that it was "not after Liszt."[14] The orientation toward Liszt in the conception of the work is nonetheless unmistakable. Though the tone poem refers to scenes in Shakespeare's tragedy (the signals and fanfares in mm. 537–544, e.g., symbolize Macduff's victory over Macbeth), it can be called a kind of psychodrama. Like Liszt in *Hamlet*, Strauss dispensed with the communication of a detailed program and merely indicated that the two main themes of the work personified Macbeth and Lady Macbeth.

Strauss prefaced the score of the tone poem *Don Juan* with three fragments of the dramatic poem of the same title by Nikolaus Lenau, and he asked the conductor Franz Wüllner, who would perform the work in Cologne in 1891, on December 17, 1890, to reprint the poem in the concert

---

Strauss. Eine monographische Skizze (Moderne Musiker) (Leipzig, n.d. [1900]), 36. And in 1909, Rudolf Louis, who aimed at a nuanced judgment, saw in 1909 the "personal strength" of Strauss in the fact "that he developed the ideal-pathetic expression of Liszt's tonal language down to a minutely detailed gestural language, which in all seriousness undertakes not only to interpret the processes of external events tonally (by revealing the music latent in them), but also to *depict* it so as to make it recognizable to the inner eye." See Rudolf Louis, *Die deutsche Musik der Gegenwart*, 2nd ed. (Munich, 1912), 177.

12 Debussy on *Ein Heldenleben*: „Encore une fois, c'est un livre d'images, c'est même de la cinématographie..." See *Monsiouer Croche*, 135.

13 See, for example Ernst Krause, *Richard Strauss. Gestalt und Werk*, 5th ed. (Leipzig, 1975), 226.

14 Max Steinitzer, *Richard Strauss*, 1st to 4th ed. (Berlin/Leipzig, 1911), 60.

program, since it was "of crucial importance" for an understanding of the piece.[15] The verses chosen do not describe any "action" but speak about "inner processes": the central idea of the poem is the pessimistic realization that the tempest that impelled Don Juan expires in the suspended animation of all wishing and hoping. That idea also dictates the end of Strauss' music.[16]

Liszt's conception of the program symphony as a "narrative of inner events" is obligatory also for Strauss' *Death and Transfiguration*. As appears from a letter to Friedrich von Hausegger, Strauss conceived the tone poem as the vision of an artist, who in the hour of his death recalls his past life, at the end of which "the fruit of his life's path" appears to him, namely "the idea, the ideal he strove to realize, to represent artistically, but which he was unable to complete because no human being could complete it."[17] Fritz Gysi justly remarked that the basic idea of the bipartite tone poem rests – similarly to Liszt's *Tasso, Lamento e trionfo*, on an "anitithesis of lament and liberation, suffering and salvation."[18]

Also sprach Zarathustra (1896), finally, readily fits into the series of works that seek to give expression to an entire philosophy. Hans Merian drew attention to the fact that the motifs in this work do not signify words or things but "symbolize ideas."[19] Strauss' proximity to Liszt, the "musician of ideas," is especially evident here also.

(To prevent any misunderstandings, we should emphasize that we are talking exclusively about the relation of Strauss' and Liszt's programmatic conceptions. We do not by any means want create the impression that we are implying a stylistic dependence of Strauss on Liszt. It hardly needs to be stressed that Strauss' symphonic music exhibits an unmistakably personal

15 *Richard Strauss und Franz Wüllner im Briefwechsel*, ed. Dietrich Kämper (Beiträge zur rheinischen Musikgeschichte, vol. 51) (Cologne, 1963), 17.
16 Cf. my *Mahler and the Symphony*, 223.
17 According to Erich Mueller von Asow, *Richard Strauss. Thematisches Verzeichnis*, vol. 1 (Vienna/Wiesbaden, 1959), 116/117.
18 Fritz Gysi, *Richard Strauss* (Die großen Meister der Musik) (Potsdam, 1934), 48.
19 Hans Merian, *Richard Strauss' Tondichtung Also Sprach Zarathustra. Eine Studie über die moderne Programmsymphonie* (Leipzig ,1899), 49.

style, and that its polyphonic structure differs fundamentally from the rather more homophonic manner of Liszt's symphonies.)

Strauss departs from the Lisztean conception of program music in *Till Eulenspiegel* (1895) and *Don Quixote* (1897), two works in which external occurrences, a succession of more or less realistically conceived episodes, are rendered into music. Typically, we find here those tone-painterly effects that are time and again cited against Strauss: the imitation of the tinkling of broken pots (mm. 135–150), and the representation of the death at the gallows in *Till Eulenspiegel*, the mimicking bleating sheep (2nd variation) and the tone-painting representation of the ride through the air (7th variation) in *Don Quixote*. Strauss seems actually to have believed for some years that it would mean progress beyond Liszt to succeed in attaining a maximum of distinctness and plasticity of musical expression. That is the sense of those utterances, cited *ad nauseam,* about the menu card that a real musician had to be able to compose, or about the glass of beer that Strauss wanted to set to music in so materially correct a manner that every listener would be able to distinguish whether what he was hearing was a Pils or a Kulmbacher.[20] It is only natural that such remarks had to reinforce the notion of Strauss' supposed mere illustrative art.

That notion, however, does no justice to Strauss' symphonic oeuvre. For the illustrative is entirely secondary and peripheral in it. Strauss' phenomenal gift for musical characterization enabled him to attain the greatest possible plasticity of expression. But musical characterization is not to be confused with mere tone painting. Strauss' music is music of spiritual and emotional expression, not mere art of tone painting. Beethoven's maxim, "More expression of feeling than painting,"[21] could serve as a motto for Strauss' entire symphonic production. Even his "realistic" tone poems – *Till Eulenspiegel, Don Quixote, Eine Alpensinfonie* – are no exception. This becomes fully clear when one considers that tone painting is possible only in the detail. But as important as the detail is in Strauss, what matters is nevertheless the central, poetic idea, which determines the themes of the

---

20 According to Ernst Krause, *Strauss* (1875), 226.
21 See Adolf Sandberger, "'Mehr Ausdruck der Empfindung als Malerei'," in *Ausgewählte Aufsätze zur Musikgeschichte*, vol. 2 (Munich, 1924), 201–212.

composition, its form and every dimension of musical technique. Two examples may illustrate this.

The symphonic poem *Till Eulenspiegel's Merry Pranks* is constructed in rondo form. The composition is based on two characteristic themes, which serve to personify Till and recur in countless variants and constellations. The couplets (episodes) are supplied by two additional themes: the pastor's theme and the theme of the Philistines, from which Strauss developed the famous fugato of the "Babylonian confusion of tongues."[22] Strauss gave the work its rondo form for the sake of its basic poetic idea, which rests on the thought that the despite all of his masquerades, the joker remains the same throughout.

The design of the symphonic poem *Don Quixote*, which bears the subtitle *Fantastic Variations on a Theme of Chivalric Character*, is likewise motivated programmatically. The subtitle is not quite accurate, as the work is erected on two themes: the first, chivalric theme, recited by the solo cello, depicts Don Quixote; the second theme, which is assigned to the bass clarinet, the tenor tuba and later the solo viola, personifies Sancho Panza. The themes undergo ten variations – one has to say, highly distinctive character variations. Corresponding to the ten different adventures they depict, the ten variations, as has not hitherto been observed, are as different as they can be. To the fourth variation, which describes a luckless adventure with a procession of penitents,[23] Strauss has aptly given a chorale-like character. The fifth variation, Don Quixote's armed vigil, has the character of a recitative; the sixth variation, the encounter with the peasant wench, is shaped as a comical dance scene (one may note the intricate meter and the sometimes false-sounding "accompaniment" of the dance tune). The seventh variation,

---

22 Strauss wrote to Franz Wüllner on October 23, 1895, that it was impossible for him to provide a (detailed) program to *Till Eulenspiegel*. Even so, he explained some details in the letter, such as the meaning of the fugato. Later on he did not shy away from entering programmatic explanations in pencil into the score of Wilhelm Mauke, who wrote an introduction to the work. See Herwarth Walden, ed., *Richard Strauss, Symphonien und Tondichtungen* (Schlesingers Musik-Bibliothek, M eisterführer No. 6) (Berlin/Vienna, n.d. [1908]), 92–108.

23 Strauss attached no program to the score of the work, but provided concrete statements about the "content" of the Introduction, the ten Variations and the Finale, which Müller von Asow published (*Thematisches Verzeichnis*, 1: 218/219).

which paints the ride through the air, is composed as a variation over a crescendo-decrescendo and a zig-zag-like rising and falling line. The eighth variation, the luckless ride in the enchanted barque, is a barcarole. Strauss managed like almost no one else to associate the programmatic with the musical, to bring the demands of the programs into line with the demands of musical form and musical logic. He was also aware of this. In his essay written down presumably in the late thirties, *Aus meinen Jugend- und Lehrjahren* (From the Years of my Youth and Apprenticeship), he notes: "A poetic program may well stimulate the creation of new forms, but where music does not develop logically out of itself, it becomes mere 'literary music' [*Literaturmusik*]."[24]

Eduard Hanslick, bitter adversary of program music as he was, was thus also opposed to Strauss. Strauss' compositions were to him "not music from the source "but "compressed literature."[25] "The characteristic of the symphonist Strauss," he opined in his review of *Death and Transfiguration*, "is that he composes with poetic, instead of musical, elements and because of his emancipation from musical logic occupies a position more alongside, than in, music."[26] After what has been demonstrated, we can say that that this verdict of Hanslick's unquestionably constitutes a miscarriage of justice.

---

24 Richard Strauss, *Betrachtungen und Erinnerungen*, ed.Willi Schuh (Zurich/ Freiburg, 1949), 169.
25 Eduard Hanslick, *Am Ende des Jahrhunderts [1891–1899]* (Der „Modernen Oper" VIII. Teil) 3rd ed. (Berlin, 1899), 270.
26 Eduard Hanslick, *Fünf Jahre Musik*, 219–222.

XVII. Hidden Program Music

> "One cannot get to know the works of nature and of art after
> they are complete. One has to catch them in the process of
> their development to be able to comprehend them to a degree."
> Goethe[1]

> "The manner of its coming about is irrelevant to the quality of a
> work of art, and a private matter of the composer's: what solely
> counts is the thing itself, not its genesis." Adorno[2]

1. Preliminary Remarks

When, in 1977, an American researcher discovered, in an estate, a copy of
Alban Berg's *Lyric Suite* containing hand-written programmatic annotations by the composer, the news caused a world-wide stir;[3] even the daily
papers covered the sensational find. True, the enormous interest of the
public in this case was due primarily to the biographical backgrounds the
secret annotations exposed, namely Alban Berg's love relationship with
Hanna Fuchs-Robettin. Even so, the find contained a great deal of explosive
matter also from a musicological point of view: a string quartet that for
fifty years had been regarded as a masterpiece of *absolute* music turned out
to be a composition with a hidden program! At the same time, it became
manifest that a composer counting among the most progressive and gifted
of his generation paid homage to program music, a genre that, since the
beginning of the 20th century was frequently deemed hopelessly antiquated
in progressive circles.

But the *Lyric Suite* is not the only case of its kind. The more intensively
one studies the music of the 19th and 20th century, the more often one can
discover that many prominent composers wrote secret program music. They
were inspired by personal experiences, by visions and ideologies, by poems,

---

1 Goethe to Zelter.
2 Theodor W. Adorno, *Klangfiguren. Musikalische Schriften I* (Berlin/Frankfurt,
  1959), 106.
3 George Perle, "The Secret Program of the Lyric Suite," *Newsletter of the International Alban Berg Society*, no. 5 (1977), 4–12. And see Constantin Floros,
  Alban Berg and Hanna Fuchs: The Story of a Love in Letters.

stories, epics or dramas of world literature, or by works of the pictorial arts, based their compositions on programs but did not divulge these to the public. There are cases of composers who prefixed programmatic titles or poetic mottos to the movements of a work in their autographs but suppressed these upon publishing the scores. Gustav Mahler initially even announced the programs of his early symphonies, but withdrew them later. There is also a considerable number of composers who made detailed statements about their extra-musical intentions in letters or in conversations with friends, pupils or acquaintances, but carefully avoided all formal disclosures about it.

A first survey of the works that are based on a secret program reveals an astonishing collection of composers of such works. Carl Maria von Weber, Robert Schumann, Bedřich Smetana, Anton Bruckner, Peter I. Tchaikovsky, Gustav Mahler, Ferruccio Busoni, Anton von Webern, Leos Janáček, Alban Berg – all of them have written such music. The number and quality of works, the circumstances of their genesis, the reasons that dictated the secrecy about the extra-musical intentions – all this raises questions that urgently require to be clarified.

2. A Survey of Works with Concealed Programs

Surprisingly many composers in the 19th and early 20th century, as indicated, have written secret program music. Let us cite some representative cases.

In March of 1815, Carl Maria von Weber wrote to Friedrich Rochlitz that he was drafting a piano concerto in F Minor. During the composition, "strangely enough," a "kind of story" had insinuated itself spontaneously into the whole in him, "according to whose thread the parts lined up and received their character, and did it in so detailed and quasi dramatic a manner" that he would be compelled to give them the following titles: "*Allegro* Parting,; *Adagio*, Lament; *Finale*, Agony, Consolation, Reunion, Rejoicing."[4] Weber completed the work, which became the well-known Concert Piece, only six years later. He communicated the "story" he had had in mind during the composition to his wife and his pupil Julius Benedict. A lady sits in her tower, thinking of her knight, who is far away in the Holy Land; ghastly visions arise in her; exhausted, she collapses and

---

4   Max Maria von Weber, *Carl Maria von Weber. Ein Lebensbild* , 1:478 f.

loses consciousness; from afar, she hears sounds; they turn out to be from the Crusaders, who are returning, her knight among them.[5] Evidently, then, Weber had envisioned a highly dramatic scene. The four merging movements of which the concert piece consists describe the several stations of this "story": the *Larghetto [affettuoso]* the sadness and lament of the Lady, the *Allegro passionato* her terrifying visions, the *Tempo di Marcia* the return of the knights, and the *Presto [giojoso]* the joy of the reunion. Typically, however, Weber neither officially communicated the program in detail, nor did he add hermeneutic indices to the expression marks, as he had originally planned.

Besides works that proclaim a public message, there are those whose message is "private, that is, works that composers dedicate to friends, patrons or persons with whom they are in a more intimate relationship. In many instances, such works contain a "private" message, which initially only the recipient can decode. The personal relationship of the recipient to the composer, the special knowledge the dedicatee has, enables him to decipher the message.

To verify this thesis, one should take a closer look at the music of Robert Schumann, whose works are replete with semantics and "private" messages. Schumann semanticizes his music by means of anagrams and cryptograms, quotations from his own and others' music and diverse allusions. Of special significance in his oeuvre are the Clara-Wieck quotations.[6] The compositions that Schumann wrote for Clara contain a rich semantic fund, which was understood by Clara but so far has been deciphered by musicologists only in small part.

The composition of Schumann's first symphony op. 38 (1841), the so-called *Spring Symphony*, was inspired by a poem of Adolf Böttger's, especially by the line "Im Thale blüht der Frühling auf," "Spring is blooming in the vale." Originally the four movements were even to have poetic titles, which were suppressed upon publication of the score. The first movement was to be called "Spring's Beginning," the Larghetto "Evening," the Scherzo

---

5   Ibid., 2:311 f.
6   Wolfgang Boetticher, "Die Zitatpraxis in Robert Schumanns frühen Klavierwerken", in: Heinz Becker und Reinhard Gerlach, eds., *Speculum musicae artris. Festgabe für Heinrich Husmann zum 60. Geburtstag* (Munich, 1970), 63–73.

"Glad Playmates" and the Finale "Full Spring": thus the titles on the title page of the autograph.[7] The motto-like horn and trumpet call at the beginning of the symphony was meant to intone the line "Im Thale blüht der Frühling auf."

No fewer than three of Tchaikovsky's symphonies are based on secret programs. Conceptually, the Fourth (1877) and Fifth Symphony (1888) immediately take up from Beethoven's Fifth Symphony, which Tchaikovsky regarded as a symphony of fate. Tchaikovsky disclosed the detailed program of the Fourth Symphony in letters to Sergey I. Tanayev and Frau von Meck.[8] The programmatic idea of the Fifth Symphony is evident from entries in the sketches for the work.[9] For Tchaikovsky, fate was an insurmountable and invincible, disastrous power hovering like a sword of Damocles over mankind's head and thwarting all human striving for happiness. This idea Tchaikovsky expressed in both symphonies by a theme of fate, which, motto-like intoned in the slow introduction, later repeatedly recurs at crucial moments and in a decisive manner. Of the Sixth Symphony, Tchaikovsky said repeatedly that it was based on a through and through personal program, which he did not want to divulge. It was to "remain a secret to all." "May they all rack their brains," he wrote to his nephew Davydov.[10]

Anton Bruckner provided hermeneutic explanations for several of his symphonies in letters and conversations, of which most refer to individual passages in the works. In several cases, that of the Fourth and the Eighth Symphony, the elucidations are such that one can speak of a coherent hidden program. In autograph scores of the Fourth Symphony, the *Romantic*, which exhibits a striking affinity with Wagner's *Lohengrin*, the Trio and the Finale have programmatic headings, which were suppressed in the first

---

7 Emanuel Winternitz, *Musical Autographs from Monteverdi to Hindemith*, vol. 1 (New York, 1965), 99 f. See also F. Gustav Jansen, *Die Davidsbündler. Aus Robert Schumanns Sturm- und Drangperiode* (Leipzig, 1883), 245.
8 Franz Zagiba, *Tschaikovskij. Leben und Werk* (Zurich/Leipzig/Vienna, 1953), 191, 183.
9 See Nikolai van der Pals, *Peter Tschaikowsky* (Potsdam, 1940), 108 f., and fig. 15.
10 Zagiba, *Tschaikovskij*, 310, 318–330; Constantin Floros, "Tschaikowskys Symphonie pathétique", in: *Hören und verstehen*, Mainz 2008, 150–157.

(1890) edition of the work. Bruckner's symphonic oeuvre, as recent investigations have shown,[11] evinces diverse relations not only to Beethoven, Schubert, and Wagner, but even to the program symphonists Berlioz and Liszt. Bruckner was familiar with the art-theoretical maxims of Wagnerism and in fact esteemed program music more highly than *absolute music*. For him the creative process was demonstrably accompanied by extra-musical images and ideas, which frequently determined the musical shape. The authentic programs of the Fourth and the Eighth Symphony, which are commonly smirked at or ignored, have to be taken seriously and can contribute materially to a deeper understanding of the works.

Oddly enough it is far too little known that Gustav Mahler started on his compositional career as a program musician. He frequently regarded his early symphonies as symphonic poems. For the first four symphonies we have fairly detailed programs, whose authenticity is beyond doubt. Mahler repeatedly communicated and explained these programs in letters and conversations. His autograph scores and sketches, moreover, contain programmatic titles to many movements and parts of movements. Several of these programs were made known to the public at the first performances. In October of 1800, Mahler distanced himself from the current direction of program music in Munich, retracted his programs and declared that henceforth he wished to be played "programless."[12]

That fact must not blind us to the true nature of his symphonic work, which is clearly confessional in character. It is unequivocally proven that Mahler made the personal, ideological and religious questions that agitated him the subjects of his symphonies. His programs give expression to central contents of his weltanschauung. Thus the First Symphony, completed in 1888, is autobiographically conceived. The cardinal philosophic idea of the work is that of transcendence, the idea of surmounting misery and suffering. *Dall' Inferno al Paradiso* reads the programmatic heading of the Finale in the autograph.[13]

Ferruccio Busoni is known to have been the most decided representative of the aesthetics of autonomy at the beginning of the 20th century.

---

11 Floros, *Brahms and Bruckner as Artistic Antipodes*.
12 For detail, see my *Gustav Mahler*.
13 In the possession of the Yale Library (Osborn Collection).

His *Entwurf einer neuen Ästhetik der Tonkunst* of 1907 can be called a manifesto of the so-called *absolute music*. What is less known is that the "young'" Busoni occasionally let himself be inspired by poems in his instrumental compositions. Thus his *SymphonischesTongedicht* op. 32a, written in 1888/1889 and reworked in 1893, bears pessimistic mottos from Lenau and Leopardi – mottos he later rejected, declaring he had added them at the advice of friends but wanted his work to be regarded as pure music.[14]

Alexander Scriabin, one of the best-known Russian composers, became famous above all through his orchestral work *Promethée. Le poème du feu* op. 60 – a work that associates sounds with colors and includes a clavilux (color organ). Intensely interested in philosophic ideas, he paid special homage to theosophic concepts. Between 1904 and 1906, he composed a voluminous poem entitled *Poème de l'Ekstase* and in its 369 lines postulates the equivalence of the sexual act and the act of artistic creation. His identically named orchestral work of 1907, which premiered with great success in New York, is based on this poem. The weighty question whether the poem served as program for the orchestral work was controversial for a long time, because the composer avoided printing the poem in the score, feeling that conductors should first come to terms with the "pure music." On the other hand, considering the public, he expressed the wish that a published brochure containing the text of the poem should be sold at the entrance to the concert hall. Friedrich Geiger has recently succeeded in proving that the orchestral work clearly belongs to the genre of secret program music. He could demonstrate meticulously that there are numerous relations between individual lines of the poem and certain passages in the music.[15]

That most of the composers of the 19th and early 20th century had a strong affinity with literature needs no further argument after what has been shown. The list of these composers is extraordinarily long. One might add in this connection only the important Polish composer Karl Szymanowski. His highly original violin concerto op. 35, for example, composed in the summer and fall of 1916, is based on the fantastic poem *May Night* by his

---

14 Edward J. Dent, *Ferruccio Busoni. A Biography* (London, 1974), 117.
15 Friedrich Geiger, "Programm und Musik bei Aleksandr Skrjabin. Zum Poème de l'Ekstase und der 5. Klaviersonate", in: *MusikTheorie*, 30, no. 2 (2015), 139–153.

friend, the poet Tadeusz Micinski.[16] The numerous expression marks of the score, like *scherzando, dolcissimo, più tranquillo, grazioso e affabile, energico, appassionato, con passione,* or *emfatico e affettuoso,* characterize the various poetic situations.

Anton von Webern has established himself in our consciousness after the Second World War above all as a brilliant constructor, as creator of a quasi- mathematically stringent music. People admire the logic of his structures and emphasize the "abstract" character of his music. Only in recent years it has gradually become known that he let himself be stimulated in his creative work by extra-musical, personal experiences, and that to an extent one would hardly have thought possible. The death of his beloved mother on September 7, 1906, was an event that left deep traces in many of his works. In a letter to Alban Berg of July 12, 1912, he confessed that, apart from a few exceptions, all his works from the Passacaglia op. 1 on referred to the death of his mother.[17] This is true to a particular extent of his Orchestra Pieces op. 6 of 1909. They give expression to psychological conditions that governed Webern immediately before and after the death of his mother:[18] the fourth piece is expressly marked *Marcia funebre* in the first version. The most astonishing thing, however, as appears unequivocally from drafts to several works (op. 22, op. 24 and op. 28) is that even in the late Webern extra-musical associations triggered the creative process and at times also dictated the formal conception![19]

A special fondness for program music, finally, also characterized Alban Berg. All of his later instrumental works, the *Chamber Concerto,* the *Lyric Suite, the Violin Concerto,* belong to the genre of secret or somehow concealed program music and need to be looked at against a biographic or autobiographic background. Like Schumann, Berg, too, semanticized his

---

16 Alistair Wightman, *Karol Szymanowski. His Life and Work* (Aldershot, 1999), 176–189.
17 Ursula von Rauchhaupt, *Schoenberg/Berg/Webern. Die Streichquartette. Eine Dokumentation* (Hamburg, 1971), 124.
18 Letter to Schönberg of January 13, 1913. Facsimile reprint in Hans and Rosaleen Moldenhauer, *Anton von Webern. Chronik seines Lebens und Werkes* (Zurich/Freiburg, 1980), 111 f. – See also Webern's own commentary to opus 6 in *Zeitschrift für Musik,* 100 (1933), 566 f.
19 Moldenhauer, *Webern,* 382 f., 390, 393, 443.

music by means of anagrams and cryptograms, allusions and quotations. Moreover, he gave it a highly significant numerological dimension.

Instructive in this respect is, to begin with, the *Chamber Concerto*, completed in 1925, which Berg dedicated to his teacher Arnold Schönberg for his 50th birthday. In his famous "open letter" to Schönberg, Berg explained various technical aspect of the work's composition but disparaged them as "externalities." He wanted to emphasize that the concerto was certainly not poorer in "inner processes" than any other music ad divulged that he had "secreted" so many "human and emotional references" into the three movements of the work that the adherents of program music ("if by any chance such still exist") would be "as pleased as Punch" by it.[20] More he did not give away.

If Berg had not made these remarks, we might never have noticed that the three tone anagrams of the motto, *a-d-e^b-c-b-b^b-e-g*, *a-e-b^b-e*, and *a-b^b-a-b^b-e-g*, stand for the names ARNOLD SCHÖNBERG, ANTON WEBEREN and ALBBAN BERG (the *e-flat*, called *es* in German, standing for the letter *s,* while the *b* and *b-flat*, called, respectively, *h* and *b* in German, stand for the letters h and b). A major role, however, is played in the concerto by a fourth anagram, constituting the cipher of the second movement, which Berg kept secret. It consists of the notes *a, h [=b], d* and *e* and stands for MATHILDE.[21] Together with other observations, it enables us to realize that that the Adagio was conceived as an homage to Mathilde Schönberg, who had died in October of 1923. The concerto additionally contains numerous allusions to works of Schönberg, which, no doubt, were immediately understood by the latter, but which are concealed and can be teased out only by laborious research. Berg did not reveal in the *Open Letter* that with the *Chamber Concerto* he wanted to set a monument not only to his friendship with Schönberg and Webern but also to the Schönberg School as a whole. To it and to twelve-tone music, he was firmly convinced, the future of music belonged.

---

20 "Alban Bergs Kammerkonzert für Geige und Klavier mit Begleitung von dreizehn Bläsern," *Pult und Taktstock, Fachzeitschrift für Dirigenten*, 2 (1925), 23–28.

21 Floros, "Das verschwiegene Programm des Kammerkonzerts von Alban Berg. Eine semantische Analyse," *NZfM*, November 1987, 11–22; *Alban Berg. Music as Autobiography*, 167–195.

As is well known by now, Berg based his *Lyric Suite* on a detailed program, which is even more personal than that of the *Chamber Concerto*. The message he directed at Hanna Fuchs is even more confidential than the one directed at Schönberg. The programmatic foundation of the work is the depiction of the "fate" of a love that undergoes "a large development" and finds its final fulfillment in a *liebestod*.[22]

Berg's Violin Concerto, finally, was composed as a requiem for Manon Gropius, the daughter of Alma Mahler-Werfel, a nineteen-year-old girl, who died tragically on April 22, 1935, and to whom Berg and his wife had been very close. The first part of the concerto is conceived as a musical portrait of Manon, the second evokes death and transcendence.[23]

3. Why the Programs were kept secret

An inquiry into the reasons for the suppression of the programs has to consider several things.

An important factor, to begin with, is that several composers in the 19th century – Liszt, Tchaikovsky, Richard Strauss, Mahler – were imbued with the conviction that the instrumental oeuvre of Beethoven was inspired by "inner" programs, which Beethoven kept secret. Mahler even believed unshakably that there had been no modern music since Beethoven that did not have "its inner program."[24] It is conceivable that Tchaikovsky and Mahler thought they were following Beethoven's example when they suppressed the programs of some of their works.

A second point is that Schumann elaborated a whole theory about suppression of the conditions under which a work came about. As his articles indicate, he thought poetic titles requisite in many cases but declared himself opposed to the communication of detailed programs. In his famous review

---

22 Cf. Floros, *Alban Berg. Music as Autobiography*, 204–261, and *Alban Berg and Hanna Fuchs. The Story of a Love in Letters* (2008), *passim*.

23 Floros, "Die Skizzen zum Violinkonzert von Alban Berg," in *Alban Berg Studien 2. Alban Berg Symposion Wien 1980. Tagungsbericht*, ed. Rudolf Klein (Vienna, 1981), 118–135; "Alban Bergs 'Requiem'. Das verschwiegene Programm des Violinkonzerte," *NZfM*, April 1985, 4–8; *Alban Berg, Music as Autobiography*, 294–327.

24 Undated letter to Max Kalbeck, GMB², 254.

of Berlioz' *Symphonie fantastique*, he expressed some reservations about the direction of Berlioz' program music and put the thesis forward that the artist had the right and the duty to keep the occasion and the process of the creative act from the prying eyes of the public. As noted earlier, he writes:

> Man has a peculiar awe of the workplace of genius; he does not really want to know anything about the causes, tools and secrets of creation, just as Nature, too, exhibits a certain delicacy in covering its roots with soil. Let the artist therefore keep to himself with his labor-pains; we would discover ghastly things if with every work we could see all the way to the bottom of its origin (I, 83).[25]

Schumann thus pleaded for keeping the secrets of creation hidden but also thought that the precise circumstances of a work's genesis would spread by oral transmission.

We can infer from Schumann's remarks that he did not reveal the subjects of some of his works because he deemed them too personal. That reflection is likely to have been a decisive factor also in the decisions of many other composers who kept their programs secret. We may recall Tchaikovsky's *Symphonie pathétique*, Berg's *Lyric Suite* and the second string quartet of Leoš Janáček, which bears the title *Intimate Letters* and was originally to have been called *Love Letters*. In all these cases, the promulgation of the program would be a violation of the private sphere. For similar reasons, Bedřich Smetana concealed the detailed programs of his two string quartets: the program to the First String Quartet he communicated only to his friend Josef Srb-Debrnov; of the second he let out at least this much, that it was to be regarded as a continuation of the first.

Another weighty reason for the suppression of programs was the fear of being misunderstood. Thus Gustav Mahler had had the sad experience that the programmatic titles of individual movements of his symphonies had led to crass misunderstandings and misinterpretations by the public and had therefore decided to withdraw the programs. Even Richard Strauss, who regarded it as an honor to be called program musician, could not be prevailed upon to provide a detailed program to *Till Eulenspiegel*: "To put in words what I meant with the individual parts would often appear damned comical and cause offense to many," he wrote to Franz Wüllner

---

25 Robert Schumann, GS, 2:83.

in 1895.[26] And Leoš Janáček changed the title of his second string quartet from *Love Letters* to *Intimate Letters* because he did not want to "expose his feelings to the mercy of stupid people."[27]

There is also this, that program music in the 19th and still the beginning 20th century was an object of countless controversies. Praised by its defenders as the only timely kind of instrumental music, it was deemed a sphere of activity for charlatans by its opponents, as "fraud" and as the undoing of young composers. To Robert Schumann, the program of the *Symphonie fantastique* seemed "unworthy" and "charlatan-like."[28] From similar considerations, Carl Maria von Weber intended to present his Concert Piece first at a location where he was already known, for he was afraid of "being misjudged and reckoned among the charlatans."[29]

Bruckner is a case *sui generis*. His authentic programs to the Fourth and Eighth Symphony, as recent investigations have shown, must not be dismissed as "ex post facto intellectualizations"[30] of a creative process; in their core they are as old as the music itself. Bruckner, to be sure, could not make up his mind to divulge these programs to the public: for one thing for fear of his critics, and for another because he was aware that his programs consisted more of individual images than that they constituted a logically progressing "action." The programs for the Seventh and Eighth Symphony concocted by Josef Schalk were, it seems, published without Bruckner's approval.

In conclusion, we still have to take the following into consideration: a program provides above all a creative impulse for the composer and is by no means always intended for the listener. In the age of the poetization of music, many composers needed the extra-musical inspiration without considering any verbalization of their intentions. They apparently proceeded much like Giuseppe Tartini in the 18th century, who in composing his in-

---

26 *Richard Strauss und Franz Wüllner im Briefwechsel*, 29.
27 Otakar Šourek in the preface to the pocket score edition of the *Intime Briefe* (Philharmonia No. 487 (Vienna/London, n.d.). See also Jaroslav *Vogel, Leoš Janáček. Leben und Werk*, 470–476.
28 Robert Schumann, GS, 1:83.
29 Max Maria von Weber, *Carl Maria von Weber*, 1:478 f., cf. 2:311 f.
30 Hans Ferdinand Redlich, "Das programmatische element bei Bruckner, in *Bruckner Studien* (1964), 87–97.

strumental works let himself be inspired by verses of Metastasio and other poets but recorded the texts in his own secret code in the scores and never published them.[31]

4. Approaches to Semantic Decoding

If one wants to fully understand, and adequately analyze, a work with a secret program, a standard structural analysis, as productive as it may be in individual instances, will not suffice. The peculiar character of this music is that its structure, the musical shape in all its dimensions, and frequently also the compositional technique are determined to a considerable extent by the extra-musical impulse. Extra-musical contents are often encoded in symbols. It is therefore requisite to include semantic aspects in the structural analysis. To put it differently: the structural analysis has to be joined by a semantic one.

How is that to be managed? To begin with, one has to free oneself of numerous widely held prejudices. It is an error, for example, to think that the extra-musical impulse is not germane to the aesthetics of the work, or that musicology as a branch of aesthetics is legitimate only if it succeeds in wholly or at least largely disregarding the person of the artist, the circumstances of his life, his spiritual world and the intellectual currents of his time. It is surely indisputable that there are periods in the history of pictorial art, literature and music in which the personality of the artist is strongly present behind his work, in which in the dialectic of objective and subjective elements the accent is on the subjective.[32] Such an epoch of art, and therefore also of music, is the 19th century.

Goethe had already realized that the occasion and the circumstances of a work of art's genesis require in-depth investigation. The genetic history of a composition is as relevant an object of research as its structure. Every document that casts light on the process of the work's creation should be

---

31 See Minos Dounias, *Die Violinkonzerte Giuseppe Tartinis als Ausdruck einer Künstlerpersönlichkeit und einer Kulturepoche* (Wolfenbüttel/Berlin, 1935), 86 ff.
32 Cf. Floros, "Weltanschauung und Symphonik bei Mahler," in *Gustav Mahler Kolloquium 1979* (Beiträge der Österreichischen Gesellschaft für Musik, vol. 7) (Kassel etc., 1981), 29–39.

utilized. This is especially true of any hermeneutic statements of the composer, which need to be scrutinized for their evidence. They are by no means merely part of the genetic history's "anecdotal" penumbra, as it sometimes maintained. Even in the case of Bruckner, the programmatic explanations must be taken seriously. The objection frequently raised that some composers were "naïve" in giving out thoughtless interpretive hints for a better understanding of their works is mostly without foundation.

Special attention is then due to compositional sketches. Not only the ultimate shape of a work must be the object of our research but the entire compositional process from the earliest drafts to the final product. It should really go without saying that the study of a composer's sketches will yield important perspectives for his way of working, his compositional plans and also his poetic intentions. Sketches of Tchaikovsky, Bruckner, Mahler, Webern and Alban Berg, for example, contain clearly programmatic key words. As yet, however, the study of sketches is still in its infancy.

How can works with secret programs be semantically deciphered? Music, of course, is a language *sui generis*.[33] As Liszt already noted,[34] it has its own grammar, logic, syntax and rhetoric, as well as a vocabulary that is subject to constant change. Tonal phonemes include above all characters, calls, signals and symbols. Characters signify compositional types and genres with prominent stylistic features and distinctive expressive values. In the symphony of the 19th century – and especially in Mahler – one can distinguish numerous characters of vocal or instrumental provenance as well as dance forms. Characters of vocal provenance include the recitative, the arioso, the chorale, the hymn and the song (without words). Examples of instrumental characters are the march, the funeral march, exequial music, the pastoral, the serenade and especially the type of "music from far-off." Dance characters include the minuet, the landler, the waltz and the valse. A category sui generis is the scherzo character. Many composers translate

---

33 Already in 1949, Erich Schenk ("Das historische Gefüge des musikalischen Kunstwerkes," *Almanach der Österreichischen Akademie der Wissenschaften*, 99 [1949; Vienna, 1950], 170–189; p. 174) pointed out that the primary unifying element of the music of the last 500 years has been its "speech character." See Klaus Wolfgang Niemöller, *Der sprachhafte Charakter der Musik* (Rheinisch-Westfälische Akademie der Wissenschaften, Vorträge G 244) (Opladen, 1980).

34 Franz Liszt, "Robert Schumann" (1855), GS, 4:162.

extra-musical contents into musical characters. It is evident that the march has a different semantics from that of the pastoral, that the chorale marks an entirely different semantic field than the dance characters. Systematic analyses of the characters in the symphonic music of Tchaikovsky, Bruckner and Mahler have yielded a semantic determination of numerous passages or sections.

Of equal relevance are tonal symbols. Not only the music drama of Richard Wagner but a major part 19th century symphonic composition resides on a highly significant symbolic level. Many symphonists – we might mention Berlioz, Liszt, Richard Strauss, Tchaikovsky, Bruckner and Mahler – frequently employ motifs, themes, rhythms, characteristic chords and even instrumental timbres with a specific symbolic intention, which need to be figured out. In the case of Mahler, three ways above all proved to be promising for symbolic decipherment.

One way leads via the vocal work. In Mahler's vocal compositions numerous tonal symbols appear besides calls and musical signals, whose meaning can be ascertained with the aid of the texts. Since some of these symbols also recur in purely instrumental symphonic movements, an identification is possible.

A second way takes off from Mahler's programmatic comments on certain symphonies. In some cases, Mahler himself drew attention to the symbolic significance of certain musical means or events. If the same or similar means appear in symphonic movements for which no commentaries have come down to us, we can, by analogy and with the necessary caution, impute a similar semantics to these means.

The third and most promising way takes off from the observation that many leitmotifs of Wagner, Liszt and Richard Strauss, whose semantics is known or decidable, occur also in symphonies of Mahler in identical or similar form. In these cases, too, one can determine, by analogy and with the aid of other observations, that theses tone formations have a corresponding meaning also in Mahler. Thus certain *Inferno* and *Paradiso* motifs can be traced in Mahler's early symphonies, which Mahler borrowed partly from Liszt's *Dante* symphony and partly from Wagner's *Parsifal*.

Lisztean and Wagnerian tone symbols also occur repeatedly in Bruckner's symphonies and offer secure grounds for interpretation.

Already from what has been said so far it will have become apparent that comparative symbolic studies have to be conducted on the broadest of bases.

Another important part of semantic decipherment is he study of quotation and reminiscence technique as well as of the technique if thematic interconnections and interweavings. Many composers quote, paraphrase or intimate motifs and themes from works of other composers, earlier works of their own or earlier movements of the same work, thereby providing us with important tips for the semantic analysis. Thus the study of the Zemlinsky and *Tristan* quotations in Berg's *Lyric Suite* greatly facilitated the decipherment of that work's secret program.

Many composers relate their personal experiences to their art. As we have stated, programs were in many instance suppressed because they were too personal. An expansion of the analysis of a work by aspects of biographic research is therefore indispensable. Above all drastic biographic experiences occurring during the time of a work's genesis or before are to be considered. Countless compositions are conceived autobiographically or have some other personal connection, which is sometimes expressed in dedications.[35] Of the advanced music of the 19th and 20th century it can be said that the much discussed thesis of the unity of living and creating was especially valid for them.

Critics who think formalistically maintain that secret program music was not really program music at all, since a major condition of the matter, namely the communication of the subject, was not given. Secret programs were thus "private matters" of the composer; they were not part of the "aesthetic matter." They might be of interest to the scholar; for the listener they were irrelevant.

The reply to this thesis is that music with a program that was kept secret does not thereby cease to be programmatic. What counts is whether a composer let himself be guided in his work by an extra-musical subject. The question whether he announced his program to the public is a secondary

---

35 See Constantin Floros, "Zur Deutung der Symphonik Bruckners. Das Adagio der Neunten Symphonie," in *Bruckner-Jahrbuch 1981* (Linz, 1982), 89–96; „Die Zitate in Bruckners Symphonik," in *Bruckner-Jahrbuch 1982/1983* (Linz, 1984), 7–18.

one. Basically, an adequate reception of a work of art having a suppressed or retracted program presupposes the knowledge of that program.

FERRUCCIO BUSONI, Symphonic Tone Poem op. 32a
Title page of the autograph
First publication
by permission of the Deutsche Staatsbibliothek Berlin/GDR

The pessimistic mottos from Lenau and Leopardi were later rejected by Busoni. He became an apologist for absolute music.

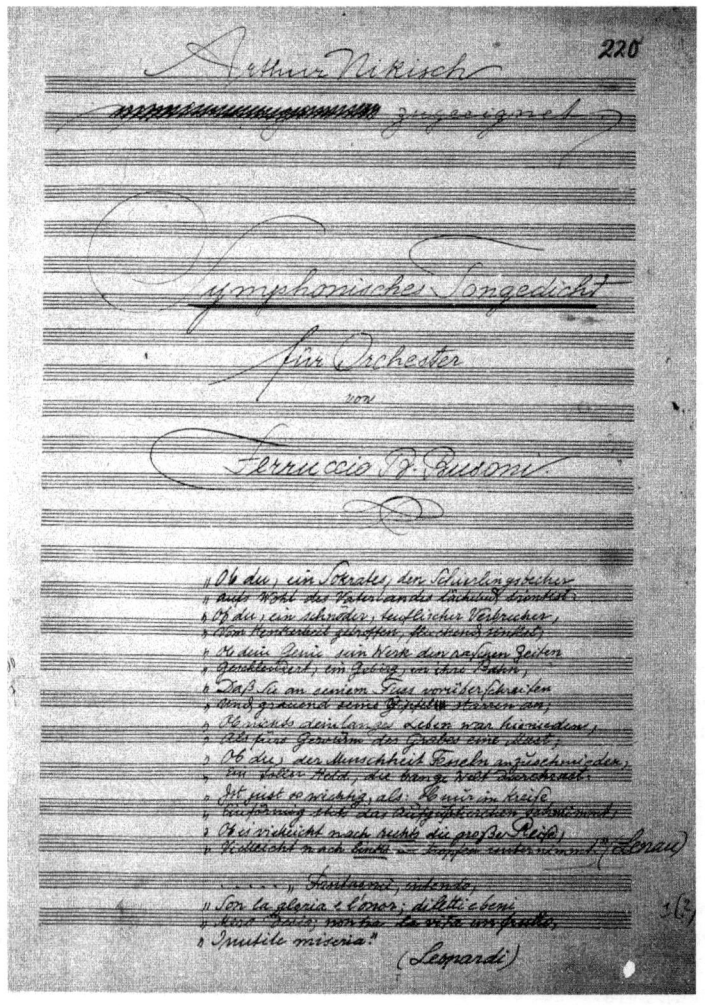

FERRUCCIO BUSONI, Symphonic Tone Poem op. 32a
Autograph, first page of the score
First publication
by permission of the Deutsche Staatsbibliothek Berlin/GDR

The poetic-programmatic headings of the tone poem were obliterated by Busoni.

287

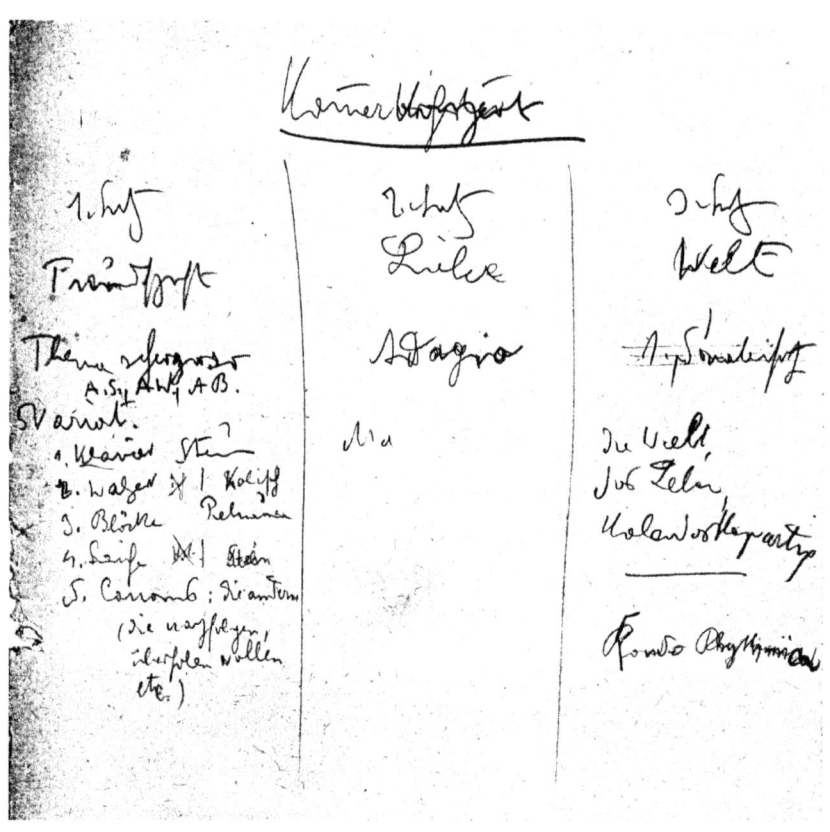

ALBAN BERG, sketches for the *Chamber Concerto*
Austrian National Library, Music Collection, Fonds 21
Berg 74/II fol.2
Published by permission of the Austrian National Library

Draft of the secret program of the *Chamber Concerto*. The three movements of
the work are characterized by the three key words *Friendship*, *Love* and *World*.
The abbreviation *Ma* in the second rubric below the words *Love* and *Adagio* is a
cryptographic abbreviation for Mathilde Schönberg, to whose memory the second
movement is dedicated.

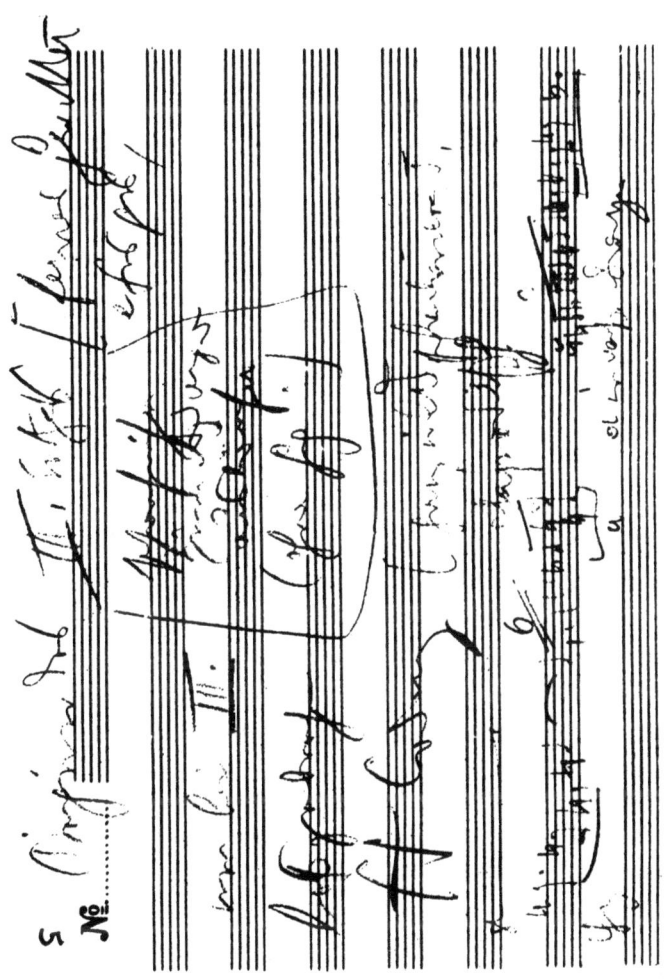

ALBAN BERG, Sketches for the *Chamber Concerto*
Austrian National Library, Music Collection, Fonds 21
Berg 74/X fol. 5
First publication
By permission of the Austrian National Library

The key word *distant thunderstorm* refers to the five bars of the piano at the end of
the Adagio (mm. 476–480) – five bars, which contain the Schönberg anagram like a
motto. At the beginning of the third movement, the "thunderstorm" – Schönberg's
grief over the death of his wife Mathilde – breaks in the form of a cadenza in fortissimo.

XVIII. On the History of Mahler Reception

Habent sua fata libelli. Terentianus Maurus

1. On Mahler's Topicality and Popularity

Not only books and art works have their fates. The stories of the reception of great artists, too, exhibit fateful aspects. This is especially clear with regard to the history of Mahler's reception, which ran a truly remarkable course. During his lifetime, Mahler, recognized and celebrated as a conductor, was controversial, even condemned as a composer. After his death, several conductors promoted his symphonic work. In the Third Reich, his music was stigmatized as *entartete Kunst*, degenerate art.[1] After World War II, it experienced an unexampled renaissance worldwide – a popularity without parallel. When the Cologne University academician Michael Braunfels ascertained the twenty composers most performed in subscription concerts in the Federal Republic during the season of 1979/1980, Mahler stood in fourth place after Mozart, Beethoven and Brahms and before Haydn, Dvořák and Tchaikovsky.[2]

To explain this puzzling vogue, one has to consider several things. Kurt Blaukopf justly spoke of a "syndrome of factors" that included text-based elements as well as performance-related and extra-musical ones.[3] Among the most relevant factors, Blaukopf mentioned the new interest in the culture of the old Austria, in the Viennese Secession, in Gustav Klimt and Sigmund Freud, secondly the discovery, spread and propagation of Mahler through records and radio, and finally the composer's being stylized as a figurehead for those protesting against the established culture. But it can

---

1 Karl Blessinger, *Judentum und Musik. Ein Beitrag zur Kultur- und Rassenpolitik* (Berlin, 1944), 130.
2 According to Heinz Becker, "Musik-Kritik," in Heinz-Dietrich Fischer, ed., *Kritik in Massenmedien. Objektive Kriterien oder subjektive Wertung?* (Deutscher Ärzte-Verlag Cologne-Lövenich, 1983), 111–133; pp. 122 f.
3 Kurt Blaukopf, "Hintergründe der Mahler-Renaissance," in Otto Kolleritsch, ed., *Gustav Mahler. Sinfonie und Wirklichkeit* (Studien zur Wertungsforschung, vol. 9) (Graz, 1977), 16–23.

be regarded as certain that there were a number of other reasons, including economic, psychological and cultural ones. Let us cite the most important ones.

In 1961, the copyright on Mahler's works expired. Mahler thus became less expensive for concert impresarios, the recording industry and the media.

A substantial contribution to the Mahler renaissance was made, secondly, by Lucchino Visconti' film *Death in Venice* of 1971, in which Mahler lends his features to the "decadent" writer Gustav (!) Aschenbach.[4] The soundtrack for this movie, the Adagietto from the Fifth Symphony, became for many the quintessence of Mahleresque music. Surely this is also the reason why the Fifth has been particularly popular since then. Most of the younger conductors, from what one hears, give it their preference.

The decisive reason for Mahler's astonishing popularity among larger sections of listeners is, of course, the strong emotional impact of his music, its stirring effect, and the broadly diversified expressive scale it possesses. It ranges, as already Bruno Walter stated in a letter to Mahler, from quietude to passion, from the old-fashioned to the novel, from humor to pathos, from irony to sublimity.[5] In view of this diversity, it must seem an inadmissible, if understandable, generalization to overemphasize the melancholy, nostalgic, the resigned or the utopian character of Mahler's music: to many it conveys the aura of the *fin de siècle*.

The Mahler reception takes a quite different direction among the composers of the avant-garde and among many musicologists. These, who represent, to speak with Theodor W. Adorno, the type of the expert among listeners,[6] are less interested in the affective qualities of Mahler's music than they are in its technical innovations and achievements. They see in Mahler a pioneer of the New Music, not only a predecessor of the

---

4   Cf. Otto Kolleritsch, "Historischer Versuch über Gustav Mahlers Aktualität," in Mahler. *Sinfonie und Wirklichkeit*, 24–39; p. 32; Monika Tibbe, "Anmerkungen zur Mahler-Rezeption," in Peter Ruzicka, ed., *Mahler – eine Herausforderung. Ein Symposion* (Wiesbaden, 1977), 85–100.
5   Lotte Walter Lindt, ed., *Bruno Walter. Briefe 1894–1962* (Frankfurt, 1969), 112 ff.
6   Theodor W. Adorno, *Einleitung in die Musiksoziologie. Zwölf theoretische Vorlesungen* (rowohlts deutsche enzyklopädie, vol. 292/293) (Reinbek, 1968), 15–17.

Schönberg School, but also a composer in whose work even germs of the much later serial technique can be discovered.[7] What matters to them is the anticipatory element in Mahler, one that was then implemented by the New Music.

What both strands of the Mahler reception have in common is that they wholly or largely ignore the programmatic presuppositions of his symphonies. Since Mahler eventually withdrew the programs of the first four symphonies, they were treated as though they had never existed. People took great pleasure in admiring Mahler as a master of the so-called *absolute music*. That view, however, is highly questionable because it cheats Mahler's music of its spiritual dimension. This point need to be clarified at the outset.

2. The Spiritual Dimension of Mahler's Music

Gustav Mahler did not subscribe to the doctrine of *l'art pour l'art* but believed in the parallelism of art and life. He was wholly convinced that art and life, art and nature, art and world were closely related. He conceived of his music as a music of experience, as autobiography in notes and as the expression of a weltanschauung. The retracted programs of the first four symphonies, the poetic-programmatic titles in the autographs, Mahler's numerous written and oral hermeneutic explanations, they all document impressively what the semantic analysis of the music confirms, namely, that Mahler's music can under no circumstances be categorized as absolute music, but has to be understood as a music that gives expression to personal, biographic, literary and philosophic themes and ideas.

Mahler, a religious thinker, was unremittingly occupied with philosophic (ontological and eschatological) questions, with the problem of the "beyond," with the ideas of return, continued existence after death, and the idea of transcending death through love. These ideas frequently form the spiritual substrate of his symphonies.[8] Some examples will illustrate this.

---

7   Dieter Schnebel, „Das Spätwerk als Neue Musik," in *Gustav Mahler* (Tübingen: Rainer Wunderlich, 1966), 157–188, esp. p. 161.
8   See my *Gustav Mahler*.

The program of the Second Symphony formulates the belief in the meaningfulness of existence, the dialectic of death and rebirth. The cosmological doctrine of the Third Symphony culminates in the message of eternal love. The subject of the Fourth Symphony, again, is neither parodistic nor classicistic but a meditation on life after death, the profound ulterior thought of the *Wunderhorn* poem "The eternal Life." In conceiving the second part of the Eighth Symphony, Mahler let himself be inspired by the ideas of eternal love, of divine mercy, of earthly insufficiency and spiritual rebirth. In the Finale of the Ninth he once again gave expression to his faith in a continued existence after death. The main idea of the Finale of the Tenth Symphony, finally, is the idea of the transcendence of death through love.

The spiritual dimension of Mahler's music becomes visible also when one considers that in three of his symphonies, the Second, Third and Eighth, Mahler further develops the Wagnerian concept of the religion of art in an original way. All three works belong to the category of the symphonic cantata. All three include the *word*, employ choruses and vocal soloists and require a gigantic orchestral apparatus. All three function in a way as mysteries of redemption. Parallels with *Parsifal* are patent in the fifth movement of the Third Symphony, where the bells and the boys' choir are to be positioned *in the height*.[9]

The chief reasons why Mahler decided to withdraw the programs of his early symphonies were, for one thing, the painful realization that the programs were misunderstood and smirked at, and for another, the fear that his symphonies might be confounded with the program music proper as represented by Richard Strauss. According to Richard Specht, Mahler would rather "be temporarily misunderstood than be understood merely rationalistically, let alone in the sense of illustrative program music."[10] He naively believed that a cultured audience would be able to guess his intentions even without commentaries. But how was the situation after October of 1900, after the withdrawal of the programs? Mahler was not understood, and he could not be understood, because the ideological premises of his

9 See my "Studien zur 'Parsifal' Rezeption," in *Musik-Konzepte*, 25. *Richard Wagner. Parsifal* (May 1982), 14–57; pp. 47–53.

10 Richard Specht, *Gustav Mahler*, 1st to 4th ed., (Berlin/Leipzig, 1913), 172.

symphonies could not, after all, be grasped merely intuitively, without the cooperation of the rational faculty.

3. Mahler and the Schönberg School

It is generally known that Arnold Schönberg and his pupils Anton Webern and Alban Berg profoundly admired Mahler's personality and music. Schönberg's commemorative oration on March 25, 1912 in Prague is one of the most moving and memorable of Mahler apologias. It opens with the emotional profession: "Instead of making many words, it might be better to say simply: "I believe firmly and unshakably that Gustav Mahler was one of the greatest of human beings and artists."[11] He wrote in a similar manner in the *Harmonielehre (Theory of Harmony)* of 1911, which is dedicated to the memory of Mahler: "It is therefore important to me to state here that I regard Mahler's oeuvre as immortal and place it next to that of the greatest masters."[12] As impressive as these professions undoubtedly are, one must not overlook the fact that our hitherto knowledge of the Schönberg School's relation to Gustav Mahler is not very extensive. There is a lack of thorough detail studies. To find out more about it, one has to sift through and evaluate the as yet unpublished correspondence between Schönberg, Webern and Berg.[13]

A study of the letters makes clear, to begin with, that, next to Schönberg, Mahler was Webern's and Berg's supreme model. In their letters, they speak of Mahler in an awed and reverent tone. They studied his scores, played them on the piano, were eager to hear the symphonies they did not yet know and traveled to performances of Mahler's works. They were indignant about the way Mahler was treated in Vienna, and were in the know about biographic details, such as the places where Mahler spent his vacations, and even the hotels in which he lodged.

---

11 Arnold Schönberg, "Prager Rede auf Gustav Mahler" (1912), in *Gustav Mahler* (Tübingen: Rainer Wunderlich), 11–58.

12 Arnold Schönberg, *Harmonielehre* (Leipzig/Vienna, 1911), 442.

13 A typescript of the correspondence is in the Music Collection of the Viennese Municipal Library. My thanks go to Dr. Ernst Hilmar, who kindly let me see the typescript.

Already during his lifetime Mahler was a guiding light to Schönberg and his pupils. After his death he became a spiritual leader to them, a human and artistic ideal. Schönberg calls him a "martyr" and a "saint" in the *Harmonielehre*. In a similar manner, we read in a letter of Webern's to Berg on September 8, 1911:

> I think of Gustav Mahler, who from this time on had wanted to live high up on the Semmering. That this is all over, or rather could never begin, is something dreadful. I saw the death mask of the saint in a number of *Musik*. Dear friend, there is only one thing: to strive with all one's might after a life here that is wholly taken up with ideals, and that is already touched by a hint of that farther, other life.

The following utterance from a letter to Berg of August 8 is likewise illuminating:

> I think a lot about Mahler. He seems ever loftier, more radiant, more wonderful. Sometimes I want to pine away with nostalgia, when I think of the times when I first saw him, first saw him conduct, his own and other works, finally got to know him personally, heard him speak, back then after the *Kindertotenlieder*, etc. All gone, over and gone.

The first work of Mahler's that Webern came to know was the Second Symphony. He was impressed by it but also had a number of reservations. He worshiped Richard Strauss at the time – it was 1902 – and wrote to the friend of his youth, Ernst Diez: "Strauss' themes are much more magnificent, ingenious, forceful. Mahler's music makes a downright childlike impression, despite the immense, extravagant orchestration."[14] Later he would radically change his opinion. His original enthusiasm for Strauss, as the correspondence with Berg makes clear, cooled in proportion as he got to know Mahler's works, until he finally acquired a regular aversion to the music of Strauss.[15]

---

14 Friedrich Wildgans, "Gustav Mahler und Anton von Webern," *Österreichische Musikzeitschrift*, 15 (1960), 302–306; p. 303.
15 Webern to Berg on May 29, 1912: "I am just increasingly sad that I shall not hear Mahler's Ninth. I look at the score of the *Lied von der Erde* more frequently now. How wonderful it is, that instrumentation. I actually do not like to use that word in this connection. For here everything is one, as in everything 'real.' (Not so in Strauss). I always start to make a stink about Strauss. But isn't it really so?"

In a letter, he peddled the rumor that Mahler had called Strauss the Lind-paintner of the present age.[16]

Of special relevance for reception history is the fact that Schönberg and his pupils had grasped and understood the spiritual dimension of Mahler's music. They were moved by its beauty, by the "plenitude of its content" and the "intensity of feeling."[17] It is true hat in his Prague address Schön-berg also speaks of the purely artistic aspects of Mahler's music, which he endeavors to shield from the charge of sentimentality and banality. But he stresses that what matters above all is the content. "But where he [Mahler] progresses," he writes, "is not so much in the forms, the proportions, the scale; those are merely the external consequences of the inner processes; but the content." And by "content" Schönberg means the extra-musical substance of the music, that is, "mankind's longing for its future shape, for an immortal soul, for dissolution in the totality of the universe, the longing of this soul for its God."[18]

Some musicologists of our time, who occupy an extreme formalistic standpoint, fight to the finish against any attempt at a spiritual interpre-tation. Oddly enough they ignore the fact that Schönberg and his pupils frequently approached this music hermeneutically. Schönberg's philosophic, even though somewhat obscure, reading of the Ninth Symphony, accord-ing to which the author in it hardly speaks as a subject any longer, is well known.[19] The subtle explication of the opening movement that Alban Berg sent to his wife in a letter has frequently been cited. A no less subtle reading that Webern attempted in a letter to Schönberg on February 26, 1914, by contrast, has hitherto remained unknown. Here he writes among other things:

> You spoke with me last year in Stettin about the [Ninth] Symphony, and I under-stood you to say that this was no longer a confession of a human experience, as, for example, the Sixth, but one from the other world, far away. That conclusion of the symphony is surely like a greeting from above. There Mahler was already far, far away from us."

---

16 Webern to Berg, August 27, 1912. – Peter Joseph von Lindpaintner (1791–1856), German musician, notable as a conductor but controversial as a composer.
17 Webern to Schönberg, September 12, 1910.
18 Schönberg, "Prager Rede," 42.
19 Ibid., 55.

However, it is time to ask how the influence of Mahler on the music of Schönberg and his pupils can be put in concrete terms. Six points, above all, deserve attention in this context.

1. Several works of Schönberg, Berg and Webern are based on programs. I will mention only Schönberg's First String Quartet op. 7, Berg's *Lyric Suite* and Webern's quartet op. 22 – three cases that some years ago caused sensations also with the general public. The three composers seem basically to have followed Mahler's example, who regularly suppressed the programs of his middle and late symphonies.

2. The inclusion of the voice in string quartets and chamber music generally was a novelty at the beginning of the 20th century. The two last movements of Schönberg's second string quartet op. 10 are based on two poems by Stefan George ("Litanei" and "Entrückung" [Rapture]). The fourth movement of the *Serenade* op. 24 of Schönberg's is based on a sonnet by Petrarca. Alban Berg conceived the Finale of the *Lyric Suite* after Charles Baudelaire's sonnet "De Profundis." Schönberg and Berg here follow Mahler, who included texts in several of his symphonies.

3. The composers of the Schönberg School were strongly critical of note-for-note recapitulations. They agree with Mahler in this, who called every repetition "already a lie"[20] and practically newly composed his recapitulations. When Helmut Schmidt-Garre once presented a sonata movement to his teacher Berg in whose recapitulation a motif was repeated "literally," he provoked the chiding remark: "How can you do something like this: consider what your themes and motifs have meanwhile 'experienced'."[21]

4. Some years ago, several attempts were made to derive Schönberg's renowned technique of the "developing variation" directly from Brahms.[22] It seems to have been overlooked, however, that this technique is al-

---

20 Herbert Killian, ed., *Gustav Mahler in den Erinnerungen von Leni Bauer-Lechner* (Hamburg, 1984), 158.

21 Helmut Schmidt-Garre, "Berg als Lehrer," *Melos*, 22 (1955), 40 f.

22 Klaus Velten, "Das Prinzip der entwickelnden Variation in J. Brahms und A. Schönberg," *Musik und Bildung*, 6 (1974), 547–555.

ready fully formed in the early symphonies of Mahler.[23] Especially Berg's method strongly reminds of Mahler. In 1905, Webern noted a saying of Mahler's in his diary according to which the variation was the most important factor of all musical work.[24] This whole complex of questions calls for a detailed investigation.

5. Like Mahler, the Schönberg School advanced the truth claim of art. Mahler's asseveration that he had not written a single note "that was not absolutely true" coincides with Schönberg's dictum: "Music should not decorate, it should be true."[25] Among the chief maxims of Schönberg's aesthetics is the conscious renunciation of ornament. In Mahler's instrumentation Schönberg praised "the nearly unexampled matter-of-factness, which only writes down what is absolutely necessary." "His sound," Schönberg says, "never consists of ornamental accessories, additions that are not, or only loosely, connected to the main matter but are merely attached as decoration."[26] Much later, Erwin Ratz spoke of the transparency of Mahler's instrumentation, which dispensed with all decorating additions and only wanted to serve the clarity of the musical construction.[27] There is to all appearances a close connection between the instrumentation of Mahler and that of Schönberg and especially Berg.

6. Mahler had a special predilection for, let us say, exquisite instruments and instrumental combinations like harps, celesta and harmonium, bells and cowbells, mandolins and guitars. He impressed Schönberg and his pupils with that, who used these instruments in turn. On September 12, 1910, Webern told Schönberg that he was very taken with a passage in the second part of Mahler's Eighth Symphony, which included harps, celesta and harmonium. It is for just this instrumentation, plus high soprano, that Schönberg in December of 1911 composed his song *Herzgewächse* (Heart Plants) after Maeterlinck's *Serres chaudes*. During

---

23 See my Gustav Mahler, vol. 3: *Die Symphonien* (Wiesbaden, 1985), 70 f., 189 f.
24 Wildgans in *Österreichische Musikzeitschrift*, 15 (1960), 304.
25 See my *Gustav Mahler*, vol. 1 (Wiesbaden, 1977), 140.
26 Schönberg, "Prager Rede," 41.
27 Erwin Ratz, "Von Leben und Werk," in *Gustav Mahler* (Tübingen: Wunderlich, 1966), 71–89.

the years 1911 and 1913, Webern's *Fünf Orchesterstücke* op. 10 were written. Their score prescribes, besides numerous other instruments, harp, celesta and harmonium, and for the third piece additionally bells and cowbells, for Mahler the idiophonic tone symbol of "otherworldly solitude."[28] As appears from a letter to Berg, Webern knew of this tone-symbolic significance of cowbells.[29] He quotes Mahler once speaking of "'The wanderer on the highest heights,' who only hears herd bells as the sole sound of this earth." The use of mandolin and guitar in Schönberg's *Serenade* op. 24, moreover, is nothing other than a reflection on the second *Nachtmusik* of Mahler's Seventh Symphony.

4. On Adorno's Mahler Interpretation

In singling out the backgrounds of the Mahler renaissance, one must not forget Theodor W. Adorno's 1960 study of Mahler.[30] Its impact on the educated world, on numerous musicologists and many composers was immense. It decisively shaped the Mahler image of many avant-garde composers – I'll mention only Dieter Schnebel, Peter Ruzicka, Helmut Lachenmann and György Ligeti.

In his "physiognomy" of Mahler, Adorno speaks as philosopher, psychologist, sociologist, aesthetician and musicologist. The powerful fascination the book produces results from its literary qualities, from the plenitude of insights it imparts, and from the interpenetration and integration of philosophic, psychological, sociological, aesthetic and technological categories. Some are immediately convincing and readily apply to the music of Mahler. Such is the case with the Hegelian category of the *Weltlauf* or world course, which indeed manages to illuminate Mahler's many perpetuum-mobile movements:[31] Mahler himself spoke of the Scherzo of the Second Symphony as of the "incomprehensible bustle of life."[32] Other of Adorno's categories, again, seem to absolutize some right elements. One might think

---

28 Floros, *Mahler and the Symphony*, 249 f.
29 Webern to Berg, July 12, 1912.
30 Theodor W. Adorno, *Mahler. Eine musikalische Physiognomik* (Frankfurt a.M.: Suhrkamp, 1960).
31 Ibid., 14 ff.
32 Letter to Max Marschalk, March 26, 1896. *Gustav Mahler Briefe* (1982), 150.

of the often quoted one of *gebrochenheit*, fracturedness, in which Adorno wants to see a regular "cipher of the content" of Mahler's music.[33] One might also think of the sociologically based thesis of the dialectic between individuality and collectivity in Mahler,[34] as well as the splendid observation of the breaking-in of the "lower" music into the "high" art. This phenomenon is given downright pictorial expression in the often-quoted sentence: "Jacobinically the lower music storms into the upper one."[35]

Beyond question, Adorno has sharpened our awareness of many a technical aspect of Mahler's music, such as the major-minor manner, the formation of variants and the technique of montage. Of serious consequence for the Mahler reception in the second half of the 20th century, however, is the fact that Adorno left Mahler's authentic programs and hence also the composer's worldview entirely out of consideration. He was aware that Mahler and the aesthetics of Eduard Hanslick were irreconcilable.[36] But he regarded Mahler's programmatic aspect as a blemish, the original programs as "embarrassing."[37] The compositions, he thought, had "swallowed up" the programs.[38]

This attitude was bound to lead to misinterpretations, because Mahler's programs give expression to central contents of his *weltanschauung*. There is unequivocal proof that Mahler made the personal, ideological and religious questions that agitated him the subjects of his symphonies. Mahler's inner biography, his world view, his spiritual world – all this was left out of consideration by Adorno. His concern was not to define Mahler's intentions but to present an interpretation that corresponded to his own philosophy and aesthetics.

Thus Adorno's philosophy of negativity became the yardstick of his Mahler critique. He was greatly taken with movements of Mahler's that met his idea of negativity, but had numerous reservations about the "positive" and "affirmative" movements. Characteristically he declared the Finale

---

33 Adorno, *Mahler*, 50.
34 Ibid.
35 Ibid., 53.
36 Ibid., 83.
37 Ibid., 9.
38 Ibid., 83.

of the Sixth Symphony – a somber vision of doom and destruction – to be "the center of Mahler's entire oeuvre."[39] In contrast, he thought the "Resurrection Finale" of the Second to be "primitive."[40] The "positivity" of the Finales of the Fifth and Seventh bothered him,[41] and he regarded the Eighth as a failure, as "the unsuccessful, objectively impossible revival of the cultic."[42]

To illustrate the discrepancy between Adorno's interpretation and the spiritual dimension of Mahler's music by at least with one concrete example: Adorno interprets the Fourth as a "children's" and "fairytale symphony," which negates at base. The listener feels taken for a fool by the bell at the beginning. Without stating it *expressis verbis*, the fool's bell says: "What you will hear now is none of it true." The symphony pictures paradise in a rustic-anthropomorphic manner "in order to announce that it was not." Thus the phantasmagoria of the transcendent landscape is at once posited and negated. Joy remains unattainable, and there is no transcendence left except that of longing.[43]

In reality, the Fourth is a symphonic meditation on life after death. This is fully manifest in the Scherzo, which is conceived as a dance of death. The third movement is based on the solid foundation of Schopenhauer's philosophy, especially the teaching that the condition of a human being who has realized the denial of the will to live was "an unshakable peace, a deep quietude and inmost serenity."[44] Mahler conceived the *heavenly life* – the *Wunderhorn* song that serves as the Finale of the symphony – indeed as a humoresque, but not as a parody. He firmly believed in the transcendence and in the transcendent mission of music. Many of his *morendo* conclusions proclaim the message of a continued existence after death.

---

39 Ibid., 131.
40 Ibid., 179.
41 Ibid., 164 f., 179 f.
42 Ibid., 182.
43 Ibid., 76–84.
44 Floros, *Gustav Mahler*, 3: 108.

5. Mahler and the Avant-Garde

For many prominent representatives of the post-WWII musical avant-garde, Mahler became a leading figure. The extent of his influence cannot as yet be fully gauged. This much is certain, however, that the expressive qualities of his music and its *tone* appealed to many composers. Both the "ideological" and the "technological" aspects of his symphonic art aroused interest.

Among the major symphonists of the 20th century, Dimitry Shostakovich, in particular, owed a great deal to, and was an outspoken supporter of, Mahler's music. Both have in common the tendency toward monumentality, the inclusion of texts, vocal soloists and choruses, the frequent departure from the four-movement norm and the predilection for programmatic elements. Krysztof Meyer went so far as to speak of a shift from the purely aesthetic to the ethical" in both composers.[45] A variety of parallels between Mahler and Shostakovich can be demonstrated, in the structure of their themes, in the use of motifs, in the instrumentation and structuration of the orchestra. Irony and the grotesque, two prominent characteristics of Mahler's music, also frequently crop up in Shostakovich.

Mahler's symphonies are rich in spatial effects. The idea of "music from far away," and that of a music that keeps coming ever closer, the use of a remote orchestra, the placing of individual instruments in the rear of the orchestra or in an elevated position, and finally the sound direction in the score of the Finale of the Second Symphony to the effect that the four trumpets that are meant to announce the Apocalypse must "resound from opposite directions"[46] – all this and more has the effect for the listener of a spatialization of sound. In a 1972 interview with Clytus Gottwald, György Ligeti accordingly spoke of an "imaginary space" in Mahler and cited instructive examples of the phenomenon.[47] There are numerous indications that in conceiving his orchestral work *Lontano* Ligeti derived decisive impulses from Mahler.

---

45 Krysztof Meyer, "Mahler und Schostakowitsch," in Kolleritsch, ed., *Gustav Mahler. Sinfonie und Wirklichkeit*, 118–132; p. 119.
46 Floros, *Gustav Mahler*, 2:117–128; 3: 73.
47 György Ligeti and Clytus Gottwald, "Gustav Mahler und die musikalische Utopie," *NZfM*, 135 (1974), 7–11, 288–295.

Another technique of Mahler's to receive wide attention was that of the montage. To many it seemed an anticipation of the collage, a technique first developed in pictorial art by Pablo Picasso and Georges Braque. The use of the "Frère Jacques" canon in the funeral march of the First Symphony prompted many to speak of working with existing material. Others adverted to the collage-like montage of heterogeneous elements in the second movement of the Ninth Symphony. In 1968, Luciano Berio created a memorial to Gustav Mahler and the collage technique with the third movement of his *Sinfonia,* by combining the Scherzo of Mahler's Second Symphony with a great many musical quotations ranging from Bach to Stockhausen and with an impressive textual collage. "I have treated Mahler's movement," Berio commented, "like a vessel, in whose walls a large number of 'musical myths' and allusions are developed, set in mutual relation and transformed."[48]

Other composers, again, let themselves be inspired by Adorno's interpretation of several form processes in Mahler, orienting themselves on Mahler's "catastrophes," fields of dissolution, suspensions and "aimlessly circling movements." One may cite in this connection Peter Ruzicka's works *In processo di tempo* ... of 1971 and *Torso* of 1973.[49]

As interesting as the technological aspects of the Mahler reception cited may seem, more important for the Avant-garde was a hardly definable spiritual sympathy with Mahler.[50] There are increasing indications that since the 'seventies a change has taken place in the New Music. The phase of a rigid structuralism seems a thing of the past. Many composers once again set store by messages and expressive qualities. I venture the conjecture that this transformation is not least due to the impact of Gustav Mahler.

---

48 Quoted from Peter Altmann, *Sinfonia von Lucio Berio. Eine analytische Studie* (Universal Edition 26225) (Vienna, 1977), 12.
49 Peter Ruzicka, "Befragung des Materials. Gustav Mahler aus der Sicht aktueller Kompositionsästhetik," *Musik und Bildung,* 5 (1973), 598–603.
50 Cf. Wolf Rosenberg, "Mahler und die Avantgarde: Kompositionstechnisches Vorbild oder geistige Sympathie?" in Kolleritsch, ed., *Gustav Mahler . Sinfonie und Wirklichkeit,* 81–92.

XIX. Music Must Become Language: On Hans Werner Henze

> "What I would like to get to is for music to become language
> and not remain this sound space, in which feeling can reflect
> itself uncontrolledly and 'emptily'; music should be understood
> like language." Hans Werner Henze

Hans Werner Henze is one of the most prominent representatives of committed music of our time. A visionary element is especially characteristic of his music. He openly proclaims himself as a socialist and a supporter of committed art, but he sharply distances himself from directions that want to abolish art, who plead for "anti-art" and so-called musical mass culture. "For culture," he once remarked," is not something one should leave behind on the way in order to advance toward forms of simplification or even barbarism, but on the contrary, beauty should be able to unfold itself in a wholly new way – in a society that is free."[1] Socialism to him, it may be emphasized, means, "not coarseness, but refinement, humanization, in term of the potentialities implanted in mankind." In his view, music is a public and a political matter, because it has to do with things that concern all human beings.[2] His politico-cultural commitment aims at making music – sophisticated music, which hitherto was a matter only for the elect – accessible to the millions, even billions.

Henze's turn toward committed art occurred in 1967/1968 and certainly signifies a new orientation. At the same time, the view that in 1968 he, so to speak, began a new life seems exaggerated. His individuality is too strongly pronounced for him to deny his artistic past.

If there were a formula to which Henze's artistic personality could be reduced, it would have to read "Versatility and Constancy," receptiveness for diverse impulses and persistence in certain fundamental principles. He commanded both a fine sensibility and a very distinctive personal style.

---

1 Hans Werner Henze, *Musik und Politik. Schriften und Gespräche 1955–1975*, ed. Jens Brockmeier (Deutscher Taschenbuch Verlag 1162) (Munich, 1976), 191.
2 HansWerner Henze, "Exkurs über den Populismus," in Henze, ed. *Zwischen den Kulturen. Neue Aspekte der musikalischen Ästhetik I* (Frankfurt, 1979), 7–31; pp. 29 f.

The influence of Stravinsky was decisive for his early work, but so was the encounter with the music of Gustav Mahler and Alban Berg. Henze confesses to have learned also from older masters – all the way back to Johann Sebastian Bach. He spent many, in fact decisive, years in Italy and got to know Italian music at the source. He knows his Monteverdi as well as Rossini, Bellini, Donizetti and Verdi. (He produced versions, inter alia, of Monteverdi's *Ulisse* and Paisiello's *Don Chisciotte*.) It is possible that the melodiousness that gives many of his works their special character was fostered by his occupation with Italian art. Already in his early works, however, the idiom of his music is unmistakable.

The leading musical encyclopedia of our time rightly praises his "prodigality of invention" as unusual for the 20th century.[3] We should add that Henze is also one of the most productive composers of his generation. His vast oeuvre is distinguished by both delight in experimentation and highly expressive qualities and, except for church music, comprises works of every genre: opera, scenic cantatas and shows, ballets, stage music, orchestral and chamber music, concertos, choruses, hymns and lieder. A special emphasis is opera. The number of his works for musical theater is strikingly large; time and again he has come back around to the theater, and he explains that by saying that his music had a strong tendency toward gestures, corporeality and pictorial qualities. But he certainly does not neglect the other genres, either.

This versatility in the cultivation of genres is paralleled by his choice of texts he sets to music. He has resorted to Euripides, Vergil, Tasso and Ariosto, Giordano Bruno, Kleist and Hölderlin, Dostoevsky, Rimbaud and Whitman. He has composed numerous texts by Ingeborg Bachmann, Wolfgang Hildesheimer and Hans Magnus Enzensberger. He derives impulses from numerous sources, he is interested in nearly every period of intellectual history, both in the present and in the past, in Greek and Roman antiquity as much as in the realm of myth. And he confronts the historical matters not for their own sake but for their relevance – simply from the reflection that certain ideas, conflicts, norms and problems have always ruled mankind and determine its thinking.

---

3 *The New Grove Dictionary of Music and Musicians*, vol. 8 (London, 1980), 489.

Independence and self-reliance strongly mark Henze the composer and intellectual. He takes a critical, non-doctrinaire standpoint. As a composer he has positioned himself outside the modish currents of our time. Even as a young man he distanced himself from Darmstadt; he moved to Italy in order to gain distance from everything. His work wholly eludes classification in terms of specific schools. He criticized both twelve-tone music and serialism, both the obsession with "pure" systems of music and the fetishism about "material." In so doing he often won insights that are beyond cavil – convincing because they hit the heart of the matter. Some examples may illustrate this.

Discussions about form, Henze thinks, are fruitless "when they are conducted in the abstract and not dictated by the need to keep interpreting art as a means of communication."[4] That is a statement that is completely persuasive. We must likewise agree with Henze's view that a method is not a language and that the use of a new technique tells us nothing about the quality of the musical piece to which it has been applied.[5] At a time when many composers ascribed major significance to construction, he rightly asked to consider that music must not be confused with musicology, and that the logic of a work referred solely "to a unique constellation of experience, encounter, knowledge, agreement," in other words, that it exceeds "the tried and true rule, the montage, the calculation."[6] He criticized the Second Viennese and the post-Expressionist School for having no "vocabulary for cheerfulness."[7] That is a rather instructive remark from a composer who aims at a broad spectrum of expressive characters. If certain followers of Theodor W. Adorno thought that symphonies could no longer be written because the "material" was *kaputt*, Henze wanted to prove, as he did in his Sixth Symphony, that a symphony could be made even of supposedly broken material.[8] Such a conviction basically expresses a faith that mankind still has a long way ahead of itself, that one had to soldier on.

Henze evaded the rigid compositional methods of our century because he wanted to preserve his freedom. Compositional freedom he understood to

---

4   *Musik und Politik*, 245.
5   Ibid., 47, 175.
6   Ibid., 77.
7   Ibid., 195.
8   Ibid., 186.

be independence and "the readiness for making decisions also outside of the established order."[9] He hated the mechanical, the automatic, the totally predetermined. "The reason why I avoided strict dodecaphony, let alone serialism," he once said, "is that these methods did not interest me for the simple reason that they appeared too 'pure' to me, and because I thought that I could not 'say' anything within those rules." And this is followed again by a highly significant statement: "I am interested in music in order to describe moods, atmosphere, conditions. I do not want any absolutely tied-up music packages."[10]

That leads directly into the heart of his conception of music. The ideal that Henze came to have in mind is not the absolute, abstract, pure music, but what, analogously to the poetics of Pablo Neruda, he called "musica impura,"[11] that is, a music that also involves the human, the allegorical, the literary. Henze postulates that music must become language, had to be understood like language. The linguisticalness of music, in which he sees a "young, highly promising means of communication,"[12] is his primary concern. So it is hardly surprising that he was intensely interested in semiotics and semantics, and especially in the semantic laws of music, from whose systematic investigation he expected important insights and discoveries. His endeavor is directed at semanticization. "What matters above all," he once said, "is that the listener learns to understand the message, the meaning of the signs that are sent out by music."[13]

How is this goal to be achieved? One means Henze cites is the use of quotations, which he deliberately incorporates in many of his compositions. They are to point where the composition is going, they form "a password, a communicative bridge."[14] In *Tristan* for example, one of his most important works, Richard Wagner, Johannes Brahms, Frédéric Chopin and the old melody of the *Lamento di Tristano* from the 14th century are quoted. In the Sixth Symphony, quotations from two Cuban folk songs play a prominent

---

9   Ibid., 77.
10 Ibid., 192.
11 Ibid., 186 ff.
12 Ibid., 242.
13 *Zwischen den Kulturen*, 28.
14 *Musik und Politik*, 188.

role, and in the *Bassariden*, Gustav Mahler and an aria from Bach's *St. Matthew Passion* are quoted.

Another possibility for semanticizing consists in the creation of analogies between extra-musical subjects and musical structures. Nearly all of Henze's more recent contributions to musical theater operate on a highly significant symbolic level. Instrument symbolism, sound symbolism, symbolisms of intervals and of dodecaphonic rows all attain programmatic significance, become shaping principles. The characters are given individual profiles and exhibit melodic and harmonic material all their own. In the music to Henze's ballet *Orpheus*, for example, Apollo, on the one hand, and Orpheus and Eurydike, on the other, represent contrary worlds, which are characterized by entirely different means. Orpheus and Eurydike are accompanied throughout by string instruments. Apollo's world, by contrast, is marked by high woodwinds, while the low register is reserved for evoking the underworld.[15]

In the *English Cat*, a pop song and a hymn are set dialectically against each other.[16] In his more recent operatic works, Henze also often works with twelve-tone-like modes, but the intervallic constellations –the way he puts intervals together – is almost always dictated by extra-musical ideas. The tone-symbolic intention covers the larger concatenations as well as the musical ur-elements.

To some extent, the introductions and commentaries Henze wrote for many of his works also serve to semanticize the music. Several of these commentaries are very detailed, and almost all read like literature. The work journal for the *English Cat* comprises about 400 pages. One stops being puzzled by the extent of these commentaries once one realizes that for Henze these introductions have a quasi-documentary character. They preserve the sensory, emotional and spiritual atmosphere that surrounded the composer when he conceived the works, record thoughts, impressions, associations and hallucinations, and fix "reactions to things experienced, read, lived through, heard."[17] When, for example, Henze refers, in the

---

15 Cf. Josef Rufer, *Bekenntnisse und Erkenntnisse. Komponisten über ihr Werk* (Frankfurt, 1979), 334–342.

16 Hans Werner Henze, *Die Englische Katze. Ein Arbeitstagebuch 1978–1982* (Frankfurt, 1983), 292.

17 *Musik und Politik*, 175.

commentary to his *Tristan*, to Goya's etching entitled *El sueño de la razon produce monstruos*[18] (the sleep of reason produces monsters), he discloses an inspirational source, but at the same time the reference can also contribute to a deeper understanding of the music. In Henze's music, truly the whole human being speaks his mind; in that sense, it is indeed *musica impura*.

Its wealth of expressive characters, nuances and facets is exceptional. Henze created musical vocabularies for all mental and emotional states: for coolness and for warmth, for gracefulness and for hardness, for euphoria and for despair, for seriousness and for parody. He, who in many of his works cultivated an insistent neo-expressionist idiom, also helped the *opera buffa* to regain its rights – as one of the few composers of the present to do so. In the score of his *Tristan*, the most diverse expression marks jostle each other: *dolce, espressivo, con grazia, giocoso, dramatico, banale*. Those are conventional marks for unheard-of sounds, for an original synthesis of piano concerto, orchestral music and tapes, for a music in which mourning can turn into madness and madness into grotesqueness, and for a composition whose most powerful eruption at the culmination of the second *ricercare* Henze interprets as the "death shriek no longer merely of Tristan and Isolde but of the entire suffering world."[19] This *Tristan* is, it seems, one of Henze's most personal works and at the same time one that gives moving expression to the crisis of our time.

Henze's turn to committed art in the years 1967/1968 clearly marked a profound caesura in his work. It divides the oeuvre into two parts. Undoubtedly the new orientation had grave consequences in ideological, politico-cultural as well as purely artistic respects. His tone language became, as it were, more concrete, more plastic. But it would be altogether wrong to reckon the early Henze among formalistically oriented composers. There are constants in his personality and in his work, which must not be overlooked. Henze was always on the side of the minorities and the oppressed, and he never made a secret of his critical position. From the beginning he had a predilection for conflicted matters in his musico-dramatic work. Even more crucial, however, is this: the motto of his entire oeuvre could well be our maxim *Music as Message*. Alongside his talent, his versatility and his

---

18 Ibid., 224.
19 Ibid., 228.

productivity, and along with his social commitment, it is this maxim that constitutes and consolidates his special position in the music of the present.

FRANCESCO DE GOYA
Illustration *El sueño de la razon produce monstruos*

Hans Werner Henze about his *Tristan*: "The sounds flit nightmarishly about like the bats in Goya's etching entitled: 'The sleep of reason gives birth to monsters.'"

311

XX. The Co-Presence of all Eras: Messages through the Ages

A message, as semiotics teaches us, can be mono- or polysemous. According to Umberto Eco, a message has an aesthetic function "when it presents itself as ambiguously structured or as referring to itself (autoreflexive), that is to say, when it wants to direct the attention of the recipient above all to its own form."[1] This definition leaves something to be desired, however, because it overemphasizes the formal side of the work of art. It can be regarded as certain that the decoding of an aesthetic message depends decisively on the knowledge, the previous education and the expectations of the recipient. There are certainly also aesthetic messages whose relative unambiguity is indubitable. As an example, I refer to the transition from the third movement to the finale of Beethoven's fifth Symphony. Most listeners will understand that the model after which this transition is shaped is the device *Per aspera ad astra*, the archetypal situation of liberation.

The music of the 20th century – like modern art generally – has an affinity with ambiguity and polysemousness. Symptomatic for it is the predilection with which numerous post-WWII composers avail themselves of the techniques of quotation, collage and montage. They quote motifs, phrases or entire passages from works of diverse composers and diverse eras and juxtapose them in multiple ways: Bach stands next to Messiaen, Richard Strauss next to Mozart and Prokofiev, Schumann next to Duke Ellington, Gregorian chant next to Debussy. In some compositions, all of music history seems to be present. Several composers, moreover, love to quote textual passages from one or several different literary works in their compositions, texts that are often spoken simultaneously in different languages. Listeners can thus not understand the meaning of the texts, and the multiplicity and connection of the musical quotations will confuse and shock them.

What is the meaning of this quotation practice, and what do the composers intend by it? In a carefully documented study, Clemens Kühn has isolated certain categories, functions and techniques of the quotation, which

---

1   Umberto Eco, *Einführung in die Semiotik* (1972), 145 f.

he regards as representative of the current practice. He distinguishes the quotation as obeisance, as grand musical gesture; the quotation as trigger of specific associations; the quotation as stimulant to the imagination, as parody or irony; the quotation as document, as contrast to, or agreement with, one's own musical language; as object of critical examination or else identification; the quotation as bearer of a certain mood content; and finally, the quotation as expression of a pluralistic idea, one shaped by a certain musico-philosophic concept of time.[2] Of these categories, the last seems to me to deserve our special attention because it can throw light on the subject at issue here.

The musical thinking of Bernd Alois Zimmermann centered on two related ideas: the idea of a "pluralistic kind of composition" and the idea of a "spherical shape of time." Zimmermann conceived of the present as the threshold between past and future. He believed that there could be no past without a future, just as there could be no future without a past.[3] His peculiar musical philosophy of time owes decisive impulses to St. Augustine, Ezra Pound and James Joyce. In his essay "Interval and Time," Zimmermann quotes some sentences of Pound's, which can tell us something about his quotation practice. There we read:

> Morning breaks over Jerusalem, while midnight still veils the Pillars of Hercules. All epochs are simultaneous [...] the future stirs in the minds of the few [...] that applies above all to literature, where real time is independent of the seeming one and many dead are the contemporaries of our grandchildren.[4]

Zimmermann's quotational practice stands in the service of his philosophy of music. In the fourth movement of his *Antiphonen*, the instrumentalists are not only to play but also to speak. They recite passages from eight different works of world literature: James Joyce's *Ulysses*, the Vulgate, the Apocalypse, Dante's *Divine Comedy*, the Book of Job, Dostoevsky's *Brothers Karamazov*, Camus' *Caligula* and Novalis' *Hymns to the Night*

---

2   Clemens Kühn, *Das Zitat in der Musik der Gegenwart – mit Ausblicken auf bildende Kunst und Literatur* (Hamburg, 1972), 98 f.

3   Ursula Stürzbecher, *Werkstattgespräche mit Komponisten* (1973), 180.

4   Bernd Alois Zimmeermann, „Intervall und Zeit" (1957), in Wulf Konold, ed., *Bernd Alois Zimmermann. Dokumente und Interpretationen* (Cologne, 1986), 37–40; p. 38.

(see the score page reproduced below). All of the passages are recited in their original languages. We hear English, Latin, Greek, Italian, Hebrew, Russian, French and German. As a rule, two or three passages are recited simultaneously.

If one asks what this Babylonian confusion of tongues is to signify, one has to consider that these heterogeneous texts all have one thing in common: they all refer to human existence and to love.[5] The composer's intention thus becomes clearer: What concerns him is not only to demonstrate the simultaneity of all epochs, but also to show that there are messages that are eternal – messages that are proclaimed time and again through the centuries.

5 Marion Rothärmel, „Der pluralistische Zimmermann," *Melos*, 35 (1968), 97–102; p. 102.

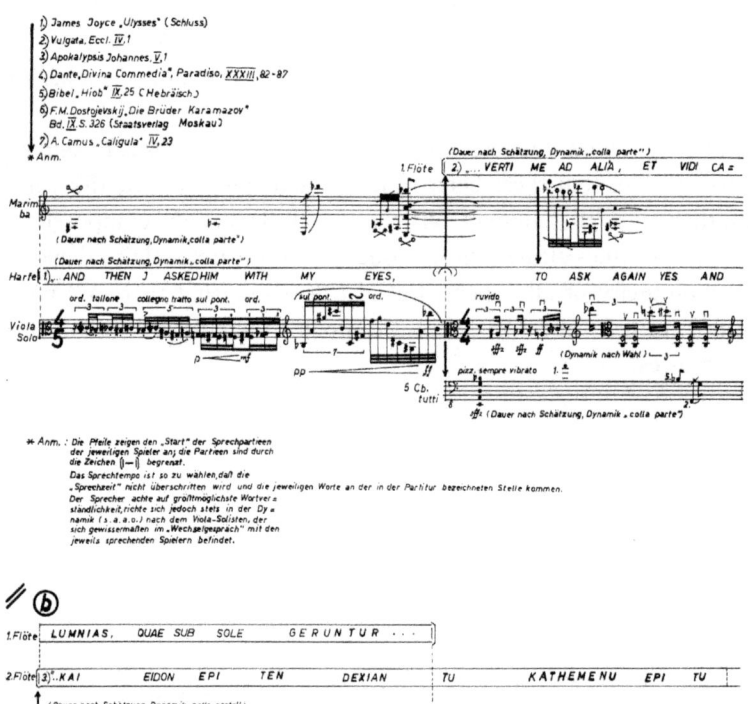

From: BERND ALOS ZIMMERMANN, *Antiphonen*
© 1962 Edition Modern, Munich
by permission

GUSTAV KLIMT
Die Musik I (1895)
Oil/canvas, 37 x 44.5 cm
Bavarian State Art Collections New Pinakothek Munich
by permission

Afterword

Gustav Klimt's first allegorical representation of music (see the reproduction on the preceding page) originated in 1865. The young woman in the long dress, who personifies Music, holds a lyre, the instrument of Apollo, in her hand. The satyr on the left edge of the picture alludes to the Dionysian element of music and to Nietzsche's *Birth of Tragedy from the Spirit of Music*. The sphinx on the right side of the picture seems to insinuate that music poses riddles, which the listener has to solve. That is the subject of this book: music – at least a certain kind of music – sends out messages, which need to be decoded. And, indeed, the enigmatic is prominent in many musical works of art. Think only of the riddle canons of the Renaissance, of Tchaikovsky's *Symphonie pathétique* or of Elgar's, yes, *Enigma Variations*.

In March of 1985, I had the honor and the pleasure of being able to hold a long conversation in Hamburg with Luigi Nono – a conversation that is unforgettable to me.[1] Early on in the exchange, he spoke to me about my publications about Brahms, Bruckner and Mahler and about my study of the esoteric program of Alban Berg's *Lyric Suite* and disclosed to me that his string quartet premiered in 1980, *Fragmente – Stille, to Diotima*, with its portentous *Scala enigmatica*, was also based on a secret program. We talked at length about currents in contemporary music, about microtonality, about world music, about silence in music – a topic that was close to his heart – about musical semantics and hidden program music. In speaking of that, he expressed his conviction that countless composers had secreted things experienced, personal, or literary into their music. It was an ancient tradition, he said, going back to the Gnostics....

---

1   See the whole text of the Conversation in my book *New Ears for New Music*, Frankfurt 2013, 97–99.

Abbreviations

AfMw	Archiv für Musikwissenschaft
AME	Alma Mahler, *Gustav Mahler. Erinnerungen und Briefe*, 2nd ed., Amsteram, 1949
BzMw	Beiträge zur Musikwissenschaft
ETP	Eulenburg Taschenpartitur
FLB	*Franz Liszt's Briefe*, ed. La Mara, 8 vols., Leipzig, 1893–1905
GMB²	*Gustav Mahler Briefe*, new ed., enlarged and revised by Herta Blaukopf. Vienna/Hamburg, 1982
GS	Gesammelte Schriften
JAMS	Journal of the American Musicological Society
JbP	Jahrbuch der Musikbibliothek Peters
Mf	Die Musikforscung
MGG	Die Musik in Geschichte und Gegenwart
ML	Music & Letters
MQ	The Musical Quarterly
MR	The Music Review
NZfM	Neue Zeitschrift für Musik
RISM	Répertoire International des Sources Musicales
RM	Revue de Musicologie
SIMG	Sammelbände der Internationalen Musikgesellschaft
ZfMw	Zeitschrift für Musikwissenschaft
ZIMG	Zeitschrift der Internationalen Musikgesellschaft

Selected Bibliography

1. Letters and Writings by Composers

BAUER-LECHNER, Natalie: *Gustav Mahler in den Erinnerungen von Natalie Bauer-Lechner.* Nach Tagebuchaufzeichnungen ed. Herbert Killian, Hamburg 1984.

BERG, Alban: *Glaube, Hoffnung und Liebe. Schriften zur Musik,* ed. Frank Schneider, Verlag Philipp Reclam jun. Leipzig 1981; English: Bryan Simms (Ed.): *Pro Mundo – pro Domo. The Writings of Alban Berg,* 2013.

BERLIOZ, Hector: *Literarische Werke. Erste Gesamtausgabe,* 10 vols, Leipzig 1903–1921.

Œuvres littéraires. A travers chants, ed. Léon Guichard, Paris 1971.

BÜLOW, Hans von: *Briefe und Schriften,* ed. Marie von Bülow, 8 vols, 2. Ed. Leipzig 1898–1911.

BUSONI, Ferruccio: *Entwurf einer neuen Ästhetik der Tonkunst.* Mit Anmerkungen von Arnold Schönberg und einem Nachwort von H. H. Stuckenschmidt, Frankfurt am Main 1974 *Von der Einheit der Musik. Verstreute Aufzeichnungen,* Berlin 1922.

CORNELIUS, Peter: *Literarische Werke. Erste Gesamtausgabe,* 4 vols, Leipzig 1904/1905.

DEBUSSY, Claude: *Monsieur Croche et autres écrits,* ed. François Lesure, Paris 1971.

German Edition: *Monsieur Croche. Sämtliche Schriften und Interviews,* ed. von Josef Häusler, Stuttgart 1974.

HENZE, Hans Werner: *Musik und Politik. Schriften und Gespräche 1955–1975,* ed. Jens Brockmeier (Deutscher Taschenbuch Verlag 1162), Munich 1976; english: *Music and Politics. Collected Writings 1953–81,* translated by Peter Labanyi, 1982.

Die Englische Katze. Ein Arbeitstagebuch 1978–1982, Frankfurt am Main 1983.

LISZT, Franz: *Gesammelte Schriften,* ed. Lina Ramann, 6 vols, Leipzig 1880–1883.

Franz Liszt's Briefe, ed. La Mara, 8 vols, Leipzig 1893–1905.

Briefwechsel zwischen Franz Liszt und Hans von Bülow, ed. La Mara, Leipzig 1898.

Briefe aus ungarischen Sammlungen 1835–1886, ed. Margit Prahacs, Kassel/Basel/Paris/London/New York 1966.

MAHLER, Alma: *Gustav Mahler. Erinnerungen und Briefe,* 1. Ed. 1940, 2. Ed. Amsterdam 1949.

MAHLER, Gustav *Gustav Mahler – Richard Strauss. Briefwechsel 1888–1911,* ed. Herta Blaukopf, Munich/Zurich 1980.

Gustav Mahler Briefe. New Edirion Herta Blaukopf, Vienna/ Hamburg 1982.

Gustav Mahler. Unbekannte Briefe, ed. Herta Blaukopf, Wien/Hamburg 1983.

NONO, Luigi: *Texte. Studien zu seiner Musik,* ed. Jürg Stenzl, Zürich und Freiburg i. Br. 1975.

PFITZNER, Hans: *Gesammelte Schriften,* Vol. I—III, Augsburg 1926/1929.

Sämtliche Schriften, Vol. IV, ed. Bernhard Adamy, Tutzing 1987.

Über musikalische Inspiration, Berlin-Grunewald 1940.

RUFER, Josef: *Bekenntnisse und Erkenntnisse. Komponisten über ihr Werk* (Goldmann Schott 33055), München 1981.

SCHÖNBERG, Arnold: *Ausgewählte Briefe,* ed. Erwin Stein, Mainz 1958.

Stil und Gedanke. Aufsätze zur Musik, ed. Ivan Vojtech (Gesammelte Schriften 1), S. Fischer Verlag 1976.

Engl. Edition: *Style and Idea.* Collected Writings, ed. Leonard Stein, trans. Leo Black, London 1975.

SCHUMANN, Clara und Robert: *Briefwechsel. Kritische Gesamtausgabe,* ed. Eva Weissweiler, 2 vols, Basel/ Frankfurt am Main 1984 and 1987.

SCHUMANN, Robert: *Robert Schumann's Briefe. Neue Folge,* ed. F. Gustav Jansen, Leipzig 1886.

Der junge Schumann. Dichtungen und Briefe, ed. Alfred Schumann, Leipzig 1910.

Jugendbriefe von Robert Schumann, ed. Clara Schumann, 4. Ed. Leipzig 1910.

Gesammelte Schriften über Musik und Musiker, ed. Martin Kreisig, 2 vols, 5. Ed. Leipzig 1914.

Tagebücher, 3 vols., ed. Georg Eismann and Gerd Nauhaus, Leipzig 1971,1982 and 1987.

STRAUSS, Richard: *Betrachtungen und Erinnerungen,* ed. Willi Schuh, Zurich/Freiburg i. Br. 1949.

Richard Strauss und Franz Wüllner im Briefwechsel, ed. Dietrich Kämper (Beiträge zur rheinischen Musikgeschichte Vol. 51), Cologne 1963.

Richard Strauss und Ludwig Thuille. Briefe der Freundschaft 1877–1907, ed. Alfons Ott, München 1969.

STRAWINSKY, Igor: *Leben und Werk von ihm selbst. Erinnerungen, Musikalische Poetik, Antworten auf 35 Fragen,* Mainz 1957.

STÜRZBECHER, Ursula: *Werkstattgespräche mit Komponisten* (Deutscher Taschenbuch Verlag 910), Munich 1973.

WAGNER, Richard: *Sämtliche Schriften und Dichtungen (Volksausgabe),* 16 vols 6. Edition, Leipzig 1912.

Briefwechsel zwischen Wagner und Liszt, 2 vols, 2. Edition. Leipzig 1900.

Richard Wagner an Mathilde Wesendonk. Tagebuchblätter und Briefe 1853–1871,11. Ed. Berlin 1904.

WEBERN, Anton: *Der Weg zur neuen Musik,* ed. Willi Reich, Vienna 1960.

ZIMMERMANN, Bernd Alois: *Intervall und Zeit. Aufsätze und Schriften zum Werk,* ed. Christof Bitter, Mainz 1974.

Dokumente und Interpretationen, ed. Wulf Konold, Cologne 1986.

2. Works of Literature and Philosophy

ARISTOTELES: *Hauptwerke,* selected and translated Wilhelm Nestle (Kröners Taschenausgabe Band 129), Stuttgart 1968.

BÄTSCHMANN, Oskar: *Einführung in die kunstgeschichtliche Hermeneutik.* Wissenschaftliche Buchgesellschaft: 6. edition, Darmstadt 2009.

BENJAMIN, Walter: *Der Begriff der Kunstkritik in der deutschen Romantik,* ed. Hermann Schweppen- häuser (suhrkamp taschenbuch Wissenschaft 4), Frankfurt am Main 1973.

BLOCH, Ernst: *Zur Philosophie der Musik,* Frankfurt am Main 1974.

CAMUS, Albert: *Der Mythos von Sisyphos. Ein Versuch über das Absurde* (rowohlts deutsche enzyklopädie 90), Hamburg 1959, 275.-284. Tausend August 1985; *Le Mythe de Sisyphe,* in: *Essais,* ed. R. Quilliot (Bibliothèque de la Pléiade, no. 183), Paris 1965.

ECKERMANN, Johann Peter: *Gespräche mit Goethe in den letzten Jahren seines Lebens,* ed. Fritz Bergemann, Wiesbaden (Insel) 1955.

GADAMER, Hans Otto: *Wahrheit und Methode* 1960.

GOETHE, Johann Wölfgang von: *Werke. Hamburger Ausgabe in 14 Bänden,* ed. Erich Trunz, 14 vols and Register, Hamburg (Wegner) 1948–1964.

HEGEL, Georg Wilhelm Friedrich: *Werke in zwanzig Bänden,* Band 13–15: *Vorlesungen über die Ästhetik* (Theorie Werkausgabe Suhrkamp Verlag), Frankfurt am Main 1970: *Phänomenologie des Geistes* (Ullstein Materialien Nr. 35055), Frankfurt am Main/Berlin/Vienna 1980.

HEINE, Heinrich: *Sämtliche Schriften in zwölf Bänden,* ed. Klaus Briegleb (Reihe Hanser Werkausgabe), Munich/Vienna 1976.

HOFFMANN, E. Th. A.: *Sämtliche Werke,* Winkler Dünndruck-Ausgabe in fünf Einzelbänden, Munich 1963–1969.

MANN, Thomas: *Ausgewählte Essays in drei Bänden,* Band 3: *Musik und Philosophie,* ed. Hermann Kurzke (Fischer Taschenbuch Verlag Nr. 1908), Frankfurt am Main 1978.

NIETZSCHE, Friedrich: *Werke,* ed. Karl Schlechta (Ullstein Materialien), 5 vols, Frankfurt am Main/ Berlin/Vienna 1979.

PAUL, Jean: *Werke in zwölf Bänden,* ed. Norbert Müler, Carl Hanser Verlag, Munich/Vienna 1975.

SARTRE, Jean-Paul: *Was ist Literatur?,* ed. Traugott König (rororo 477 9), Reinbek bei Hamburg 1981.

SCHLEGEL, August Wilhelm: *Kritische Schriften und Briefe,* ed. Edgar Löhner, Vol. I, Stuttgart 1962.

SCHLEGEL, Friedrich: *Kritische Schriften,* ed. Wolfdietrich Rasch, Munich 1971.

SCHOPENHAUER, Arthur: *Zürcher Ausgabe. Werke in zehn Bänden,* Diogenes Verlag, Zurich 1977.

3. On the Subject of Music as Message

ANTOVIC, M: *Towards the semantics of Music. The twenthieth century. Language and History* 2009.

BEN, Arnold: *The Liszt Companion,* Greenwood Press 2002.

BLAUKOPF, Kurt: *Musik im Wandel der Gesellschaft. Grundzüge der Musiksoziologie,* Munich/Zurich 1984.

BITTERLI, Peter: *Und immer wieder Abschiede. György Kurtágs Botschaften.* http:/www.beckmesser.de/komponisten/kurtag.htm.

BRUHN, Siglind: *Encrypted Messages in Alban Berg's Music*, London 1998.

COOKE, Deryck: *The Language of Music*, London 1959.

DÜRHAMMER, Ilija: *Geheime Botschaften: homoerotische Subkulturen im Schubert-Kreis, bei Hugo von Hofmannsthal und Thomas Bernhard*, Böhlau Verlag Wien 2006.

ECO, Umberto: *Einführung in die Semiotik* (Uni-Taschenbücher 105), München 1972.

FALTIN, Peter, und REINECKE, Hans-Peter, (Eds): *Musik und Verstehen. Aufsätze zur semiotischen Theorie, Ästhetik und Soziologie der musikalischen Rezeption*, Cologne 1973.

FLOROS, Constantin: *Gustav Mahler*, Vol. I: *Die geistige Welt Gustav Mahlers in systematischer Darstellung*, Wiesbaden 1977; Vol. II: *Mahler und die Symphonik des 19. Jahrhunderts in neuer Deutung*, Wiesbaden 1977; Vol. III: *Die Symphonien*, Wiesbaden 1985.

Gustav Mahler and the Symphony of the 19th Century, Peter Lang: Frankfurt am Main /New York 2014.

Gustav Mahler. The Symphonies, Amadeus Press 1993.

Gustav Mahler. Visionary and Despot. Portrait of a Personality, Peter Lang: Frankfurt am Main 2012.

Beethoven's Eroica. Thematic Studien. Peter Lang: Frankfurt am Main/ New York 2013.

Mozart-Studien I, Breitkopf & Härtel: Wiesbaden 1979.

Anton Bruckner. The Man and the Work. Peter Lang: Frankfurt am Main/New York 2011; 2. edition 2015.

Johannes Brahms. "Free but Alone". A Life for a Poetic Music. Peter Lang: Frankfurt 2010.

Brahms and Bruckner as Artistic Antipodes. Peter Lang: Frankfurt am Main/New York 2015.

"Die Faust-Symphonie von Franz Liszt. Eine semantische Analyse", in: Musik-Konzepte 12. *Franz Liszt*, Munich 1980, 42–87.

„Studien zur „Parsifal-Rezeption", in: Musik-Konzepte 25. *Richard Wagner. Parsifal*, Munich 1982, 14–57.

Peter Tschaikowsky (rowohlts monographien), Reinbek bei Hamburg 2006.

Humanism, Love and Music. Peter Lang: Frankfurt am Main 2012.

Alban Berg. Music as Autobiography. Peter Lang: Frankfurt am Main 2014.

New Ears for New Music. Peter Lang: Frankfurt am Main/New York 2013.

György Ligeti. Beyond Avant-Garde and Postmodernism. Peter Lang: Frankfurt am Main/ New York 2014.

Hören und verstehen. Die Sprache der Musik und ihre Deutung, Schott: Mainz 2008.

„Die Musik soll nicht schmücken, sie soll wahr sein". Zur Ästhetik der Zweiten Wiener Schule, in: Malecka/ Pawlowska (Ed.): *Music as a Message of Truth and Beauty*, Kraków 2014, 65–74.

Wagner als Vegetarier und Pazifist, in: Frankfurter Allgemeine Zeitung vom 22. Mai 2013, pag. 28.

FLOROS, Constantin/GEIGER, Friedrich/SCHÄFER, Thomas (Eds): *Komposition als Kommunikation. Zur Musik des 20. Jahrhunderts* (Hamburger Jahrbuch für Musikwissenschaft Vol. 17), Frankfurt am Main 2000.

FLOROS, Constantin, MARX, Hans Joachim, and PETERSEN, Peter, (Eds.): *Programmusik. Studien zu Begriff und Geschichte einer umstrittenen Gattung* (Hamburger Jahrbuch für Musikwissenschaft Vol. 6), Laaber-Verlag 1983.

GEIGER, Friedrich (Ed.): *Musikkulturgeschichte heute* (Hamburger Jahrbuch für Musikwissenschaft Vol 26, Frankfurt am Main 2009.

Programm und Musik bei Aleksandr Skrjabin. ‚Zum Poème de l'Extase' und der 5. Klaviersonate, in: Musik-Theorie 30, Issue 2 (2015), 139–153.

GRABOCZ, Márta: *Musique, narrativité, signification*. L'Harmattan: Paris 2009.

HALLER, Silja: *Wort-Ton-Gestaltung in der Sinfonik Gustav Mahlers*, Universitätsverlag Potsdam 2012.

HEERO, Aigi: „Poesie der Musik. Zur Intermedialität in Robert Schumanns frühen Schriften", in: Trames 2007 (11/61/56), 15–34.

HRCKOVA, Nad'a: *Hudba ako posolstvo*, Bratislava 1995.

INTERNATIONAL REVIEW FOR THE AESTHETICS AND SOCIOLOGY OF MUSIC JOHNS.

Keith T./SAFFLE, Michael: *The Symphonic Poems of Franz Liszt*, New York 1997.

KARBUSICKY, Vladimir: *Grundriß der musikalischen Semantik* (Grundrisse Band 7), Wissenschaftliche Buchgesellschaft Darmstadt 1986.

KOELSCH, Stefan: *Music, Language and Meaning: Brain Signatures of Semantic Processing*, Max-Planck-Institut für Kognitions- und Neurowissenschaften 2004.

KOLLERITSCH, Otto (Ed.): *Verbalisierung und Sinngehalt. Über semantische Tendenzen im Denken in und über Musik heute* (Studien zur Wertungsforschung Vol. 21), Vienna/Graz 1989.

KRONES, Hartmut: „Rhetorik und rhetorische Symbolik in der Musik um 1800. Vom Weiterleben eines Prinzips", in: Musiktheorie 3 (1988), 117–140.

„Geheime Botschaften in Gustav Mahlers ‚Lied von der Erde'", in: Nachrichten zur Mahler-Forschung 51 (2004), 38–50.

„Konzepte semantischer Musikanalyse in der österreichischen und deutschen Musikwissenschaft", in: Markéta Stefková (Ed.): *Konzeptionen des musikalischen Denkens in der europäischen Musikwissenschaft des 20. Jahrhunderts* (anlässlich des 100. Geburtsjahres von Josef Krésanek), Bratislava 2014, 109–136.

KURET. Primoz: Die Bedeutung der Musik in der slowenischen Widerstandsbewegung, https//www.gko.uni-leipzig.de.

LEVI-STRAUSS, Claude: *Mythologiques I. Le cru et le cuit,* Paris 1964. German Edition: *Mythologica I. Das Rohe und das Gekochte* (suhrkamp taschenbuch Wissenschaft 167), Frankfurt am Main 1976.

LOOS, Helmut (Ed.): *Robert Schumann. Persönlichkeit, Werk und Wirkung*, Gudrun Schröder Verlag: Leipzig 2011.

MÄCKELMANN, Michael: *Arnold Schönberg und das Judentum. Der Komponist und sein religiöses, nationales und politisches Selbstverständnis nach 1921* (Hamburger Beiträge zur Musikwissenschaft Vol. 28), Hamburg 1984.

MALECKA, Teresa/PAWLOWSKA, Malgorzata (Eds.): *Music as a Message of Truth and Beauty*, Kraków 2014.

MALECKA, Teresa (Ed.): *Teoria muzyki*, 6 vols. Craków 2012–2015.

MEYER, L. B.: *Emotion and Meaning in Music*, University of Chigaco Press 1956.

MICHAELY, Aloyse: *Die Musik Olivier Messiaens. Untersuchungen zum Gesamtschaffen* (Hamburger Beiträge zur Musikwissenschaft Sonderband), Hamburg 1987.

PERRAKIS, Manos: „Die intime Botschaft der Musik", in: Tà katoptrizómema Issue 53.

PETERSEN, Peter: *Alban Berg. Wozzeck. Eine semantische Analyse unter Einbeziehung der Skizzen und Dokumente aus dem Nachlaß Bergs* (Musik-Konzepte Sonderband), Munich 1985.

PETRI, Horst: *Literatur und Musik. Form- und Strukturparallelen*, Göttingen 1964.

RATHERT, Wolfgang: *Charles Ives*, Darmstadt 1989, 2. Ed. 1996.

REDEPENNING. Dorothea: „Botschaften hinter Klängen. Überlegungen zu musikalischen Kommunikationsstrategien",in: Sprachen ohne Worte ed. Thomas Pfeiffer, Heidelberg 2009, 91–110.

REVERS, Peter: „Allan Pettersson: 7. Sinfonie", in: Melos 46 (1984), 103–125.

RÖSING, Helmut: „Heavy Metal, Hardrock, Punk: Geheime Botschaften an das Unbewußte?", in: Rösing (Ed.): *Rock, Pop, Jazz im musikwissenschaftlichen Diskurs*, Hamburg:CODA-Verlag, 163–185.

SCHAFFLE, Michael: *Franz Liszt. A Research and Information Guide* (Routledge Music Bibliographies), 2013.

SCHIEDERMAIR, Ludwig: *Die Gestaltung weltanschaulicher Ideen in der Vokalmusik Beethovens*, Leipzig 1934.

SCHNITZLER, Günter (Ed.): *Dichtung und Musik. Kaleidoskop ihrer Beziehungen*, Stuttgart 1979.

SIRMAN, Berk: *Music vs. Words. Exploring the problematic State of Semantic Meaning in Music,* Uppsala 2009.

STAIGER, Emil: *Musik und Dichtung*, 5. Ed. Zurich 1986.

STEGEMANN, Michael: *Franz Liszt. Genie im Abseits*, Piper: Munich/Zurich 2011.

TARASTI, Eero (Ed.): *Musical Signification: Essays in the semiotic Theory and Analysis of Music*, Mouton de Gruyter 1995, Reprint 2011.

UNSELD, Melanie: *Biographie und Musikgeschichte. Wandlungen biographischer Konzepte in Musikkultur und* Musikhistoriographie. Böhlau: Cologne/Weimar/Vienna 2014.

WECHSLER, Julia: "Music as a message and music as an autobiography: On the topicality of "old" musical hermeneutics" (Russ.), in: Musikalnaja semiotica 2015.

WECHSLER, Julia: "Die drei W". Zu einem Opernplan Alban Bergs, in: Jahrbuch des Staatlichen Instituts für Musikforschung 2000, 234–258.

Index

Ingram Content Group UK Ltd.
Milton Keynes UK
UKHW020958130623
423332UK00006B/207